STEADY AS SHE GOES

Women's Adventures at Sea

EDITED BY BARBARA SJOHOLM

SEAL PRESS

STEADY AS SHE GOES: *Women's Adventures At Sea*
Copyright © 2003 by Barbara Sjoholm

Published by Seal Press
An Imprint of Avalon Publishing Group Incorporated
161 William St., 16th Floor
New York, NY 10038

Grateful acknowledgment is made for the right to reprint material from the following sources:

"Sailing with Steinbeck" copyright © 2002 by Andromeda Romano-Lax. All rights reserved. Excerpted from *Searching for Steinbeck's Sea of Cortez* by permission of Sasquatch Books, Seattle WA.

"Whale Watching Me" copyright © 2001 by Jennifer Hahn. Reprinted with permission of the publisher from the book *Spirited Waters: Soloing South Through the Inside Passage* by Jennifer Hahn, The Mountaineers, Seattle WA.

Excerpts from "The Pull of Rowing" from *Rowing To Latitude* by Jill Fredston. Copyright © 2001 by Jill Fredston. Reprinted by permission of Farrar, Straus and Giroux, LLC.

From *Untamed Seas* by Deborah Scaling Kiley and Meg Noonan. Copyright © 1994 by Deborah Scaling Kiley. Reprinted by permission of Houghton Mifflin Company. All rights reserved.

"Swordfish" from *The Hungry Ocean: A Swordboat Captain's Journey* by Linda Greenlaw. Copyright © 1999 by Linda Greenlaw. Reprinted by permission of Hyperion.

Library of Congress Cataloging-in-Publication Data

Steady as she goes : women's adventures at sea/edited by Barbara Sjoholm.
   p. cm.
    ISBN 1-58005-094-8 (pbk.)
     1. Women and the sea. 2. Seafaring life. I. Sjoholm, Barbara.

  G540.S74 2003
  910.4'5'082—dc21   200305728

9 8 7 6 5 4 3 2 1

Designed by Paul A. Paddock
Printed in the United States of America
Distributed by Publishers Group West

Are you afraid of your boat sinking? Try this if you are: Watch a paper carton or cup float around on the surface of the bay hour after hour. Watch a tin can float around in much the same way. Now these materials do not naturally float, but the shape of them, with the hollow inside, causes them to stay above the surface, so to speak. We have this hollow shape in boats too, plus another good factor: boats are usually built of wood and wood naturally floats which, in itself, will keep your boat from sinking.

Now place a tin can in the bathtub and start filling it with water. Notice how full it must be before it will sink. A boat may be awash and still it will not sink if there are flotation tanks (tanks of air) or enough empty cans, etc. aboard. You can prove this to yourself by taking a toy wooden boat and filling it with water. No, it will not sink. Now put enough weight on it so it will be just beneath the surface. The weight you add may be easily counteracted by attaching a balloon or like object filled with air. Your little boat will float itself.

—*from* The Fearless Sailorette *by Fran Westfall*
(a self-published pamphlet from the 1960s)

Contents

Introduction

Barbara Sjoholm

Some years ago I lived in a house on the shores of Lake Union in Seattle. Built on pilings, it wasn't quite a houseboat. You entered on land, through a conventional door that faced a grassy lawn and picnic table, but by the time you'd walked through the former bootlegger's boat shed, you were over the water, in a narrow room with windows on three sides. Through these windows I watched a continuous parade of vessels of all sizes. Sculls and rowboats, canoes and kayaks, rubber rafts and wind surfboards, battered dinghies, gleaming-white sailboats, and restored two-masted wooden schooners all went by my windows. Sturdy tugs pulled barges five times their size; tourist boats—blasting golden oldies—showed visitors cityscapes they couldn't see from downtown hotels; dot-com millionaires drank champagne with friends on lavish cruisers. For someone who likes all things salty, it was heaven, the closest thing to being at sea myself.

I have liked ships since I was a girl, growing up in the port city of

Long Beach, California, visiting the huge harbor full of container ships on school field trips. Although I tended, as a child, to be more *in* the water than *on* the water, that changed when I found a job one summer in Norway, working as a dishwasher on the coastal steamer. I spent several months on the *Kong Olav*—with its poky little cabins and cramped public spaces, its sonorous horn that wailed arrival and departure, its splendid, gold-barred captain on the bridge, and its fixed itinerary that took us up and down the ragged coast from Bergen to the North Cape, the Russian border, and even, every third trip, across the wild Norwegian Sea to Svalbard. It was my idea of the perfect vessel: big enough to live on but not to get lost on, small enough so you felt the movement of the ocean, sturdy enough to carry you and its cargo in rough seas.

Later, in the Pacific Northwest, my notion of ship-sized perfection focused on the kayak, a simple way of floating water-tight and soundless along a shore or across a bay. The kayak allowed me to paddle hard at times and at others lean back, watching for seals and eagles. The kayak was a boat I could drag to the water's edge and step into, a boat that glided under wharves so I could see anemones and sea stars, a boat that made me a movable island, powered by my arms and the tides, with a flexible 360-degree view of the world. Most of the time, in my kayak, I feel stable and secure, even knowing there are fathoms of cold salt water below me. It's the same way I felt on the coastal steamer: at home, yet afloat.

The stories in this collection gather together essays by twenty sea-going women. Some of them are working gals—deckhand, assistant engineer, captain, kayak expedition leader. Thorough salts, they make a living from the sea. Others are on quests, by sail or paddle, to test their mettle or learn new skills. Sailing or kayaking is meant to be recreation, but sometimes, drenched by waves and at the mercy of the weather, these seafarers wish they were on dry land again. Whatever their experience at sea, one thread unites them, whether they're working or "relaxing": they are, to a one, boat-crazy.

In "Below Decks" Jessica DuLong works down in the engine room, among the dials and knobs of an old New York City fireboat, now a sightseeing vessel. Her fascination is the machinery; you'd hardly know at times she was on water. Ginni Callahan has built her own kayak; in "Fourteen" she tells us its particulars with affection and pride. Jill Fredston, whose lovely book, *Rowing to Latitude*, recounts a lifetime spent pulling oars, here describes the process of finding the right vessel for her wilderness explorations. The sailboat *Tethys*, which carried Kaci Cronkhite around the world, is a real personage in her story of rounding Cape of Good Hope. Dodo Danzmann gives us a fascinating glimpse of the tradition-bound life in Hamburg Harbor as she and her friends tool around in the *Antoinette*, their beloved cruiser from the twenties. Jennifer Karuza Schile's essay, on what the Alaskan fishing boat *Vis* meant to her, captures the heart-felt sense of joy when a ship is part of the family, while Melinda Tognini writes movingly of the loss of her beloved sailboat *Evergreen*.

Many of the writers describe with equal affection (and occasionally exasperation) the people who accompany them on their journeys. We suspect that Sue Muller Hacking might not have survived the difficulties of the passage from South Africa to New York without her husband, while Bernadette Bernon, whose adventures cruising with her husband appear weekly on the Web, describes the adjustments any relationship has to make at sea. Family connections are a large part of the essays by Penelope Duffy, who has to steer the sailboat through a storm while her father and another crewmate are incapacitated below, and Dawn Paul, who takes her elderly mother out kayaking. Andromeda Romano-Lax is brave: She has her two young children with her on a sailboat in the Sea of Cortez, as well as a husband and a depressed brother-in-law.

Some of the contributors are seasoned seafarers, like Holly Hughes, a Seattle writer who's spent many exhilarating and grueling summers fishing in Alaska, or Linda Greenlaw, who has to keep her male crew toeing the line as they catch swordfish in some of the roughest waters on the planet. Others, like devorah major, whose essay about a first sail on San Francisco Bay limns themes of prejudice and welcome, are saltwater beginners. Tania Aebi, well-known as the youngest person to make a single-handed circumnavigation, weighs in with a tale of having to learn a new skill, that of mooring a sailboat full of students in a crowded Greek harbor. Moe Bowstern's fresh and funny take on how she learned to be a skiffman on a fishing boat in Alaska contains both humility and courage, while Pamela Powell's tribute to "Captain Lou," the Boston ferry captain who taught her the ropes when she was a young deckhand, shows gratitude for how a female seafaring lineage was passed on.

These women find themselves having to make decisions in tight corners, to rely on others and sometimes only on themselves. A tempest at sea is no time to lose your wits; to weather it out and survive is, in fact, to build enormous confidence. While Deborah Scaling Kiley and Meg Noonan's true tale of shipwreck is a heart-stopper, several other blustery pieces collected here are equally teeth-chattering. Holly Hughes, in fact, finds a way to transcend fear during a terrible storm at sea, as does Kaci Cronkhite, battered by winds at the tip of Africa. We need more stories of women's nerve and spunk, to teach us and inspire us. I might not ever find myself on a raft in the Mid-Atlantic, but I now know to keep my legs up, well away from shark jaws. Conversely, if I found myself, like kayaker and naturalist Jennifer Hahn, eye to eye with a surfacing, barnacle-encrusted gray whale, I'd like to think I wouldn't break a paddle trying to get to safety, but would come even closer, to carefully observe the patterns on the beast's skin.

Although maritime writing has been part of world literature for centuries, this is, believe it or not, the first collection of women's adventures at sea. The essays are contemporary, but they rest on a foundation of earlier, mid-twentieth-century narratives about seafaring women, including the classics *My Ship Is So Small* by Ann Davison, *At One With the Sea* (previously titled *Alone Around the World*) by Naomi James, *Woman Alone* by Clare Francis and, from even earlier, *My Year Before the Mast,* by Annette Brock Davis, which tells of a working voyage on one of the last great four-masted vessels in 1933. These stories, in turn, have a precedent in long-out-of-print novels and memoirs by women who grew up in maritime communities or accompanied their husbands or families back and forth across the Atlantic or around the Horn at the turn of the century.

In recent years, historians have been looking into the suspect notion that women never went to sea, and have been unearthing diaries of whaling wives and sea captain's children, as well as doing original research on women sea tars, who passed as men in the merchant marines and navies of several countries. For further reading, take a look at Joan Druett's popular but scholarly books, *Hen Frigates* and *She Captains,* and Suzanne J. Stark's *Female Tars* to get a sense of how present women have been throughout maritime history.

"Steady As She Goes" is one of the many nautical phrases that have become a part of the English language. It particularly refers to a ship leaving harbor, to instructions to keep her steadily moving forward as she leaves her mooring. Although many of the authors in this anthology refer to their boats by name, or as *it* rather than *she* (even the august Lloyd's Shipping Register fairly recently decided that they would no longer refer to ships as *she*), the phrase still fits.

Welcome aboard.

Big Storm, Small Boat

PENELOPE S. DUFFY

Slowly up and then slowly down. Slowly up and slowly down again. It got to all of us, not to mention the cold. I had on long underwear, a T-shirt, a turtleneck, a wool sweater, two pair of insulated socks, a full set of foul-weather gear, a wool hat, knee-high rubber sailing boots, and I still felt the cold on my face.

Everyone wanted to stay on deck, and we argued over who got to take the first watch until we admitted that none of us could so much as look at the cabin without throwing up. Around 1:30 A.M., we thought a bit of hot soup would take the chill off and give us some strength. I opened the jug of Ma's minestrone, a talisman against the elements, a reminder of hearth and home. The aroma of tomatoes and beef broth wafted up.

Johnny was the first to go—in one movement turning, grabbing the gunwale, and letting forth all he had over the side. I was next, followed by Dad, and, finally by the soup itself. I poured the entire batch into the ocean. Johnny even asked me to toss the jug over.

"So much for soup," we said.

We were hungry and we were tired. Two hours earlier we'd fired up the diesel and headed out under bare poles into a starless night. The moon raced in and out of fast-moving clouds. As soon as we hit the ocean swells, the moon disappeared, and with it the horizon. *Kestrel*, our thirty-three-foot Tartan Ten, was loaded to the gills and somewhat sluggish in the chop. We were on the first leg of a trip that would take ten days and cover more than one thousand miles from the southern coast of Nova Scotia home to the Chesapeake Bay. It was my first time sailing out of sight of land.

The night had started the day before with my father's pronouncement that he was "fit as a fiddle," and ready to head out. No one else thought he was fit as a fiddle. We'd been delayed two weeks by his bout with a kidney stone, a raggedy thing that had returned with him in a jar from the hospital in Halifax. Prior to its removal, he'd spent ten days in writhing agony. We were told it would pass. It did not. We finally dragged him, loaded with morphine, over rough coastal roads to Lunenburg, a town with a thirteen-bed hospital. Take him to Halifax, they said. By the time we did, we were told he should have been there days ago. A day or two later, relieved of the stone, he was nearly dancing. He was told the trip home should not be made for another two weeks. He was told he was old. He was told he was weak. He didn't like being told any of those things. So Johnny, me, and fit-as-a-fiddle Dad were suddenly packing up the *Kestrel*.

A racing sailboat, she was hardly designed for off-shore cruising. But someone had to sail her up and down the eastern seaboard so we could spend our summers racing in Nova Scotia and then back home to race on the Chesapeake. She had a fairly high freeboard. The deck was almost flush, so there wasn't much headroom below. It didn't matter. The cabin was bare bones anyway. No refrigeration, no gimbaled stove, and no head. Just some bunks, a chart table, a single-burner alcohol stove lashed to the mast should seas be calm enough for cooking, and a galvanized bucket to answer the call of nature. She had neither roller reefing nor a self-furling jib. But she was fast. And that's what mattered. Outside of the occasional picnic, sailing was just another word in our family for racing.

My father, an expert sailor, had an exaggerated sense of invincibility, or perhaps a death wish. In my twenty-five years of sailing with him, we'd been through our share of disasters—broaching under spinnaker, running aground on granite ledges, wrestling huge storms in little open-cockpit boats, masts breaking, sails ripping, random pieces of equipment flying off into the wind only to turn on us and fly back again at our heads. These are the sorts of things that instill in sailors a respect for the elements. My own respect was particularly fine-tuned.

During an emergency, Dad acted as if nothing at all was happening, and afterward, as if nothing at all *had* happened. He was Magellan, Columbus, and Horatio Hornblower rolled into one. He was also an Episcopalian minister, and he either had great faith or great denial when things went bad.

Once we took several dowager ladies from the congregation out, an expedition no doubt arranged by my mother. Dad held his course even as dark clouds grew up ahead. Suddenly, the keel struck hard, not once, but twice, flinging my three-year-old,

Melanie, out of my arms, knocking the wind from the sails, and everyone except my father off their seats. Arms and legs stuck up out of a tangle of dresses, hats, lines, and life jackets on the cockpit floor. "Dear God, we're sinking!" came the muffled shrieks. My father said not a word other than, "Gee, looks like this must be Sheep's Ledge." Followed by, "Tide must be going out."

The ladies sat in frozen, wild-eyed silence all the way back as my father sang sea shanties and betrayed not the slightest distress.

When not dealing with disasters, we were having fun. My father knew the lyrics to every popular song since World War I. We told tall tales and reveled in the camaraderie that comes from working hard, winning or losing. But there was more. From the moment I felt the lift of the sea beneath my feet, the heel of a boat, the power of wind and sail coalescing, I was in love. And have been ever since.

But I'd never been tested on the open sea. Now we were headed in a straight shot from Nova Scotia to Plymouth, Massachusetts, in what we hoped would take about three days, most of it about two hundred miles off shore. Dad hadn't instructed me on either the radio or the loran navigation system. You'll learn on the way, he'd said. On a boat, learning by doing is best, as long as there is room for mistakes.

Of course, in a race there is no room for mistakes. My sisters and I learned that fast enough. Dad was such a gentle man he'd carry little insects outside in his hand to free them. In a pair of baggy khaki shorts, a holdover from his missionary days, he'd wander in and out of his study, thinking great thoughts, rescuing insects. We'd never heard him raise his voice, let alone use profanity. Never, that is, until the fateful day when he decided we'd try racing.

"Let's try racing," he said with an excited grin. I was ten, my sisters in their teens. We hopped innocently aboard the old hag of a boat we were renting. He headed for the starting line. The gun went off, and he asked Patty to "ease the jib sheet." She blithely let it go entirely. The boat stopped dead. Amid the whipping rope and flapping sail, the gentle father we had known shouted, "Jesus H. Christ! *Whatahyadoin*? Get it in! Get it in!" about fifty times. But we were stunned to paralysis with that first "Jesus!"

Jesus H. Christ? Did Jesus have a middle initial? And where was Daddy? Who was this crazed man?

We recovered. Everyone yells during a race. I soon did it myself. I was good at racing, committed to winning, and yet never quite had the confidence I needed when I was skipper of my own class boat—a boat I'd sold to help buy the Tartan. I always felt better as crew than skipper, which suited my father just fine.

I was confident now, though, even if Dad wasn't up to par. Johnny, our great friend and fellow racing crew, would be with us. He was strong, healthy, in his twenties, and had made the trip before.

On the evening of our departure, Johnny came over and we sat by the fire and listened to NOAA weather radio. Storm coming in about twenty-eight hours. "Hmm," my father said, "we'd be better off leaving tonight and out-running it rather than getting socked in here."

"That's the stupidest thing I ever heard of," Ma said. "After all that packing, you're exhausted." She and Melanie would be driving home sometime after we left, but she was worried about Dad.

"What do you think, guys? We're tough, huh?" Dad said, the maniacal gleam appearing.

"We're tough," we responded.

So around 11:00 P.M. we pushed off, thermos of soup in hand, waving good-bye to Ma and Melanie on the wharf, and forgetting entirely that our motion-sickness medicine takes twelve hours to work.

At 3:00 A.M. I went below. Dad stayed on watch. Johnny, sick as a dog and not dressed warmly enough, was already below. It was the last we'd see of Johnny on deck for the next two days.

As dawn approached, Dad and I felt better and didn't bother with Johnny, now resting after spending a night retching into the galvanized bucket. Dad finally agreed to get some sleep, and I took over, heading southeast on an easy, uneventful watch, my first ever.

When Dad got up, we raised the main to steady the boat and take advantage of the freshening breeze coming now west-southwest. Johnny remained incapacitated. I helped him drink some water, after which he sank into a heavy sleep.

I caught some sleep, too. Dad refused to go below. By late afternoon the wind was a stiff twenty knots with heavy gusts. The seas were kicking up and knocking the boat around. Periodic rains were heavy. *Kestrel* had a huge mainsail. Shouting that we'd better take a reef, Dad tied a line around his waist and crouched along the deck. He was a big man, his progress hindered by his jacket. Its insulated folds contained a giant flashlight, a pocket knife, a radio beacon, a couple of flares, and enough flotation to fill several life jackets.

I slowly hauled in the main and pointed us into the wind. Dad fought his way to the mast, grabbed hold, and heaved himself up. His hood was blown back, his knit cap lost quickly to the seas, and his jacket, like an anchor, kept him in a sort of bent-knee position.

Holding on with both hands, he nodded for me to release the halyard. He wrapped his arm around the mast and tried to pull the sail down with his free hand to no effect. Finally, raising himself to a wide-legged stance, head down, he grabbed the sail above his head with both hands and pulled down with his full weight until he bent to a crouch. He then struggled to raise himself up against the yawing of the boat. I continued to lower the halyard as I watched him lurch around in the cacophony of flapping sails, spray, and a now driving rain. When it was finally down to the first reef point, I could see the glazed eyes. Either he was weaker than I'd realized, or his jacket weighed more than I thought. A knot of fear began in the pit of my stomach. By silent agreement he took the helm while I furled and tied the sail along the boom. Reaching the boom from the aft deck I was occasionally lifted off my feet and left swinging as the boat dipped and leaned.

That done, we headed off on a close reach, and caught our breath. The boat was heeling over, so heavy she was pounding, rather than cresting, through the waves. From a perch on the companionway, I managed to pour a cup of coffee, still hot, from the thermos. Dad leaned in as I passed him the cup. Not quick enough. It whisked in a lateral sweep past his outstretched hand, hovered momentarily above the waves before dropping into the deep. We stared in stunned silence.

"So much for coffee," I shouted.

We needed more to eat. Above the sink only coffee, dry soup, hot water, and crackers. The bulk of the food was in a laundry basket under the forward bunk. I needed to check on Johnny, so I went below.

As my foot left the last step, I was instantly knocked to my knees and slammed against the port bunk—conveniently face to face with Johnny. Still breathing, I noted. Every time the bow pounded off a steep wave, the mast shuddered. The whole cabin shuddered. Bouncing around, crouching up and down, I felt sick again. I inched forward, and, with one hand around the mast, groped blindly in the basket. I shoved a couple of cans of peaches in my pockets and grabbed a bag of apples, then crawled back, dragging the apples with one hand, holding the leeward bunk with the other, and hoping all the while that I wouldn't throw up.

Near dizzy with hunger, I stood in the companionway. I held up the cans. "Peaches," I shouted. Oh, those succulent little peaches. Can opener! Ha! I spied it among the dishes. But I couldn't make my hands work. Stiff with cold. "Please open," I implored the opener. "Please, please open." Finally, turning the can upside down and willing my fingers to squeeze, I punctured it! Slowly, slowly I twisted the key until it was open. I grabbed the spoon I held in my teeth, popped it into the can, and passed it to my father's waiting hand. The boat lurched in a wave, knocking me off balance, and the little can scooted down the deck in the wash, its lid and spoon standing at attention until it disappeared merrily off the stern.

Dad stared after it for what seemed minutes. My heart sank.

"So much for peaches," Dad shouted.

"So much for peaches," I shouted back.

I hauled the second can out of my coat and felt the round ring of a pop-top. I pulled the top off so fast, Dad's eyes shone with greedy delight. After a successful pass, he shoveled in the peaches with his fingers. I ate just as quickly.

"Johnny," I said. Dad nodded in sad agreement. I opened a third can, crawled back down and knelt next to Johnny. I raised his head, and up and down we went trying to match the spoon, his mouth, and the rocking of the boat into a single coordinated movement. One tiny spoonful after another I managed to get the juice in his mouth.

He was so weak, he barely opened his eyes. It took forever, and the cabin quickly felt hot and steamy in the two tons of clothes I was wearing. Johnny fell back on the sweaters with a thud. I was about to throw up.

On deck, Dad looked sodden and heavy as he stared ahead through rain speckled glasses. I made mugs of soup with green apples for dessert. The wind was increasing. At 7:00 P.M. we mentioned a second reef, but Dad said he had to go below.

"We don't need that now," he said. I agreed, wanting to believe it.

As I steered the boat, I could see him below, struggling with his jacket. He couldn't even manage the zipper, so I tied the tiller and helped him out of his clothes. He quite literally could not undress himself—a bit of frightening information that, along with his two previous heart attacks, haunted me as I headed back into the storm.

It was raining hard. Waves were smacking around and breaking up against each other in chaotic frenzy. Probably the remains of an earlier storm breaking against the one we were in. A huge wave broke green water over my head from the stern. Knocked forward by its force, I looked in horror at water swirling almost to the tops of my yellow boots. Again I leapt into the cabin.

"Daddy! Are you sure the cockpit is self-bailing? There's a ton of water in there," I shouted.

Eyes closed. "Yup," he said. "Just make sure the life raft doesn't wash away." He lay there as if dead.

I flew up to see if he was right. He was. Water was pouring out of the sea cocks. With the next gust the boat slammed over and was slow to recover, despite my efforts at heading her up. I knew I couldn't reef or haul down the main alone and decided to wait till Dad was rested to ask for help. Maybe after dark. Then I noticed it was dark.

I switched on the running and compass lights and settled into a rhythm of spilling wind by letting out the main sheet then hauling it in, hand over hand, leaning my backside against the tiller. The wind was so strong that the tiller never moved an inch to windward against my 125 pounds.

A few gusts later, I tied the tiller and went below. A glance at Johnny's pale face and I knew he was out of commission. My father was asleep and ashen. Dripping water, I was forced to a sitting position by the pounding of the boat. I shook his shoulder hard. We needed to get the sail down and go under bare poles, I told him.

"I can't do it," he said weakly.

What?

"No, I mean it!" I shouted.

No response. "Seriously, Dad, we're taking knockdowns. Come on!" The boat pitched wildly.

"Can't," he whispered. "Can't move. Must be the morphine. I really can't get up." He seemed both amazed and resigned.

"But I need you!" If those words got from my brain to my mouth,

I do not know, because we hit a wave that felt like a rock. *Kestrel* was over and foundering. I raced back up and ripped the main sheet out of the jam cleat. The sail whizzed out and the boat slowly righted herself on a cresting wave that foamed white teeth. I untied the tiller, held the main sheet in my one hand, and stretched my leg out straight so I could anchor my foot against the forty-five-degree heel of the boat, a huge luff in the main. Spray showered off in green plumes against the glow of the starboard running light.

"We're okay," I told the boat. "I can do this," I said, pulling the main back in. But when another wave slapped green water against my shoulder, I countered that my father was going to die, that I didn't know CPR, that I didn't know how to use the radio, and that there was no one to call even if I did. "Johnny," I thought, "I could get Johnny if something bad happened." Adrenaline might rouse him, but I knew he'd be more of a danger than a help. Strength and balance were needed, and he could barely sit upright.

Okay. Steady. The sail was not ripping and the mast was not breaking. Guiding the boat and keeping her upright in this wind, with this much sail, as heavy as she was, would require energy and concentration, admittedly in short supply. Easing the main sheet meant hauling it back in with two hands, a procedure sure to sap my strength. Spilling wind by heading the boat up required skill to prevent the boat from going into irons. If I headed up too far into the wind so that the wind was on either side of the sail, the boat would lose momentum and start slipping backwards fast. That meant no steerage way, and she'd be completely vulnerable to the force of the wind and waves, beyond control—the most frightening and dangerous thing of all.

Besides sinking, of course, which is what would quickly follow. As the gusts shrieked through the rigging, I was forced to both head up and let out the main.

I reminded myself that I was a good heavy-weather sailor, but I was fighting tears and consumed with the thought that I was alone. No Daddy. No Johnny. I couldn't believe it. Suddenly, I was joined by a small bird, a land bird blown out to sea. He clutched his position on the life lines, gathering breath and courage for further flight. He cheered me briefly, then took off without warning.

Under the sail the tiny red light of a fishing boat appeared, then dipped into the trough of a swell and out of sight. "I could call that boat on the radio," I thought. "If I knew how to use the radio."

The waves were wild and unpredictable. They'd sneak up from behind and lift the stern so high that the bow would hover momentarily, and then either crash down hard and flat or point straight to what was surely the bottom. My only guide was the light cast by the running lights. Not much, but it gave me enough time to try to steer my way through the chaotic seas. I guessed the swells were growing to some thirty feet because I had to course down their backsides at an angle.

From the crest of the next swell, I could see my fishing friend had turned due south. What did he know that I didn't? Should I follow? I watched over the stern quarter as the light appeared and disappeared in the waves until it was out of sight forever. "Hold your course," I told myself, and I stared at the compass, feeling ever more bereft, uncertain, and abandoned.

"Oh, God," I thought. "I can't do this alone. What's up ahead?"

Pretty soon I found out exactly what was up ahead, and behind, and all around. The full moon took a turn out of the clouds and cast a cool white light on the scene. My mouth fell open at the revelation: a black sea, screaming with whitecaps. On the peak of a swell, I stood and slowly turned around. In every direction, I was greeted by a vast, dark, never-ending ocean churned into a fury. Everywhere sharp, saw-tooth waves cracked and crashed against each other, flinging foam off their tops before curling over in folds of roiling surf. I had been operating in the dark. How I longed to be in the dark again. Oh, for the innocent illumination of the running lights! I shut my eyes and wished the moon back to its cloud cover. When it slid back, the scene was indelibly imprinted on my mind: black waves so jagged and swells so huge that I could not see how we were still afloat. I was no more than a bit of flotsam tossing about.

I sat down, frozen. I tied the tiller and leaned into the cabin to grab a cigarette off the shelf above the sink. Yes, I was going to smoke. I huddled out of the wind to light it with trembling hands. One puff, two. Oh, it tasted so good. Then a third. *Whap!* A side wave crashed green water over my head, water pouring down my neck. I stood up, water to my calves, and raised my fist. I cursed the seas and the wind, and slid with the washing water to the tiller, untied it, and held on.

Fearful and angry and more alone than I thought possible, I kept thinking our lives were in my hands. I felt weak. "Don't think about that now," I said aloud. The wind howled. I began to sing hymns. The one that came to mind was "Nearer, My God, to Thee," sung by those sinking on the *Titanic* which went down off the coast of Nova Scotia. I replaced hymns with a nursery rhyme, which then reminded me of the daughter I might never see again. I thought of home and my mother and how even minestrone would taste good. I found myself laughing for no reason. Tears mixed with the salt spray on my face. I thought of things I hadn't done and things I should have said. I thought of how deep the ocean was, and how cold.

I searched for my watch under my foul-weather gear, and by the compass light saw it was 11:20 P.M. I had been handling the boat for hours with God-knew-how-many-more to go; we were at least a day and a half from Plymouth. How long would these seas keep up, and the wind? How long was a night? How long could I endure the strain of holding on and hauling in? How long could I maintain my concentration as the never-ending seas piled up on top of each other? My arms felt numb. The seas became a wall of water that I had to climb up over.

A huge gust hit and I couldn't free the sheet from the jam cleat. My hand wouldn't work. My arm wouldn't work. I was crying. Bending to yank it, I came eye level with black water rushing past the gunwale. Watching it come over the gunwale, the leeward deck awash, I shoved the tiller hard to leeward and finally jerked the line free. Then the tiller felt useless. I'd gone into irons! I looked back. The stern was out of the water on a wave. We surfed the downside. The rudder caught, and the tiller worked, and the shaking sail caught the wind again.

The words, "Oh, God, thy sea is so great and my boat is so small," came to me. I repeated them out loud once, then whispered them again and again. Without realizing it, I was praying. It was difficult to realize it because my father had schooled me to believe that it is simplistic and ignorant to pray for concrete things. God was not "up there" granting wishes. But those words, *thy* sea, *my* boat, opened me to an awareness that I was not alone. Sea so great, boat so small. I sensed my own limits, but somehow was less frightened by them. I saw that all the rage and fear I felt amounted to nothing. Were nothing. I saw I might not make it. The boat might founder. The ocean might rise up around me. The boat might sink.

Mile after mile, hour after dark hour, rising and falling, I steered the boat, let out the main, hauled it back in, hand over hand. How I did it, I do not know. The seas remained crazy; rains came and went, cold wind screamed around me, and the moon raced through the clouds. Waves hit, the boat pounded, near knock-downs came, and I kept going. The boat, the storm, and I became one. My boat was small, but I was not alone. And in that awareness had come the courage to find peace.

$$\text{\textbf{\textbeta}} \qquad \text{\textbf{\textbeta}} \qquad \text{\textbf{\textbeta}}$$

Many hours later, the sky, still dark with storm clouds, began to brighten. Dawn had come, but I didn't know it. The wind had dropped a bit and the seas were less ragged. Suddenly, against the southern horizon, I saw a campfire on a beach. An island appeared about a mile off the starboard bow. And someone had lit a fire on the beach. I rubbed my eyes. "They're having a cookout!" I shouted. "Johnny, Daddy, come quick!" I looked around wildly. Where were we? What had happened in the night?

My father flew up in his long johns and skidded in sock feet to

15

the stern. Johnny tried to rise, but in his haste hit his head on the bulkhead and was thrown back to his bunk.

"Oh, God!" Dad said as he stared at the bright crimson center of what surely was a campfire and at the surf breaking on the shore of what was surely land. "Where on earth have you taken us?" He grabbed the tiller and began to turn the boat around without even looking at the compass.

I threw myself against him, clutching his arm. "No!" I pleaded. "Don't! Let's just beach her on the island. I bet they're cooking hot dogs on that campfire!"

The stern to the island, I almost started to weep. Then as we looked back, the island changed shape in a cloud formation. There was a small break in the dense clouds along the horizon allowing the light of dawn to pierce through in a flickering beam. So much for the campfire. The shoreline was whitecaps flashing against the line of light, giving the illusion of surf. So much for the beach.

Dad shook his head. We both did. "You almost had us going over there for hot dogs," he said. Johnny joined us. I hugged him, and we all laughed. I laughed a lot and couldn't stop. Then I began to shake.

"It's been a long night," I said.

"Really?" Dad asked, looking around at what was now a calmer ocean.

"Yeah, really."

He went down to gear up and take over. I went below and sank into dreams, still steering the boat as I slept.

Years later we still laugh about the morning Penny wanted to beach *Kestrel* on a phantom island to get some hot dogs. But no one talks about the storm. I never said much about it. Had no words to explain it. What had come over me that night in the storm wasn't just courage or confidence. No, it was a peace. A peace that truly exceeds understanding. Peace in the face of whatever was to come, sinking or sailing. Peace in howling wind, in raging seas, in the quiet of dawn. I was skipper of my own little boat at last. And I was not alone.

Maiden Voyage

I have crossed the Atlantic on a steamer, cruised down the California coast, ferried across the Bosporus, the Hudson, Hong Kong Bay, and rowed in rivers and creeks whose names I have forgotten. Oh, the excitement and humility those journeys taught me. But sailboats seem to hold a particular magic in their sway. For years and years I watched those boats as I crossed the bridge, as I sat at a pier or looked out a window to see the bay fan out in an arc of blue dotted by tiny white sails that seemed to skate across the water. How free they appeared, disciplined but not regimented or uniform, free in a way I wanted to be. The dream held a specific flavor: the damp of the fog, a scent of salty air on your cheeks, a shadow cast over an ocean cove, a certain feeling that I was sure I would find, an affirmation of my mediation on freedom: how to get it, how to hold on to it, how to spread it, how to be it.

Not that I wanted to sail only to feel free. The fact is, I have always been attracted to water and boats; although this is a reality that lies in direct contradiction to my meager swimming skills. But then it has been the boats that drew me; from canoe to rowboat, motorboat to ocean liner, summer camp raft or pedalboat on a park lake, there is something about riding the current of river, the undulation of lake, the shifting tides of ocean. There is something in the sounds, the way the wind changes its personality when you are surrounded by the water. It is there that I can feel the roundness of the earth and have a palpable sense of its size.

§　§　§

Until the morning of my first sailing adventure I had forgotten how many years I had wanted to sail. Andre, my generous friend who introduced me to the wonders of sailing, walked me down the gangway to the slip where his twenty-four-foot, single-mast sloop was housed, telling me about his lifetime love of the sport. When we reached the berth where his boat was tied, I began to remember my own. I was maybe ten years old, and going out with our small family, my parents and brother, on a motorboat owned by someone my father knew. It was a late afternoon, and chilly. I recall digging my hands deep into my pockets only to pull them out again as I leaned over the side and looked down at the churning water. The boat was larger than I expected, and the engine made a lot of noise as it growled its way through the water. As we huffed out of the harbor we passed a few sailboats, bending side to side with the wind as they tacked left and right across the bay. Most of those boats were smaller than the boat we rode on, and all were quieter.

As much fun as the ride on the larger, faster, far-sturdier motorboat held, it was one of those sailboats that I actually wanted to board. When my father had told my brother and me that we were going on this adventure, I had decided that we would be on a sailboat. It was not that my father had for a moment said *sailboat*. It was that I had assigned all boats and ships, pulled from my limited knowledge of types of watercraft, to a particular body of water. Rowboats and rafts were for rivers, steamers and freighters were for the ocean, ferries were for canals and inlets, and barges, sailboats, and tugboats were for the bay. Since tugboats only pulled other boats, and barges only had freight, that left sailboats. My little dream stayed buried for years, forgotten in the imperatives of raising children, keeping the lights on, struggling for peace. Then the history of my dream made a serendipitous reappearance, as I grabbed on to the lifeline as I had been directed, climbed on to the boat's edge, and crossed over the few feet to the bow.

$$\ \text{\textgravedbl}\ \ \ \ \ \text{\textgravedbl}\ \ \ \ \ \text{\textgravedbl}$$

I sat down. Andre moved his long limbs across his boat, with more ease than he had ever shown on solid ground, then began to unpack, roll out, and bend-on the sails. As he explained some basic rules, I noticed that, despite his neatly trimmed beard and carefully barbered head, he had a certain handsome cragginess that was cut into his jaw as much by ocean winds as by time. He started with the chain of command—he was the captain, and I was the mate. This was not an order given by a commandant with a penchant for maintaining absolute control at all times, but a matter-of-fact survival strategy presented by a seasoned mariner. Then he quickly provided me with a minimal sailing vocabulary lesson and a series of basic safety instructions. Andre asked me to do a few very minor tasks involving feeding the mainsail into the mast slot and helping to hoist it. As the large triangular sail began to fill with wind, the boat restlessly pulled at the rope that kept it tethered to the dock. "We're sailing," Andre chortled as he took care of the smaller sail, the jib, by himself, allowing me to look at the many boats docked around us and realize that, although the materials have evolved, and the engineering has more nuance and shade, sailboat technology is still essentially the same as it has been for hundreds of years. Wind, cloth, wood, rope, anchor, rudder—hewed in the same shape, hoisted and dropped with the same requirements, steered with the same considerations.

❧   ❧   ❧

I know that I came from a long line of boat people, stretching centuries back to the west coast of Yoruba land. Before we were stolen, my people fished and explored river and ocean waterways. Later when forced to make the West Indies home, they still were close to boats, regularly rowing from Bahamian islands to American soil. Most fished, and some, including my grandfather, were also briefly involved in bringing a kind of rum concentrate into Florida during Prohibition. The liquor was suspended from the back of the boats from nets that were supported by floats. One day my grandfather rowed to America and stayed, returning home only for brief visits. My father, too, held sailing in his blood. The few joys he experienced in the navy were found diving off a boat into the clear South Pacific waters. So, I was at home in this boat; though new to the craft, I could feel a history of sailing etched into my genes.

We cast off into the postcard afternoon of soft-blue, cloud-punctuated skies, through the Oakland estuary, past the cargo ships, close to the gigantic steel crane beaks, lifting up and setting down low, long square containers on and off the anchored freighter's bellies twenty-four hours a day. On the other side were dry-docked boats, hulls being opened and examined, and sterns being refurbished. The sun was still high in the sky, its heat soft against my cheeks as we slid though the channel. My heart was beating faster as the same gentle wind that filled the sails painted a broad smile on my face. The water, like the city that embraced it, teemed with commerce. Ferries, tugboats, freighters, water taxis, and armed and constant Coast Guard joined with the sailboats crossing out, under, around the Bay Bridge.

As we piloted through the estuary, my friend explained the etiquette of sailing, not just the rights of way, not just the manners, the respectful acknowledgment of each other, but the imperatives to help anyone who requires it. By avocation my friend races sailboats, both his own and others. In racing too, despite the competition and one-upmanship, there was still, he explained, a highly respected code of ethics. One would always forsake a race to help a fellow sailor who was compromised.

§ § §

After demonstrating how quickly and tightly the boat could turn, Andre showed me how to steer, placed my hand on the helm, and pointed out how to evenly push it to left or right to direct the prow the opposite way. Then, as if handling a clumsy flat-bottomed barge, I timidly headed toward the bridge. He was back at the helm when we finally rolled under the bridge, and the bay opened its mouth as we moved a small distance from the clang and whistle of profit and loss. Suddenly around me there was nothing but balance and peace and quiet.

At that point a Coast Guard motorboat came closer. It was then that Andre shook me out of my reverie. He explained that the Coast Guard could and did board boats at will, with or without cause. When a Coast Guard captain decided you were to be boarded, you were boarded. They might check that you had the required number of life jackets and other emergency supplies. They might search for contraband. They might just be checking who was on the boat, and where. One, he said, would board while another stood at the edge, gun at the ready. "On the water," he smiled wryly, "there are not the same rights as on land. Not really." He said that he had been boarded several times. It came with the territory. I was not sure how much was the territory of sailing and how much was the territory of sailing while black. We changed course, steered around a small island, and the Coast Guard boat that had been headed in our direction watched us move away.

$ $ $

For parts of each day my mind wrests around the implications of a globe in a state of unending war. My own neighborhood, with its guerilla skirmishers and midnight sirens, is a daily reminder of the persistent harshness of these times. Somehow I am to craft phrases and punctuate rhythm and make poems that are more than a relentless bray, more than a reiteration of the madness. Somehow I am to continue to meet classrooms of children or adults and, with courage and faith, try to have them find the words for vision, and resistance, and justice, try to help them find the memory of freedom. Every day I am crowded with images of carnage and despair, houses mowed over, waters polluted, hungry children, abandoned elders, problems that are not easily excised by surgeon's knife, or herbalist's tea, situations that are not upturned simply through fervent prayer. My shoulders ache from the weight of these days, my eyes are red with tears, my voice hoarse. All of this falls away as the boat skims across the rising ripples in the water, as Andre maneuvers it to a quiet cove and we stop and let down the anchor, come to. We rest there for a time, as pelicans wing overhead and then hover close to the waves, balancing on the air compressed between their large outspread wings and the water, before dipping their long beaks into the waves and catching fish that have come to the top in the quiet of the afternoon bay. Sea gulls squawk and settle on this boat's helm and that one's bow.

We were the only African Americans I saw sailing that day, although my friend had pointed to a boat berthed near his, and told me that its captain was also black. Yet, with a friendliness I have not found evidenced at the theater, or many a fancy restaurant, people waved and greeted us as I know they never would have, had we simply been walking down the street. I joked with my friend that it was too bad that all this civility and peacefulness would not translate to the land once we all debarked. It was sad, he responded, that so many would tie up their boats and forget it all, go back to a world too often lived in go-for-self, king-of-the-mountain scenarios. I wondered how soon they put it aside. Did it happen before they had walked far enough to shake off the ripples of sea in their legs and feet? Was it, as my friend indicated, an almost instant amnesia—lost, the wonder we shared, by being part of, not dominator over, nature and community—immediately forgotten, like yesterday's reheated dinner or last week's tepid embraces. If anything, he had said, some of the increasing harshness of human relations on land were becoming a growing part of the life of the sea. We both became quiet as the wind sang a song with fall's chill in its trill.

🦌   🦌   🦌

As the sun set we put about and Andre once again handed me the helm, as we traveled on a waterway that was now mostly empty and mostly quiet. Cormorants flew in patterns, swooping toward the water and then arcing back into the skies. Brown pelicans pointed toward the North Bay in small triangular flocks. Sea otters bobbed and curled around the rising waves, and the wind laughed softly as the boat eased back toward land. Life for me, at that moment, was so incredibly sweet. Not that sailing was giving answers, creating solutions, or making change. But that the balance that I found being held by the water's rhythms, the space that I was afforded while steering through its ebbs and eddies, provided room to refuel, to recompose, to breathe, to feel for a moment free, and to find more energy to walk and, when need be, help to clear the rocky road that lies ahead.

When we returned to the harbor and tied up the boat, I alighted with peacefulness and clarity that has stayed far longer than that one afternoon, than that one small daydream could have presaged. Sometimes it seems that we always focus on the big dreams, the life achievements, the accomplishments that could someday fill some lines in the pages of a funeral obituary, as measures of getting where we are supposed to be going; but I sometimes think that it's the simple dreams, the ordinary but special deeds that make up our lives, that can clear the spirit, help us breathe, help move us closer to who we want to be. For some people, the little dream is finally clearing and planting that plot of dirt and then watching buried seed sprout, bud, flower, become crap. For some it's that perfect bowling score, that foreign country finally visited, that letter written and sent and then answered, that moment forgiven. For me, on that cool November Sunday, it was my first journey into the world of sailing. However, truth be told, we never left the bay, and my new dream of a longer voyage will have to wait for another day.

Fourteen

GINNI CALLAHAN

D amn, you're sexy.

Doesn't everyone say that to their boat? I love this boat. I know in my cells the way it moves. I know its every smooth and graceful curve; heck, I made its every smooth and graceful curve.

It's the way the wood bends from vertical at the stern to almost horizontal for the hull in the space of two feet and is still mirror-smooth. Mirror-smooth with this latest coat of varnish. It's hard not to run your hand along it. But don't—it's not dry. See how the scars still show underneath? That's history. It has, gouged and scratched into its very being, memories of our journeys in the Sea of Cortez and an encounter with a particular rock in the Pacific surf. It's the fiberglass that bruises white on impact or when it's ripped by a rock. Epoxy keeps no secrets, but it sure is strong.

There are a few boats in here; let me show you around. See that red Falcon against the wall? That was my high-adventure kayak before this one. That Falcon is a fast, dicey boat. You gotta pay attention to stay topside. My first boat was this thirteen-and-a-half-foot Merlin. I guided my first two Baja seasons in this sweet little thing. That seventeen-foot wooden one I made, too. It's good for tall people and lots of gear. Personally, I'm not crazy about how it handles. I like a small boat, like that sexy fourteen-footer on the varnishing rack.

I just made her last year. She's been to Baja once and already has some tales to tell.

At night when a boat hull slices bioluminescent water, the wake off the bow glows a welding-torch blue and paddle strokes make swirling galaxies. Microscopic animals with a super-sized glow express their body heat in a different dimension: light.

Fourteen's first dip in the Sea of Cortez was a night paddle in Bahía Concepción where I stopped to sleep during my fifth annual drive south. I seemed to recall good bioluminescence created by dinoflagellates (marine plankton) in this bay from a few years ago, so the first thing I did after parking was throw a handful of sand in the water. A trail of stars swooshed across the surface. No choice but to take down the *Fourteen* and see if I could find that island I remembered.

Panicked fish flee from a glowing hull in a variety of ways, all revealed in neon by the dinoflagellates they agitate. Some leap like frogs, leaving rings. Some blaze straight away across the surface. Some zigzag for the depths. In the dark, the fish are invisible, just the light patterns show.

I left a candle lantern burning on the beach so I'd know where to return in the moonless dark. It blazed clear and bright from a half mile out. I found the island, a dark hulk stealing the stars from the horizon and serrated from its underwater base by glowing blue. Invisible birds rustled feathers overhead. Silhouettes of sentinel cardon cactus slid across constellations. Paddling in the Sea of Cortez for the first time each year is always like a long exhale; the air you breathe after that has a different quality.

Being rocked on the ocean feels like belonging. It's both a nurturing embrace and the steel that sharpens your skills. It's easy to fall in love with the boat that takes you there.

🖒　🖒　🖒

I guess she won't dry any faster if we stand here staring at her, and the varnish fumes are probably destroying my last brain cell. Let's go out on the porch. We can watch the tide come in.

One of the most exciting moments in building the *Fourteen* came when I wired the four hull panels together and it began to look like a boat. That moment came so early in the process it was almost cruel because I had no idea how much work lay ahead. I had no idea either how little woodwork is involved in building a stitch-and-glue kayak. It's mostly epoxy work—fiberglassing, filling, sanding, finishing.

Yes, I built it from a kit. I'm a bit defensive about that, but it was my first homebuilt boat and I wanted to ensure success. Quick success. The instructions call for creating a six-foot-long handle and plunger for a little syringe that allows you to fill the seam between the deck and hull from the inside. That extension lets you reach the bow and stem from the cockpit. I did my best with a PVC tube, a dowel, zip ties, wire, and tape, but the tool was far from accurate.

I set the kayak on the floor on its chine so gravity would help the epoxy find the seam. I donned the Darth Vader mask, mixed the epoxy, thickened it with wood flour, poured it into the syringe, and stuck my head into the cockpit, knocking off the clip light and breaking my fourth and last light bulb. You have a matter of minutes to work with thickened epoxy before it sets, so I groped my way into the kayak, felt for the seam, and pressed the dowel. With a flashlight I hastily grabbed out of my truck, I saw that the epoxy glob had completely missed its mark. In desperation, I grabbed a tongue depressor and dove headfirst into the kayak.

It's tight in there. I could reach the glob with one arm outstretched and tiptoes on the cockpit opening. I just couldn't see it because the flashlight was in the other hand. The kayak pressed against my ribs and amplified my heartbeat like a drum. I backed up, memorized what the glob looked like and where it needed to go, and launched into the operation by feel. I thought I got it and was feeling proud of myself when the kayak fell over, cockpit down.

If you'd have walked into the room at that moment, you would have noticed a radio quietly playing to a kayak upside down on the floor, twitching and grunting. People assume a lot of pride goes into building your own boat. Only after the fact.

My longest trip in the *Fourteen*? That would have to be this year's two-week Baja adventure with Matt down the coast from Agua Verde, almost to La Paz, and back.

Let me set the scene for you. Fifty coastal miles south of Loreto, and about seven hundred miles below the United States/Mexico border, Agua Verde is the end of the road. Not the highway, but a dirt turnoff one takes only to get here—an eternal, cliff-edge, stomach-in-your-throat kind of road that descends down the precarious Sierra la Giganta Mountains with nothing but prayers for guardrails.

The mouth of Agua Verde cove is marked by a thirteen-foot, guano-encrusted pinnacle of rock. To the east Punta Marcial juts three miles into the Sea of Cortez before letting the coast fall back to its southerly direction. Viewed from the north, from my guiding territory of five years, Punta Marcial is a dividing line, marking the edge of my knowledge. On clear days, the distant southern islands beckon as hazy silhouettes off a hidden coast.

In the morning, Matt and I load an amazing amount of gear into those two wooden kayaks, promising faithlessly to remember where we put everything. The *Fourteen* handles a lot of gear for a kayak its size, and Matt's seventeen-foot kayak is a packhorse. The tent doesn't fit, which is what I secretly planned. I like stars as my ceiling.

We round Punta Marcial, getting a feel for how the boats handle loaded, and how to trim them better. Home again, in the saddle, feeling the sea alive beneath me. Something inside uncoils, relaxes, slips into place.

There is a peak south of Punta Marcial that looks like Neapolitan ice cream: a chocolate base maybe sixty feet high, then a creamy French vanilla layer, topped with pink strawberry. Up close, the amazing part is the sea cave carved from a fault in the chocolate. The relentless sea worked the fault into a passage, which, at the next tectonic shiver, could slip and slam shut with pyroclastic ice cream.

Giant barnacles and sea fans grow in the triangular entrance to the cave. My pulse quickens as we cautiously paddle in and let the surge lift and lower us. From the darkness ahead comes a crashing *gal-oop!* We proceed. Around one turn my paddle no longer fits without wedging between the sides of the cave, and my fingers make for blind, timid bumpers on the walls and ceiling. The kayaks grind against rock once or twice, and the darkness swallows the beam from my headlamp without giving up any secrets.

We camp on the next beach, Ensenada la Ballena. Whale cove. But we call it Pirate Panga Playa. *Playa* is Spanish for beach. *Pangas* are open motorboats, about twenty feet long, painted white with blue gunwales. All the fishermen use them. This pirate *panga* was burned at the water's edge. Its crime, we discover later from soldiers in green uniforms and face paint patrolling the brown desert waterfront, was running with the *narcotraficantes* and transporting drugs. A lone palm stands guard over its carcass.

After a bean burrito dinner, I walk the beach to digest and gain perspective. To the south, a rugged, fading coastline beckons. Sunset plays light and shadow along it, picking favorites. Back toward camp, the Neapolitan peak dwarfs the palm and two golden kayaks sitting parallel to each other. Between them is an insignificant pile of gear and a diminutive person sitting on a sleeping bag, thoughtfully smoking a pipe. In the vastness the heart clings to such little things.

There's lots of wildlife in the Sea of Cortez: magnificent frigate birds, blue-footed boobies. Fin whales. They're the second biggest animals on the planet, after blue whales. Dolphins every day. Little grebes sport golden "ears" of breeding plumage and peep so quietly you have to stop paddling and hold your breath to hear them. The entire flock dives together, leaving nothing but wrinkled water. For several days the sea is a mirror. Our arms and torsos motor the kayaks past sheer cliffs at least one hundred feet straight up enlivened by giggling swallows. We paddle close in to steal afternoon shade and watch fish. Brilliant parrotfish, turquoise on top with rose bellies.

"Barracuda," Matt warns. I don't believe him. He's prone to dramatization. The more of them he announces, the less I believe they even exist in the Sea of Cortez.

A talented surfer, gifted board-shaper, sailor, commercial fisherman, and boatbuilder from southern California, Matt somehow looks out of place in a kayak. He's a slender 6'2" with a long back; he likes to recline a bit in the seat and motor by bending his elbows. He paddles like the sport is beneath him, which is exactly how he considers it. Torso rotation is for sissies.

But he looks good under his faded-blue wide-brimmed hat. A few days' worth of salty gray stubble on his chin has a rugged appeal. He puffs along on his pipe like he's steam powered.

I am passionate about kayaking; in five years it has become my livelihood. Kayaks are my surfboards of choice, the vehicles of my travel fantasies, they are what I build in between the Sea of Cortez guiding season and the Lower Columbia River instruction season. I find long solo trips deeply satisfying and relationships difficult, although I see the need for the latter every time I haul a loaded kayak onto a challenging beach by myself.

As Matt and I relax on shore in the shade of another cliff, two enterprising fishermen sell us a pair of lobsters. When they motor off, a boatload of soldiers hails them and hassles them for selling seafood without a license. The fishermen buy off the officials with six lobsters.

We have been sharing the coast with these soldiers since day one, when they walked right past us like we were lizards on a rock to go patrol the shrubbery for illegal substances. At each beach, a few more pleasantries are exchanged, until Playa San Mateo.

"Do you know the name of this beach?" I ask. The tall soldier scrutinizes us, suddenly suspicious. Matt and I sit beneath a cliff eating our egg-salad sandwiches, and two soldiers take a break in the shade beside us. The midday desert sun forces unlikely unions, as if Cormac McCarthy were inventing our trip. I try to explain that our maps aren't very good, and we were looking for Playa San Mateo because Matt wanted to see his beach. They lighten up and agree that this must be his beach. Crazy tourists.

They ask about the boats, are they wood?

"*Si*. She made them," Matt says as we all walk to the waterfront. The soldiers' boat approaches.

"*Ella?*" the tall one repeats, looking at me, disbelieving. I nod and smile. I describe the process of tying the wood panels together with wire, gluing it, laying fiberglass cloth over it, and soaking it with epoxy resin.

Where do you put everything, the young man with the family back in mainland Mexico wants to know. And how can they possibly be safe to row?

Matt points out the bulkhead behind the seat and lifts the rear hatch cover off *Fourteen*. I catch a skeptical look from the tall soldier, as if he's wondering where the hidden compartment is. Where are the drugs?

Moving the conversation along, I say, "Paddling isn't bad, once you learn how. The boats are safe. The danger I worry about is from *la gente*." I've heard stories from my Mexican co-workers about drug runners killing people for gas or water on remote islands.

"*No se preocupe*," the family man assures me as he stands a little taller. We are protecting you.

What he couldn't fathom, though, was that we would do this for fun.

Some days further down the coast I give my favorite minnow lure a tour of the Sea of Cortez, having pushed the morning's paddle well past noon in search of lunch. Matt leads the way to a sandy landing, but I, in my tired stubbornness, do not want to follow with an empty hook. Slowly I drift in to the beach behind Matt when the line goes taut. The fish council has elected to send a sand bass to improve our menu and my attitude. It makes four lovely fish tacos.

A family walks by as we eat. That could seem strange here, miles from any road, but they seem to belong. It's a Mexican couple in their thirties. He carries a three-pronged spear and is wet to the thigh from hunting lobsters. She lugs a burlap bag of his success. Of the four kids, two wear life jackets like tuxes with tails that are oversized. The coyote-like dog wants to taste a taco, but the man hisses at her—*psssht!*—and she slinks away.

Los Dolores, a mile south of where we lunch, is a place poignant in its vastness. Mountains flank a wide valley and tease the sun with bold palisades. Palm groves line the sandy beach. Something in the heart responds by opening. We land here, knowing it's the last reliable pull-out for a while, and the last place to get water before San Evaristo, twenty miles south. It's our fifth day. Camp routine is comfortable and the sight of matching kayaks on the beach is familiar like your front door.

There is a large concrete house in the valley surrounded by a fence of wire and crooked mesquite posts. The house is obviously used, though nobody's home when we visit with empty water bags in hand. We return the next morning and recognize the family, back from their lobster hunt and now shooing cows into a pen.

Lucio, his wife Loreto, and their kids are the only people in Los Dolores. She's from the next fishing village up, he's from the next one down, and this house was abandoned when its owner died, so they moved in. That was twelve years ago. There are the ruins of a mission up the valley and a good well nearby. It's nice to know such fairy tales exist, and even nicer to know this one is only accessible by boat or foot.

We launch early the next day with full water bags and a round of cheese from the family's cows. An orange horizon blooms into day as we push off. To take advantage of a building tailwind, we skip from point to point past a zone of neck-craning cliffs. On a wide open section, my lucky lure's leisure cruise of the Sea of Cortez is curtailed by something big and hungry. The line *zizzes* out, then stops. I reel in. No lure, no leader, no nothing. No more trolling for today. "Shark," says Matt.

The waves are making him nervous. They are building to exciting proportions, demanding actual attention be paid to paddling. In these conditions the kayak comes alive. It takes on a personality. Sometimes playful, sometimes unruly, depending partly on the design of the boat, and partly on the mood of the paddler.

Fourteen is frolicking. She surfs down little three-foot wave faces, taking a few at an angle to the east, then a few back to the west. I want to whoop and catch all the rides I can, but Matt isn't happy. The seventeen-foot packhorse is being unruly. It refuses to keep true to a heading like a respectable boat. Somehow we manage to land together at San Evaristo, nearly twenty miles downwind.

From the San Evaristo beach the next day, Matt hails a couple rowing out in a funky dinghy. He wants to know if their forty-foot cat-ketch is homebuilt. Sure enough. No doubt he wishes he could trade right now—boats, partners, it doesn't matter. The French couple designed their boat after sailing for a few years and not finding anything that met their needs. Matt and Gerard discuss construction methods and designs while Corine and I swap fish stories. One time off Spain, she says, something really big cleaned off not just their leader and lure, but the line, rod, rod holder, and base mount. Now they wrap a line around the winch to fish.

Matt has tried to lure me into sailing, but I've been reluctant. I find the pace of human-powered travel agrees with me. The pace. The exercise. The simplicity. The intimacy with the coastline that kayaking necessitates. Besides, doing something different would mean change, and change is scary.

Eventually, we paddle out to Isla San Jose, and I fish through sunset. Dolphins leap and lunge after their dinner. Off the sandy spit with the lighthouse, two fin whales operate giant bellows. Refraction paints atmospheric particles salmon and turquoise, as predictable as science, as fluid as music. I paddle *Fourteen* in ever-hopeful circles. A twelve-inch leopard cabrilla takes my lure and I take him for dinner.

A *Norte* is the notorious Sea of Cortez weather pattern to watch out for in the months between November and early March. Usually a hard three-day north blow, sometimes longer, I've seen it turn a beach into a river of blowing sand and whip foam off the wave tops. The morning we want to cross back from Isla San Jose, we both sense a *Norte*. They're hard to predict and even harder to explain how one senses their approach. The waves just seem nervous. We set our paddles to full steam ahead and bounce our way northwest to the peninsula.

Paddling a long crossing, Matt once commented on the similarities between sanding and long crossings. You're scratching away forever with no visible progress, then suddenly you notice a change. Bit by bit you get there. I think, too, that there's hidden technique and skill to both. Gracefully done, someone would never know all that went into it.

The glassy waters of the previous week are gone, and we paddle an uphill treadmill for a few days. The slog inspires us to siesta on a steep cobble beach south of the fishing village Timbabichi and sun ourselves. It's one of those landings that makes relationships worthwhile as we stagger over ball bearing–like rocks to a ledge where the boats won't slide back into the water. It's one of those afternoons made for being lazy.

There's an international convention of surf-worn rocks at the water's edge. Representatives of all shapes, textures, and colors attend. Some are flecked or marbled with their own mysterious history. A study of all the cobbles on this small beach would take years. Assessing their lineage would take . . . well, I don't know what it would take, but it would be interesting. No two are even the same color. I want to take them all home. Matt says I need a bigger boat. And where is home anyway?

Asked of an itinerant kayak guide, it's a good question. Home is where you like the rocks.

To feed oneself from the sea almost becomes a compulsion on the two-week trip. After the third day, I fish every day and for several days catch nothing. Sometimes I accept this gracefully and give up before dark.

It's near the end of the trip; the sun is getting low. Just one pass around Punta San Telmo, I promise. The krokadile fishing lure wiggles enticingly behind me in the current, past the shallow rocks that make standing waves. I circle back, torn between keeping my word and taking one more pass, when the line comes to life. A short, intense struggle leaves me drifting toward the rocks with my paddle pressed against my belly, the rod falling overboard, and a Mexican barracuda flopping on my spray deck. In a kayak you can't just toss a fish in the cooler and motor away. If you remove the hook first, the fish is liable to flop overboard on the final hook-freeing tug, so I always secure it on the stringer before removing the hook. After getting out of the current.

I hold the fish down with one hand and paddle with the other, paddle shaft tucked under my arm. The barracuda rubs its white scales off on my black spray deck with its thrashing. Matt was right: there are barracuda in the Sea of Cortez. I see that now. Feeding the stringer through that angry mouth requires the combined skills of a surgeon and a lion tamer. The metal tip is not long enough to pass from the mouth out the gills without sticking my fingers in the mouth, which seems unwise on account of the profusion of pointy teeth. So I open the gills, reach in the back, and pull the stringer the rest of the way through.

The hook is deep, and all three points are embedded. I'm thankful for my ninety-nine cent hook-removal tool, but I'm still not fast enough. By the time I remove the hooks, the fish is dead and I have no choice but to keep it.

I remember Matt saying he didn't like barracuda, so I try meat-fishing for his dinner. I gut the barracuda on my deck—guts and blood christening the wood, chumming the waters. I cut chunks of meat from just behind its head, string them on a gangion of hooks, and bounce them toward the beach. A four-pound bullseye puffer, a stubborn box of a fish, puts up a better fight than the barracuda, but it's deadly to eat unless you've brought along a specially trained fugu chef, and even then the odds are not convincingly in your favor. I decide not to feed it to Matt.

All told, we covered only 120 miles in thirteen days, but the days were full of living. Existing at a simple level—eat, travel, observe—one loses the protective busyness. Out here one lives and moves viscerally, seamlessly. On the final morning, I found the thought of returning to civilization unbearable. I wanted to hide, just me and my kayak, and whoever wanted to paddle out for a visit. I mean, I actually buried myself in the sleeping bag and cried. Matt had to dig me out and usher me back into the insanity commonly perceived as everyday life.

So here we are; she's almost ready. Let me pull the masking tape off. The tape ensures a clean line where the deck and hull meet. No drips.

That big scar on the hull is a souvenir from a training course off Washington State's Olympic Peninsula. We were practicing rescues in the turbulent zone around offshore rocks. The moment our water dummy went over, I took my attention off my immediate surroundings and a swell lifted me up, carried me over to a sharp rock, and set me down on it, where I teetered and slipped, trying to think light thoughts, until the next swell relieved me of the perch and I could go help with the rescue. That gash penetrated the wood, but she's all better now.

With this last coat of varnish my sexy little *Fourteen* is ready for another season in Baja. So am I.

Happy Jack and the *Vis* Queens

JENNIFER KARUZA SCHILE

Mom tiptoed over to my bed and quietly shook me awake, then went to wake my sisters, Cassandra and Stephanie. Although I'd been sound asleep, I woke easily. A nervous twitching filled my stomach, and my heart raced.

It was time.

In silence, we pulled on our sweat pants, sweat shirts, tennis shoes, and bulky winter coats. We crept out the front door into the frosty early March morning and slid into our red Subaru station wagon.

I placed my hands inside my coat pockets and stared out the window as we pulled out of our driveway, turning right on Meridian Street and left onto Squalicum Parkway. It was a three-minute drive we routinely made, but this time was different. It felt deliciously strange to be awake and driving at one in the morning.

We parked at Bellingham's Squalicum Harbor boat launch. We got out and stood shivering in the cold, waiting.

"Ooooh. They're coming," Mom whispered excitedly. The procession had started. Dad inched down Roeder Avenue in his black, three-quarter-ton Ford truck. Trailing behind him, with yellow revolving lights on top of the cab, crawled a green army-style truck, slowed by the cargo it towed—the weight of thirty years' hard labor, the weight of one man's dream. A fifty-eight-foot, eighty-four-ton dream made of steel.

We were here to celebrate the conception, birth, and launch of our newest family fishing boat, the *Vis* (rhymes with "peace" and named after the Croatian island that our family, and many other Bellingham-based fishing families, hailed from a generation earlier). Dad had hired a local maritime welder to build the boat he'd been researching and drawing for years; it had taken two years to build and cost just under one million dollars. And now Dad's reward for decades of time spent away from home, chasing elusive fish in Alaska waters, lumbered toward us. It crept along tortoise-like to the launching pad.

The only sound was the rumble of diesel engines as our eyes locked on the boat, which stood over twenty feet high. It seemed like twenty stories, towering over us as it approached.

The procession came to a stop. The green vessel rested proudly on her trailer, commanding respect and reverence from her loyal subjects. She got it. All of us—crew, builders, family—circled around her in the dark and stared up at the magnificent sight.

It was time to christen the *Vis*, a combination vessel that would fish several different fisheries all over Alaska, by smashing a champagne bottle or two against the sharp edge of her bow. My mother, who's not quite 5'2" and yet holds court as the steadfast matriarch of our fishing family, clasped her little hand around the neck of the first bottle and, swinging hard, crashed it against the hull. Glass and liquid flew in all directions, accompanied by cheers and clapping. It looked like fun, destroying a bottle like that. I wanted to try.

I took the second bottle and gave it a good swing. Nothing. The bottle was heavier than I'd expected, too heavy to break against the steel with my self-conscious and tentative fifteen-year-old-girl swing. No matter. I looked over to Dad.

Dad laughed as he came over and grasped the bottle. He gave it a swift, strong swing, slamming it against the bow. It splintered into thousands of pieces and the spray splashed us both.

🦌   🦌   🦌

A month later, we gathered at the harbor to send the *Vis* off on her maiden voyage to Alaska for the longline halibut and black cod fishery. There wasn't another boat like her anywhere, and she seemed to know it as she bobbed against the dock, sitting tall and mighty. She seemed to know how massive she was, how beautiful, how loved by her family. We waited giddily as the crew untied the lines holding her to the dock. The stout boat moved slowly away from the dock and, as if on promenade, glided toward the breakwater. Just before the boat disappeared around the corner and into Puget Sound, Dad leaned outside the wheelhouse door and blasted the foghorn. We laughed and gave wild, two-handed waves.

❧   ❧   ❧

Two years later, I graduated from high school.

"I won't write you a blank check for college," Dad had informed me early in my senior year, "but you can have a spot as deckhand on the *Vis* and pay for it yourself."

So, June 1992, I joined Cassandra, also working her way through college, on the back deck of the *Vis*. A few years later, Stephanie joined us. My sisters and I had grown up as daughters, granddaughters, great-granddaughters, nieces, cousins, and friends of fishermen. We became the fifth generation of fishermen in our family.

We hauled web, piled corks, coiled lines, and sorted salmon in Southeast Alaska as part of the *Vis* crew. We worked twenty-hour days and flopped into our bunks exhausted at night. In a purse seine fleet made up of mostly men, we were a novelty. The fleet dubbed us the *Vis* Queens: three sisters who "worked the pile," with their blonde hair braided and tucked underneath fluorescent pink baseball hats. Dad was known as Happy Jack. He had a brand new vessel and his three daughters fishing with him in the summer. The rest of the year, he had a solid crew of men for the halibut, black cod, and crab seasons.

I was the "leads and web gal." I worked in the stern under the power block, separating the leads from the web as the 250-fathom purse seine net was hauled on board. I worked two-day fishing openings that began at 3:00 A.M. the first day and went until 8:00 P.M. the second day. I worked the cold and rainy days, the sunny and warm days, and I worked the days when the ocean swell was so rough I clung to the web I was trying to pile, got swung around the stern, and slammed against the bulwarks.

I stood in the middle of 130,000-pound deckloads and posed for pictures, smiling wide as I held up prized sockeye, already contemplating how I'd spend the $2,500 I'd made in two days alone. I began researching the best way of dressing to avoid the biting, painful sting of the blood-red jellyfish that plopped down directly on my head as they rolled through the block.

Each year on our way up the Inside Passage, Dad called my sisters and me to the tophouse, where we'd have our annual lesson on chart and barometer reading, longitude and latitude, radars and radios. We were expected to know how to take a wheel watch and understand the markings on a chart, know when to pass a boat and when to get out of the way.

We drew straws for each two-hour watch. The ideal watches, while on an opening, were the first and last shifts. The worst was the watch in the middle. The unfortunate crew member who drew that straw would sleep in his bunk for two hours, get up and take a two-hour watch in the middle of the night, then go back to his bunk for two hours before waking up at 3:00 A.M. to go fishing.

I regularly drew the short straw and got the middle watch. If this was the case, Tim would take the first watch and I would follow him. Tim, a sandy-blonde haired former athlete and family friend, was a career fisherman three years older than me. He ran the skiff for Dad during the salmon season and also longlined on the *Vis* for halibut and black cod. Tim worked on the boat nearly eight months a year and, next to Dad, knew the *Vis* better than anyone. He was also a very patient person. He could explain things. Things I needed to understand, like which direction we were going, and obstacles—other boats, the shoreline, rocks—I should stay away from.

"The tide's pulling us over this way," he'd say, gesturing. "You'll need to keep a watch on this point," he'd instruct, pointing to a blob of green mass on the radar. "Don't get too far away from that spot."

"Piece of cake," he'd say, smiling, perceiving the terror on my face. Being put in charge of an expensive boat, being responsible for the safety of my crew and family, not to mention other boats making their way, was nerve wracking. "Come get me or Cassandra if you have any trouble," he'd say before disappearing down the wheelhouse stairs and into his bunk.

To calm myself, I listened to music from the only tape on board, which we called the "wheel-watch tape." Our wheelhouse CD player had never quite worked. The tape was somebody's home-made recording of a local oldies station back home. I passed the time doing calf raises to "Green-Eyed Lady," and smoking ciga-rettes just outside the wheelhouse door to the tune of "Little Red Riding Hood."

"You're up!" I'd call gleefully to Cassandra, two hours later. She'd glare at me from her bunk. If Tim took the watch before me, Cassandra usually took the watch after me. I think it was so she could get us back on course.

"Here's where we are," I explained, pointing to the blob of green on the radar. I mimicked Tim's explanation of the location of rocks, other boats, and the shoreline. "Bye!" I'd shout on my way back down the stairs, racing for my bunk.

I loved my bunk and I went there often to lie down and relax. It was the one place on the *Vis* I could go to gather my thoughts and enjoy some peace away from the constant rumble of engines. I day-dreamed, planned my future, and fell asleep to the music I played in my Discman—Natalie Merchant, Indigo Girls, Anne Murray—and read books until Cassandra or Steph hollered at me to turn off my bunk light.

I slept in the starboard bunk closest to the floor for the first five years. I chose it because when it got rough and the boat rocked and rolled, rising with wave crests and crashing down into valleys, the low bunk didn't feel the impact as much. I slept there for five years until Cassandra's boyfriend, Danny, came on board and swiped it from me. That year, Cassandra chose the low port side bunk across from him. They plugged two sets of headphones into his Discman and fell asleep to David Grisman each night.

The only time we sat down to eat a meal while fishing was after the last set of the second day had been hauled aboard. After the fish had been pushed into the hatch and the deck was rinsed, we'd sit down to eat the dinner Cassandra, as cook, had prepared. After dinner, it was time to clean the boat.

Steph and I would stow away the ketchup, butter, salt, pepper, bread. She'd set the pan of roast beef on the galley counter for me to package up as a leftover, and she'd hand me a pot of yellow corn that I'd take outside and toss overboard. Out from under the sink came the bottle of 409 and a couple rolls of paper towels. Steph squirted the green galley table and matching green vinyl cushions, and I tackled the galley counter until there was not a speck of anything, anywhere.

We doused the white cupboards, white drawers, white walls, and the white refrigerator. Gone was the black soot from the stack that always seemed to creep inside. Gone were the dried red jellyfish bits stuck to walls and cupboard doors that we inadvertently tracked inside on quick dashes to the bathroom or for a snack.

Our job took about two hours. When we finished, we peeled off our gloves, threw the blackened paper towels into the garbage, yanked off our boots and stored them away underneath the galley step, jumped into the galley booth, looked at Cassandra, and laughed.

We laughed because our cleaning was done and hers wasn't. We laughed because she wore blue, elbow-length rubber gloves. We laughed because of the mop and sponges she held, and because of the sickened expression on her face. We laughed because it was her job to clean the shitter.

Cassandra had the horrible job of peeling long hair off the bathroom walls and scraping pubic hairs out from under the shower grate. She had to scrub a stained toilet bowl where the guys' aim had gone astray.

Sometimes, Steph and I would complain.

"We have to clean the *entire galley*," we'd cry. "It takes us forever. Cassandra only has to do one job."

Cassandra froze there in her stinky wool socks, black sweats, and the dirty black baseball cap she wore to hold her curly hair back. Her rubber-gloved hands clenched the mop handle in a sort of death grip.

"Do *you* want to clean the shitter?" she'd ask.

Steph and I looked at each other, then back at her, and laughed.

After the floors had been swept and mopped and the carpet vacuumed, we were done. We popped a big bowl of buttery popcorn, filled a small plastic bowl with peanut M&M's, and hauled out the Tillamook Rocky Road ice cream. We handed it all up to the tophouse, then one by one, climbed up the stairs to the wheelhouse and Dad.

"All done down there?" he'd ask as he navigated the boat toward town, still a good three hours away.

With the *Vis* polished and shined, ready for our visitors in town, we flopped into the entertainment area of the wheelhouse and turned on a movie.

The *Vis* was built to accommodate and encourage social activity among crew and guests. Instead of building a separate captain's quarters in the wheelhouse, Dad put his stateroom on the main level. He left the tophouse spacious enough for movie watching and general congregating. Our galley was three times the size of a normal purse seine galley, and our back deck was double the size of most.

"This isn't a galley, this is a *kitchen*," exclaimed our friend Ken. Another friend, Ed, stood outside and said, "You could play basketball on this deck!"

While tied up in Ketchikan's Bar Harbor, the *Vis* was full of young men dropping by at all hours to see what the *Vis* Queens were up to and which bar we'd be frequenting that night. Little John from the *Favorite* would come aboard with a pizza from the Harbor Lights restaurant, sit down at our galley table and invite us to dig in.

We'd wake up on the *Vis* in the morning to find Joel from the *Nikki Lee* already at our galley table. He'd have walked to Carr's supermarket for coffee and the *Ketchikan Daily*, then walked back to our boat, and let himself in. We'd stumble out of our bunks, groggy and grubby from the two previous days of fishing, and stare as he sipped his coffee and read his paper. "Good morning!" he'd call cheerfully. "Door was open!"

One morning, Dad woke me up.

"Where's your sister?" he asked sternly.

"I don't know," I said. I'd last seen her at the First City Saloon the night before. Apparently, she had not returned to the boat.

Dad walked up the dock ramp to the pay phone and placed calls to the police station and the hospital. I had orders to knock on the door of every boat in the harbor.

"Have you seen my sister?" I asked Ken on the *Chinook*, John on the *Favorite*, and Troy on the *Resolute*.

Nobody had seen her.

Cassandra came prancing up the ladder about mid-morning. She bounded over the railing and practically hopped across the deck to the galley door. A battle of wills ensued.

"But I'm twenty-three years old," she wailed. "Tim's stayed out all night before. What's the difference?"

Dad quickly pointed out the difference. "You are a girl in Alaska," he said. "Tim is a guy; it's different. You're my daughter. I worry."

We found out later she'd spent the entire night dancing, eating, and playing with some guy she'd met. Some guy named Danny. A guy who, less than two years later, would become her husband.

Cassandra spent the rest of the summer with Danny, a twenty-five-year-old crewmember on the *Nikki Lee*. He had brown eyes that sparkled with mischief, an impish smile, and a boisterous spirit. He was a professional rock climber who also made a living as a fisherman.

In town, Steph and I would pass Cass and Danny on the street. We'd be rushing to McDonalds, and they'd be headed back to Bar Harbor. They'd walk hand in hand, laughing, almost skipping down the road.

"Hi!" they'd call as we passed.

"Hi!" we'd call back.

They ambled on, lost in their own world of new love and possibility. Steph and I looked at each other with a look only a sister could behold—one of disgust, judgment, and skepticism.

"Pathetic," we'd agree.

Cassandra and Danny pranced and danced through the rest of that summer, and Danny bought me a beer on my twenty-first birthday that August. The next year, he'd be our new cork piler on the back deck of the *Vis*.

%   %   %

After they married in October 1996, Danny left on the *Vis* to fish the winter tanner-crab season in Southeast Alaska. Cassandra was the only one who made it down to the harbor to wait and wave as the boat left with Danny, Dad, and Uncle Mark.

I wish I'd made the effort.

Danny's wrist would get caught in a loop of fishing line as he pushed a crab pot overboard. As the 350-pound crab pot sank toward the bottom of the ocean, the line would tighten against his wrist. As he stumbled along the entire length of the boat, Danny would struggle to loosen the line. His efforts would fail, and he would finally be pulled back to the stern where he'd flip over the end of the boat and into the bone-chilling Alaska seas.

Although they would stop the boat immediately and rush to haul up the line that held the crab pot and Danny, only the crab pot would come back aboard. Danny would vanish beneath the dark green surface of Excursion Inlet. The last and only sign of Danny would be his black Vis Seafoods baseball cap, which floated to the surface.

Escorted by an old family friend, my devastated father flew home the night after the accident. Upon arriving in Bellingham, he was taken immediately to the hospital and met by a crisis team that attempted, unsuccessfully, to treat my inconsolable father for shock and trauma. I sat in a chair at home and watched out the dining room window, waiting for Mom's car to pull up with Dad inside.

I was not prepared for what I saw. My youthful, independent father—Happy Jack—had been transformed into a man I didn't recognize. Overwhelming grief had turned his hair white and rendered him unable to walk. I ran outside. He shuffled across the lawn to our front door, supported heavily by my mother and me. Once inside, I realized he could not speak, either. He sat in a chair and cried.

৯   ৯   ৯

The *Vis* came back to Bellingham from Alaska a few days later, brought home by some of the longline crew who'd flown up to retrieve her. A small group of us shuffled with stooped shoulders down the dock with Cassandra, headed toward our boat. We were here to collect Danny's things. We found his sleeping bag still unrolled on his bunk, as if he'd just hopped out. We stared at his Winnie-the-Pooh pillowcase, where he'd last laid his head. We fixated on the way his knit hat and purple fleece coat spilled out of the duffle bag that Cassandra had helped him pack two months earlier.

My sister knelt at his bunk and sobbed. I walked out to the back deck and lit a cigarette. My heart ached and my throat was so tight it hurt. I stood in the middle of the deck, where six months ago I'd made faces at Danny, trying to make him laugh as I worked across from him. I envisioned, over and over, the accident. How I imagined it happened. *Danny,* I thought. *Dad.*

৯   ৯   ৯

A month later, in March, the *Vis* left Squalicum Harbor on a cheerless and dreary day, bound for another halibut season in Alaska. For the first time, not one member of my immediate family was leaving with her. My sisters and I huddled near Mom, but Dad stood alone, gray and stone faced. The *Vis* pulled away with—instead of us—an eight-foot-tall, steel cross tied to her tophouse. The longline crew—Dave, Tim, Uncle Mark, Mike, Bill, Steve—were going back to Excursion

Inlet, to cement the cross into the shoreline near where Danny had drowned. We'd given them trinkets of Danny's favorite things—a golf ball, golf tee, a can of 7-Up—to cement in at the base of the cross. I wrote Danny a letter, which I asked Dave to tie to a rock and toss overboard.

That day, the *Vis* made a somber cruise out of the harbor. I watched her hulking mass glide sadly around the breakwater to silence instead of the usual cheers and waves. No foghorn blasted. I looked at Dad, hunched over under the weight of grief and shattered dreams of boats and sons.

We never fished on the boat again. Dad refused to step one foot on her deck. He said he didn't care. He said he was done. The longline crew pulled together, with Dave as skipper, and kept the boat running for the next six years. They took care of her mechanics and did the maintenance. Tim took her seining. Dad hired a skipper for the crab season. I went down to the docks with Dad a couple of times to send Tim off on the salmon season. We stood apart from a crowd of family and friends we didn't know. They didn't know who we were. They wondered aloud why we named the boat *"Vis,"* and mispronounced her name. Dad and I got into our separate cars and drove off in separate directions long before the *Vis* got around the breakwater.

It was difficult to accept the manner in which five generations of fishing had come to an end. I tried to forget the *Vis*. I moved out of state, returning home only for brief visits. On one of those trips home, I brought George with me. George, my new boyfriend, was a Bering Sea fisherman and the proud co-owner of a brand new, fifty-eight-foot steel longliner. I'd told him all about my own beautiful fifty-eight-foot vessel. I wanted him to see her.

We drove with Mom and Dad to the dock, where George and I got out. Dad stayed in the car with Mom. I clamored down the ladder to the boat, excited.

My excitement was short-lived. The sparkling white linoleum galley floor I remembered was now black with grime. There was a crack in it. The green vinyl seat cushions were torn and hastily patched. The head was filthy and it reeked. I went upstairs. The tophouse carpet was trashed. The cushions in the entertainment area were stained. Yellow foam spilled out of a bad gash in Dad's captain's chair.

I climbed, defeated, back down the tophouse stairs and up to the car. I sat and tried not to cry.

"It's bad, isn't it," Dad said. It wasn't a question, but a statement he waited confirmation on. I nodded.

George reappeared a few moments later. He didn't seem impressed. I attempted to tell stories of our glory days, the same stories he'd heard before. This time, my stories fell flat. I stopped talking.

"Well," said George, trying to make it better. "The *Vis* is a good work boat, and she's been working for ten years straight. There's going to be some wear and tear after a decade."

He didn't help, and I didn't want his pity. He had a shiny, brand-new boat. We did not. Not anymore. What we did have was a boat in need of cosmetic repair, in need of her captain. But her captain didn't want her.

I wasn't surprised when Dad announced shortly after that visit he was selling the *Vis*. I'd already given up hope and resigned myself to the fact that it was over. There was nothing I could do.

A year later, the boat was still on the market. Times were, and continue to be, tough in the commercial fishing industry, and nobody had $2.5 million for a boat and her gear. I saw the ad for our boat in commercial fishing magazines, including the magazine I wrote for. Vis *for Sale*. It began to sicken and anger me. We have to do something, I decided. I had to do something. I had to find a solution.

I asked George if he would take over the *Vis*.

"I wish I could," he said. "Believe me, I would if I could." He already had a new boat. He was a Dutch Harbor fisherman, not a Southeast Alaska fisherman. He had partners he couldn't abandon. I bypassed George and appealed to his mentor and partner, Nick. One of Nick's other boats had recently sunk in Alaska and I figured he was in the market for a solid, seaworthy boat.

"I wish I could," he said. "It's just more boat than I need."

I prodded and schemed for a year. Finally, our ebb tide began to flood. And it was more rapid than I ever imagined.

Dad went fishing with George, on George's boat, in Alaska for a month in the spring of 2001. George told Dad he was planning to propose marriage to me. Dad told George he ran a tight ship. He liked George's fishing style and work ethic. Dad was a captain, George was a captain. Dad liked what he saw.

In April, George proposed. In May, we sat in my parents' family room. George and I had discussed the *Vis* at length and decided it was time to take her on. George was tired of partners and co-owners.

He wanted to fish on his own terms. We talked about how we'd approach Dad with our plan for the *Vis*.

All of our rehearsed speeches flew out the window. I had no time for formalities.

"Dad," I said from the couch, "can we take the *Vis*?"

Dad's face got flushed. His eyes sparkled. His mouth and cheeks stretched into the beginnings of a smile, like he was holding back laughter and relief. The more he tried to stay calm and composed, the redder his face became. Mom's cheeks also turned pink, and her eyes expressed the same mix of joy and relief as Dad's. We had our answer.

Dad began restoring and repairing the *Vis* that summer. Riding on the wings of rediscovered energy and hope, lost seven years previous, he went to Squalicum Harbor each day. He had the galley cushions replaced. He put new carpet in the wheelhouse and bought new linoleum for the galley floor. He added new electronics, worked on the refrigeration, and had the entire boat repainted. He repaired the gash in the captain's chair.

George and I got to work on the *Vis* in October 2002, after returning from our honeymoon. We began by sending in the paperwork for our new corporation, Fifth Generation Fisheries, Inc. We set up shop temporarily in Tim's covered shed amidst thousands of buoys and six hundred crab pots. Dad joined us and we painted the buoys a bright, fluorescent yellow. We worked day and night, in freezing winter wind and rain. George's crew hauled, pounded, drilled, and rigged the crab pots for the Washington Dungeness crab season.

Dad decided to make the November voyage to Westport with George on the *Vis*. A month later, he'd make the first crab trip with them. At the end of that trip, he'd go out again, "just to make one more."

I drove to the sawtooth dock at Squalicum Harbor the morning they left. The weather was warm for early winter and the sun beamed for the first time in weeks. George stood at the wheel while Dad untied the bowline. George's crew grabbed the spring and stern lines. The *Vis* pulled away from the dock, hundreds of crab pots stacked on her deck.

She made a slow, tentative push away from the dock and out toward the breakwater. Once there, she lingered for a while, turning neither left nor right. She idled. I stood at the end of the dock and heard an engine's rumble behind me. It was Tim. He pulled up next to me, his new baby girl, Megan, giggling in the back. Out on the breakwater, the *Vis* continued to loiter. We watched.

Finally, she made up her mind. She turned sharply to the right and blew a decisive puff of black smoke out of her stack. She steamed out of the harbor into Puget Sound, sparkling under that unexpected December sun.

Mediterranean Mooring

TANIA AEBI

My first visit to Greece was an unplanned pit stop, which has taken on special significance in my memory as the first taste of a country that has since become very dear to me. It was July 1987, and I was alone on my sailboat, as I had been for two years already, motoring from the Suez Canal to Malta on a windless Mediterranean Sea and burning up fuel like an SUV. By the time the fuel-gauge needle neared the empty mark, the southern coast of Crete wasn't far off and my small-scale Mediterranean chart showed a little cleft marked by the name "Loutra," just east of the sizable town of Palaiokhora. It seemed like a clear shot with plenty of deep water all around. Sure enough, on the approach, there were no navigational surprises and Loutra ended up being the quaintest cluster of buildings nestled at the foot of some pretty steep Cretan real estate. After a week at sea, I anchored in the light-blue water near a beach covered with young sunbathers and looked around. Umbrellas advertising different brands of *ouzo* shaded the tables in front of *tavernas* and rooming houses teeming with bodies, and the smell of mingled suntan lotions wafted over to me along with the sound of voices at play—summer in Greece.

Having just emerged from more sober and far-flung lands east of the Suez Canal, I inflated the dinghy and threw in the diesel jerry cans, eager to do some European-people-on-vacation watching. I wasn't disappointed. Settling in at a weather-worn, bleached out, and salty table, I watched the latest fastidiously maintained fashions parade by, and ordered up a plate of sautéed string beans to satisfy a craving for fresh vegetables. The innkeeper was very chatty, curious about where such a scruffy creature had come from and where I was going, which quickly led to the fuel question. As it turned out, Loutra's main attraction was that it was only accessible by ferry. No roads led to the cove, therefore, no cars —a romantic ideal for tourists, but absurdly inconvenient for me. No cars meant no fuel, and after a brief respite in this oasis, I motored over to Palaiokhora and filled up there before pointing the bow to Malta.

The two-day Cretan sojourn is a blip on the screen of memories from my circumnavigation, a reintroduction to a world completely different from the Middle East and Asia I had just left in my wake. Eight years went by before Greece came back onto my radar, and stayed there; I was land-bound in the U.S. and got a job working with a sailing school that organized overseas trips. Greece was the school's most popular destination, as it has been with many people for as long as tourism and travel have existed, and after skippering a week-long cruise of the Saronic Islands, I was hooked.

Stepping off the airplane from New York to Athens for the first time was just the beginning of my adventure as a throng of smokers yelled back and forth and hugged each other, surrounding me in a cacophony of sound, smell, and energy. Ever since, the contrasts between beauty and ugliness, frivolity and austerity, and the high passions and fierce love of life that is Greece have added connections and substance to my own world. Its own nautical history is a richly relevant background for some of the yarns I can tell about sailing and how I have learned the skills of my skippering trade. Greece is home to my greatest tactical accomplishment— mastery of the Mediterranean mooring—as well as my most miserable failure—an unfortunate encounter with a rock. With every trip, the pile of memories has grown, but these two incidents stand apart as milestones in my career, the stories I tell the most often.

I love Mediterranean moorings now, but this wasn't always the case. In 1995, with my first boat full of clients, I eyed my first mooring on the island of Hydra like a sky-diver faces a first jump. It was ridiculous. I had already sailed around the world single-handedly, weathering storms, navigational problems, mechanical failures, and knockdowns. I had written a book about it and traveled around the country giving lectures and advice to potential sailors. I had even given birth naturally to two large boys, and yet, to drop an anchor, pay out rode and squeeze in between other docked boats, all at the mercy of the entirely fickle response of a keel boat under reverse power, was a feat of unimaginable difficulty to me. It was a maneuver only the most skilled pilot could attempt. I knew how easily stanchions and pulpits bend, how fragile two colliding hunks of fiberglass can be, and as we passed Hydra's breakwater and took in the sight, nothing in the pilot book could have prepared me for this minuscule harbor, and no amount of deep breathing could steady my nerves.

Under different circumstances, Hydra's harbor would have been beautiful to behold. Donkeys and mules are the only form of transportation on the island, and the loaded beasts of burden lined the cobble-stone quay framed by colorful stone buildings, tiled roofs, bougainvillea, and striped *taverna* awnings. Hills towered above the diminutive village as we entered a small basin—a square of sorts—chock-full of boats. The entrance side is reserved for ferries and hydrofoils, and one of them was holding its length along the quay, the wash from its engines churning the water around us into something resembling a whitewater rapid. Across from the ferries, a cluster of local fishing boats was crammed off a shallow-water quay. Perpendicular to these two quays were the sides of the square reserved for pleasure craft. On one side, boats were backed stern-to against the inside wall of the jetty. On the opposite side, they were backed to the waterfront with sterns facing the storefronts and *tavernas*.

In neutral, we bobbed on the ferry wash while I had to make a difficult decision: Where do we dock? There was one small opening on the jetty side and, judging from the yelling coming from that direction, this was the spot for us. Okay, I thought, all we have to do is get the boat into a position directly ahead of our slot, drop the anchor, and back up. Simple, except I knew that keel boats never back up easily. I signaled, the anchor was released, and as I put the engine into reverse, the stern yawed in the opposite direction from where the wheel was telling it to go. Then it came back again, too far, and went over to the opposite side. Swinging wildly, the forty-five-foot-long boat heaved her big bottom back into the general vicinity of the spot we were aiming for, until we were close enough to throw the lines and get warped in and secured by helping hands on the other boats. *Oof.* My first Mediterranean mooring. I didn't feel proud, but at least it had been only mildly embarrassing; we didn't foul any other anchor lines, the boats next to us remained unblemished, and we were safe, for now. The next harbor and docking belonged to another day.

We still had a week of harbor hopping to go, and I knew that unless I had some great epiphany, it was just a matter of time before we became the center of some very undesired attention. Salvation came that very evening from a Greek captain named Nick who was working on another boat from the charter company we were using. I had watched his seamless docking and how he had then helped many other boats, knowing just what to tell the helmsmen to do, and when to do what, without hollering too loudly.

I had long ago learned how to ask for advice when it was needed, so I will always remember and be able to use the lesson I got in broken English from Nick on the dockside. With a cigarette clenched between stained teeth, he slid matchboxes, lighters, and cigarette packs around on a *taverna* tabletop to illustrate the steps of a Mediterranean mooring until I thought I understood.

The next day, on the island of Spetsai, in the even tinier harbor of Palaio Limani, I placed the bow of the boat in a line directly ahead of the spot we wanted. Obeying and visualizing Nick's instructions about propeller effect, thrust, and speed, I felt my boat respond accordingly as it slid smoothly in between two others, stern to the dock, just like the pros. As soon as the lines were heaved ashore, I put the engine into hard forward and stopped the boat, three feet shy of the quay.

Imagine the exultation! I finally understood how to execute the granddaddy of maneuvers under power, the Mediterranean mooring. After this first trip to Greece, propellers, rudders, and docks never intimidated me again. In fact, backing up and docking has become something I look forward to. The more crowded the harbor, the smaller the spot, or the stronger the wind, all mean the better the challenge, and to be able to embrace with such glee something that once terrified me was an incredibly liberating feeling.

The thing that still makes me squirm, however, is the idea of hitting a rock. Thanks to Greece, a country full of rocks, I also know what facing this particular nemesis feels like; it is terrible, and, knock on wood, it'll never happen again. The biggest boat I have ever skippered and my first rock met on another trip—the first day of a ten-day excursion with nine lives in my allegedly competent hands. Several hours out of Athens, under the watchful shadow of Poseidon's Temple, boat and rock came together and, as is usually the case with this sort of thing, there was no warning.

The boats were freshly provisioned and checked out and we were taking a shortcut I had used in the past between an island and the mainland, setting a course for Kea, our first landfall in the Cyclades. The chart was on my lap as we carved a wake through the calm waters at a cool seven knots, leading the way for a second boat carrying the other half of our group. Keeping an eye on our position and the marks that surrounded it on the chart, I pointed in the direction we needed to head for the helmsperson and blithely continued with the small talk, answering the questions typical of the first day out with a group of strangers getting to know each other. It was another beautiful Sunday in Greece; the sun was shining on the cerulean blue sea, burning off the damp chill of morning and warming up the red rocks and cliffs around us.

The crisp clarity of the perfection surrounding this moment will always be there in my memory, and so will the image of it shattering into a thousand shards of broken light as the boat hit a very hard rock, one place where a mass in motion will always come to a full stop. The crash was all encompassing—fiberglass on rock, wine glasses on the cabin floor, contents of lockers thudding up against the walls, and the alarmed cries from everyone on board combined to provide the soundtrack for a skipper's nightmare. It all happened very fast; one second everything was good, the next everything wasn't.

I looked overboard as the keel thudded across a menacing rock that had appeared under our port side, a mass of liquid browns and reds under the swirling water. We glanced off its side and slipped back into the deeper water just as what had happened registered. Shipwreck! I leaped to the helm, pulled the engine throttle back into neutral, and ran to the VHF radio to warn the boat directly behind us while the others pulled down the mainsail. No water was gushing up through the floorboards, but still, I jumped overboard with a pair of goggles to assess the damage. On the starboard side, a small piece of fiberglass was missing from the leading edge of the keel, but it didn't look too serious. Before I could swim around to the other side, an enormous dark blob loomed way too close for comfort. Shark! What next? In a panic, I scrambled for the ladder and back onboard.

The shadow ended up being the keel of our companion boat that had swung close to see if we were okay. With my underwater findings and a still-dry bilge, it seemed we weren't about to sink, so I gave them the thumbs-up and we continued on across the placid waters toward Kea. I kept checking the bilge—it remained shipshape—and I began to breathe easier. Perhaps the rock's bark was worse than its bite. The next day, though, Mediterranean-moored safely in the clear, shallow water, I dove down to check out the port side of the keel and found the damage was much worse there. It was nothing I could gloss over and describe as a dent or a chip. Major chunkage was missing.

I had hit my first rock and I had done it good, but the hardest part was yet to come. The boat could be fixed, but what about my pride? How does one handle such a failure? The rock was inevitable. Earning a living with sailing and all its attendant risks, it would have been asking too much for my record to remain blemish-free forever. After the blunder happened, it wasn't the force with which I kicked myself that mattered as much as how I handled it professionally and personally.

The next day, I was sitting on a wall on the island of Siros, waiting to use the phone to make the dreaded confession to the charter company, eyeing an enormous cross that was perched on a distant peak. If it could have turned back the clock, I would have climbed up and carried the cross down to the harbor. No matter how my feverish mind tried to cut and paste the possible excuses into something else, I was still responsible for the one thing a boat was never meant to do: hit a hard, stationary object. Period. The damage was done and I had to come to terms with the ugly emotions that followed—guilt and self-criticism. That day, I wrote in my journal, "I can't help but relive that awful shock, the pounding as we hit, over and over again. I think I'll remember it forever, how I sat there, chatting gaily in the cockpit, oblivious to what was about to happen."

On the bright side, there is no place like Greece to recover from such a blow, where making mistakes and learning from them is as old as the country's myths. For the Greek, arguing about the specifics of life lessons is the spice of life itself, a social act, and a human right to be engaged in, not avoided. It means milking the details of an accident for all its worth, sharing stories, opinions, ideas, and if necessary, speaking louder than the others to be heard. All the ribbing and personal anecdotes I got in the following week from my Greek skipper friends scattered around the islands finally managed to put the whole experience into a better light.

All manner of other real-life nautical nightmares were relived for me in commiseration, from flaming instrument panels, to entire sets of teeth being knocked out, gaping head wounds, and boats being completely lost. The best consolation came from an older, seasoned guy who said that, as we age, our pride takes so many knocks the inflated importance we have vested in it eventually

deflates. It comes with the territory of acquiring experience. "Pride,"
he said, when I complained that mine had suffered more damage
than the boat, "is overrated. Get over it, Tania."

A healthy respect and awareness of the inevitability of the unexpected is not overrated. My friends in Greece are hard-core sailors,
taking groups out on charters all summer long, year in and year
out, often in the howling Meltemi winds. They sail hard, sleep
little, and party down, and my casual impression of them is of a
modern-day, Odysseus-like bunch of guys commanding the wine-
dark seas. After the rock, though, a couple of them let me see past
this veneer of bravado as we talked about our fears. The ease with
which the men were able to relate to the way I was feeling belied
how very close to the surface this fear lives. I had been meeting the
anticipation of every trip with more and more apprehension in
previous years, waiting for something to go wrong, and I wasn't
alone. "How long can the gods keep smiling on me?" one friend
asked. How long?

If he's lucky, they'll be smiling on him as long as Greece has been
answering to them. I had already done several Greek trips, figured
out the Mediterranean mooring, and felt the edges of the rock incident memory dull by the time I went back to school, spending a
semester exploring the foundations of western literature. This was
when I first realized how much the Greek thread connected the stories I had lived and the ones I was still creating to an ancient tradition and history of navigation, exploration, and human experience.
Argolis, Sparta, Achaia, Rhodes, Kos—these were all names I recog-
nized from poring over the charts, not just mythological places. The

ancient Greeks, on the mainland and among the islands of their melting-pot nation, were the first to articulate exploration, travel, debate, tragedy, and humor. Whether a two-thousand-year-old joke or a theme I had used in my own writing, this connection with the ancients was still making each trip to Greece so special for me. I read tragedies that started in Corinth, philosophy that was first explored in the agora of Athens, drama from the Peloponnese, poetry from Lesbos, and the adventures of the original Odysseus who wandered all over the map just to get back to his faithful Penelope.

In the Saronic Islands, I had sailed to and past Aegina many times, an island named for a nymph who eloped with Zeus. When her father pursued them, Zeus turned himself into a rock, her into the island, where the temple of Athena stands. Hydra, the site of my Mediterranean-mooring lesson, shares a name with the nine-headed creature Heracles had to kill as one of his labors. On the passage from Athens to Kea in the Cyclades, boats can pass directly beneath the temple of Poseidon where my rock lurks, one that Theseus managed to skirt on his triumphant return from Crete. Dhilos, in the Cyclades, still has the ruins of a trading civilization, from a time when the island was considered the center of the Mediterranean and Aristotle was proving the earth is round.

A stone's throw away from Dhilos is Rhinia, birthplace of Apollo and Artemis, as well as one of the favorite anchorages to relax in following a whirlwind on the nearby party island of Mykonos where hedonism is still being reinvented. Epidauros, on the Peloponnese, has the ancient amphitheater where, throughout the ages, these stories have been playing on the stage—from Euripides to a performance by Greek diva Maria Callas. Further south on the peninsula, there is Monemvasia, a medieval village carved into a rocky hillside where everything is still functioning, mostly in its original capacity, making for a spectacular backdrop for sailing pictures.

In almost every port, roads—designed to get invaders hopelessly lost—wind, intertwine, and double back on each other as they lead up from waterfronts, no surprise in an area that is famous for its labyrinths. For thousands of years, in times when not many other people dared to confront the unknown, the adventurous and bold Greeks have been sailing the Mediterranean, between the islands and beyond. Since boats need to park when they get to land, Greece, over millennia, has been uniquely organizing itself and arranging its culture to accommodate sailors and their craft. Odysseus, Theseus, Helen of Troy, and so many other familiar names with stories that still influence us today, are characters who got around by boat, in fiction and reality, just like I am doing thousands of years later on all the oceans of our planet. But, it all started in Greece.

Today, the islands and the mainland are linked together with cruise ships, high-speed ferries, and hydrofoils, but they all need docks. Every single island, unless it's just a pile of cliffs sheering away from the water too steeply for anything but sheep and goats, has a harbor. And it is a safe harbor with a jetty for mooring, a substantial breakwater for protection from Aegean winds, fishermen with fresh catches, grocery stores, and plenty of *tavernas* on the waterfront.

When you step ashore, day after day, you are greeted by sights everyone recognizes from postcards and calendar pictures of a land known for its whitewashed homes, blue doorways, temples, and donkeys. The ruins and museums that lie everywhere are reminders of a history that began the documentation and instruction of the human journey through art and words, by land and sea. The beauty is there, alongside perpetually unfinished buildings with rebar sticking out of the walls and roofs, the litter, and the chaos, which, to me, is precisely the beauty of Greece. The combination of contrasts makes Greece feel real. This marriage of human passions and flaws can transcend and strip away the clutter of the ages, allowing us to embrace life for what it is today, for better and worse.

The opportunity to follow in the wake of Greece's established legacy of sailing was what first brought me, by chance, to that Greek harbor fifteen years ago, to a tourist spot with no facilities for any transportation but a boat. Since then, by way of my own unfolding history with her, Greece has found a rock-solid place in my life, and I know she will keep calling me to her mooring for as long as there is wind in my sails.

Boat Knowing

Dawn Paul

I n our landlocked kitchen, my mother taught me to swim, moving my arms and legs while I lay across a chair. I was three. Her palms were cool and dry on the backs of my hands as she held my fingers together to make a paddle.

She had grown up on the water, with a salt creek across from her house and Tenean Beach down the street. Spring days were full of the tapping of hammers from the boat yard, where fishermen readied their boats for the season. There were few pleasure boats—it was the 1930s, the Depression. Hot summer nights, she and her brother Joe would slip out after supper to wade in the shallows under the pier, a place scary with hanks of wet, dark seaweed. Mr. Kerrigan, the old Irishman across the street, allowed her, and her alone, to row his heavy wooden boat. In the familiar brogue of that Boston neighborhood, he said she was "a gi'l who knows her boats."

When the war came, she joined the navy. Her family was scandalized. Sailors had a bad reputation, and worse was the reputation of women who associated with them. But my mother did not enlist to chase uniforms, she signed up to wear one. She was full of romantic notions of the sea, but women in uniform did not go to sea. They did shore duty. Seaman First Class Mulkern was assigned to a transport pool outside Washington, D.C. She never set foot on the deck of a ship.

On a northbound train to Boston, she met a sailor, a career navy man. They fell in love and married. But a navy marriage did not get her on shipboard, either. She raised my siblings and me on shore. I was named via a series of letters between her and my father overseas.

After twenty years, my father retired from the navy with no sentimental attachments to the sea. We retired with him, to an inland suburb in his home state of Rhode Island. He bought a long ranch house, painted it battleship gray, and affixed brass anchors to the window shutters. That was as close as my mother got to being at sea.

Years later, just before my father died, he bought a house on an island near Newport. Whether he felt the pull of the sea at the end or wished to finally give my mother what she always wanted, I do not know. When he died, my mother sold that house of sorrow and moved back to our family's town. In time, the upkeep of that house became too much for her, so she decided to move into housing for the elderly. Against all advice, she moved from her familiar town to a place called Shoreside Apartments, a short drive from the coast. She admitted to being drawn to the name. I was glad to see her free of the cares of home ownership. I had visions of her strolling the decks of the cruise ships advertised on the bulletin board in the lobby.

Shortly thereafter, I noticed that she was becoming forgetful and uncertain about small details. Then there were physical problems—pains, dizziness, fatigue. The problems came steadily, a rising tide of limitations and frustration. There were no cruises. Looking back on it now, I see that we might have done things differently and better, my mother and I. But there were days we got it right. One day in particular.

The day I took my mother sea kayaking, I woke at sunrise and clicked on the weather radio for the NOAA forecast. Winds less than ten knots, clear and sunny. Perfect. I hauled my new sea kayak, stowed in its pack-bags, out of the shed. I loaded it into the station wagon with paddles, PFDs, and a lunch bag. It was my first boat, a beamy and sturdy Klepper folding double. It had a snap-together wooden frame and a skin with a red canvas deck and a black rubberized hull. A five-thousand-year-old design made with modern materials. From my seat in the stern, I steered with a pedal and rudder set-up, while my passenger paddled in the bow. It was very seaworthy and, with two paddlers, surprisingly fast. I loved sitting below the waterline, feeling the hull flex with the motion of the waves.

I drove two hours south to Mom's apartment. She was waiting on the bench outside, in pastel-blue knit slacks and new walking shoes. She had her gray windbreaker over her arm, "in case of a change in the weather."

I drove to the local boat launch, a steep, stony beach with a crumbling ramp. I unloaded the bags and began assembling the kayak. Mom examined the wooden pieces lying on the beach and the rolled-up canvas and rubber skin. She looked doubtful. It was not, she said, like old Mr. Kerrigan's rowboat.

As I snapped the pieces together and slipped the frame into the skin, I tried to figure out the best way to get Mom into the kayak. Lowering oneself into the narrow cockpit while the boat rocked in the water required flexibility and balance that Mom no longer had. I'd watched friends of mine half her age teeter and fall. If I helped her into the boat on the steep beach then pushed it into the water, I knew from hard experience it would pivot around the stern and capsize.

I finished hooking up the rudder cables and gave the boat a gentle shove down the steep beach. The stern hung up for a moment then slipped into the water. I wrapped the bowline around a rock. It was low tide and no one else was launching. The collector of launch fees dozed in his booth. I thought I would ask him to steady the boat while I helped my mother into the cockpit. I approached and he waved away my five-dollar launch fee with disdain, as though two women and a boat without a motor were not worth his waking time. I could not bring myself to ask for his assistance.

I turned from the booth to see Mom, new shoes in hand, hook a leg over the cockpit rim and lower herself slowly into the bow seat. She did this with calm assurance, keeping her weight low and centered. Summers of sixty years past had given her sea sense, and she had it still.

I waded in and showed her how to draw the paddle at a low angle across the surface. I told her to feel free to rest as often as she liked, and showed her how to lay the paddle forward across the gunwales, out of range of my paddle strokes.

I got in and lowered the rudder. The water was shallow and clear in the small inlet. We leaned over the side and watched hermit crabs lightly make their way across the bottom. A horseshoe crab ploughed along like a tank.

Mom had a natural feel for the water. She knew how to move the blade of the paddle to slow down or turn and was nonchalant about leaning over the side. She had a confidence on the water that I had not seen since she had moved into elderly housing, since she had mentioned she was "not quite myself lately."

She was wearing a sleeveless blouse and I watched her bony freckled shoulders working as she paddled.

"You're my best paddler yet," I told her.

"I know boats," she said. She gave mine a look from bow to stern, as though accepting that this unusual craft was indeed a boat.

We paddled down a salt creek under banks of black mud and marsh grass. The creek came out into a shallow cove. There we startled a flock of small sandpipers. They rose, all flashing wings, then touched down. Mom laughed as they bent their heads again to the serious business of getting their fill before the tide rose.

We headed across the cove to East Greenwich Bay. A half dozen sailboats cut lazy circles and a lobster boat chugged out toward open water. Mom watched the boats and smiled. I pointed out landmarks on shore—a seafood restaurant where we once had lunch, a foot-bridge—but Mom was not interested in land. She was looking out where the bay opened to the sea. She exclaimed over the sun sparkling on the water "like liquid gold."

We shipped our paddles in the middle of the bay and let the boat drift. I passed Mom grapes, crackers, and almonds from the lunch bag. The bow turned west with the incoming tide. The distant shoreline was crowded with tall trees and a bank of dense white clouds massed just above them. Most of our weather comes from the west in summer, so I made a mental note to keep an eye on that bank of clouds. I didn't want anything to spoil Mom's day.

We picked up our paddles again and I hit the rudder to turn us back toward the mouth of the bay. Mom's strokes were slow but steady. She was small and had to lift her arms high to clear the gunwales.

"You'll sleep well tonight," I said. That was always her line when I'd come in after a long day outdoors.

Mom rested on her paddle and I suggested we think about turning back. I reminded her that we still had the return trip to the launch site. But Mom had a goal. She wanted to paddle out to the mouth of the bay. She picked up her paddle and dug in.

I looked back over my shoulder and was shocked to see that the low clouds bunched in the west had piled up into a high black thunderhead. I felt the wind shift and rise, as though an enormous door had opened. On the boats out in the bay, sails went slack, flapped, then caught the wind. The sailors hiked out and let their boats fly.

I pressed the rudder pedal hard and the kayak came about quickly. Mom looked back to watch the sailboats. A fork of lightning dropped soundlessly out of the clouds. Then another. There was no thunder.

I floundered. We were in the middle of the bay, a long way from our launch site, a long way from anything. The wind was kicking up whitecaps. Mom was resting again, her bird-like shoulders hunched over her paddle. Her head was bent and the back of her neck looked thin and fragile. I considering waving a paddle to attract the attention of the sailboats, but they were far off, speeding away toward shelter.

Mom saw the next flash of lightning. She turned her head around slowly to look at me. Her face was confident and calm. We know boats, her eyes said. A wave splashed over the bow. I hoped she was right.

"Let's head for shore!" I yelled. There was a public beach along the southeast edge of the bay. It would be the safest place to land in rough water. Landing a boat on a public beach is illegal but I thought our predicament qualified as an emergency.

I steered for the beach. The wind pressed on us broadside. The half of the bay under the thunderhead was gray-green and churning. Ahead of us, the beach gleamed in sunshine. Tiny figures stretched out on blankets under umbrellas. They splashed in the shallows. It seemed unreal to be paddling through whitecaps, my head cocked toward a gathering squall, while on the beach people strolled and tossed Frisbees.

Mom worked hard, but she was tired. We had to paddle in unison to keep our blades from clacking together, and she was slowing us down. Finally, I asked her to ship her paddle so I could get us in faster. I felt bad asking her to give up, but she complied without protest. I imagined her in her navy uniform.

Lightning flashed again and the air had the buzzy feeling of a squall ready to break. I heard a soft muttering then a tremendous boom. Suddenly the beach ahead of us was full of motion. People swept up towels and umbrellas and fled the beach like a huge flock of gulls. The beach was empty when our hull ground up onto the sand moments later.

I helped Mom out of the cockpit and together we hauled the boat out of the waves. We half-dragged, half-carried it up to the wrack line. Mom grabbed her jacket and the bowline and stood looking for something to tie on to. I yelled over the wind for her to drop the line and run. Thunder was coming hard after the lightning over the wide open beach. I had never felt so exposed to danger. We headed across the empty beach to the bathing pavilion as the squall roared in. Mom hitched along on her stiff knees, clutching her jacket, telling me to run ahead. I jogged along beside her with the hair rising on the back of my neck, waiting for a lightning strike.

We made it under the roof of the pavilion just as the rain started. Heavy drops kicked up sand like bullets. We stood at the railing and watched the squall sweep in.

"I'm sorry," I said, "I listened to the forecast . . ."

"I like a storm like this," she said. She pointed to the waves and the silver-white flashes of lightning. "It's beautiful, now that we're out of it." She laughed.

I leaned over the railing and looked fondly at my boat, a small dash of red down the beach. Right then, a gust caught it and rolled it over and over across the sand. My eighty-pound boat, rain-soaked and full of gear, blew like a leaf before the wind.

Thinking only of my new boat, I leapt off the pavilion deck and ran across the empty beach. I tackled the rolling kayak, dragged it with adrenaline strength well past the tideline, and tied it to a half-buried lobster trap.

The run back across the sand felt like miles. My hair and clothes were soaked with cold rain and the muscles between my shoulder blades cramped. The squall was right overhead and I watched a bolt of lightning hit the water. This is how people get killed, I thought. I cursed myself for my cavalier run down the beach, for ignoring the signs of a summer squall, and for forgetting that my mother was old.

I looked ahead through the rain. Mom was standing on the deck of the pavilion, leaning over the railing, watching me. She raised her hand, waved, and smiled, as though I might have forgotten she was there. As though her daughter, caught up in the excitement and beauty of a storm, might keep running across the open beach.

Midterm Reflections from a
Semester at Sea

BERNADETTE BERNON

Seventy-two hours after Douglas and I landed at Isla Mujeres, off Mexico's Yucatán peninsula, I jumped on a plane and traveled in one day the distance it had taken *Ithaka* half a year to cross by sea. The next morning our year-old niece, Hannah, would go in for open-heart surgery. My brother had delivered this news by SSB as we meandered westward along the necklace of isolated cays on Cuba's northwest coast, and Douglas and I determined that I'd fly home as soon as we got to Mexico. Now, here I was, relieved to be en route to Rhode Island but anxious about Hannah and about leaving Douglas to fend for himself in an anchorage with notoriously poor holding ground.

I ordered a stiff drink.

When the flight attendant arrived, her colorful manicure momentarily riveted my attention. I had to smile; you just don't see that kind of thing on a cruising boat. In contrast, since moving aboard, my own knuckles and knees are perpetually skinned. "It's hard to believe you ever took ballet," Mister Tactful declared one day last fall, after pulling a Mario Andretti off an Intracoastal Waterway gas dock. I'd had to leap back aboard, landing in a heap on *Ithaka's* icy coachroof, scarring my shin in the performance. We've come a long way since those ungainly days, and we still have a long way to go.

Cruising is a rugged life, demanding a high price for stupid mistakes, and we made plenty our first year. But the rewards have been enormous: renewed feelings of possibility, pride in all we've learned, awe over the staggering beauty around us, and an intensification of our relationship that's come from sharing and working the extremes. When we're not loving the intense highs, we're hating the lows—together.

$$\text{\$} \qquad \text{\$} \qquad \text{\$}$$

Within a year after Douglas and I decided to quit our jobs and go cruising, we'd bought a 1992 Shearwater 39 cruising cutter, unloaded the house, and shipped out. We named our boat *Ithaka*, after the mythical island to which Odysseus endeavored to return, and hoped she'd convey us on our own odyssey of adventures. That, she's doing. For our summer shakedown, we cruised New England and Maine. Then, one crisp October morning, we waved good-bye to our loved ones, including five-month-old Hannah, and cast off.

Like puppies galumphing along, we sailed overnight down the coast to Atlantic City, around foggy Cape May, inside Prissy

Wicks Shoals, and up Delaware Bay, dodging tankers. *Ithaka* entered the Chesapeake and Delaware Canal and rode its rushing tide at ten knots into the Chesapeake's kaleidoscopic fall foliage. Unaccustomed to being unemployed and unscheduled, we lingered too long, lured by the hubbub of Annapolis, by friends, by a hideaway in the Magothy River, and by the solitude of Spellman Creek. We looked up from our daily feeding of crab one afternoon to find the days growing colder faster. Then the winds came.

We beam-reached past hay-covered duck blinds and around half-mile-long fish weirs to Mobjack Bay, anchoring alone among golden marshlands. In the East River, the list of things on *Ithaka* that needed fixing or replacing got too long to ignore, so we stopped at a boatyard and rolled up our sleeves—paying our dues for setting off without first getting all the kinks out. A sweet surprise awaited us: Cruising friends and ex-colleagues from Newport, Michel Savage and Germaine Adolphe, had anchored their beautifully refinished Westsail 32, *Dharma III*, in the East River to rendezvous with us. As we fixed a leak in the water tank, got new jibsheets, did some electrical work, and installed a new dripless packing gland, we also hung out in Mathews, Virginia, with Michel and Germaine, eating hush puppies and barbecue, following the election debacle from a bastion of southern conservatism, and talking about all the possibilities that lay ahead. While Douglas and Michel did boat projects, Germaine and I borrowed a truck from the yard and careened through the countryside running errands, passing scrawny hounds wearing electronic sensors on their collars signaling hunters who followed in pickup trucks. At the local coin-ops, we shot the breeze with the black ladies during spin cycles. As I loaded a dryer, one rushed over and pulled my laundry back out. "This chile don't know enough to pick a dryer," she said. (She got that right.) "Girl, lay your hand on 'em. Find a hot one, and save yourself twenty-five cents!"

Ithaka and *Dharma III* set sail in mid-November for Norfolk, our debut on "The Magenta Line," that path on the charts that signifies the Intracoastal Waterway as it snakes down the U.S. East Coast. We arrived in Norfolk in a gale of snow and ice, wearing every piece of warm clothing we had. There wouldn't be another day without frost until we pulled into Florida a month later. We didn't have a heater, so we hugged Michel and Germaine good-bye-for-now, picked up the pace, and looked for a weather window to escape the ICW and go offshore.

֍   ֍   ֍

We awoke every day to dour predictions from the National Weather Service. I started baking muffins, bread, cookies—anything to keep that stove humming till lights-out. Douglas began sleeping in his fleece jacket and earmuff hat.

Every morning we set off at 7:00 A.M. and connected the dots between the mile markers; at five knots, it was like walking to Florida. The serpentine waterway—here as wide as a bay, there as narrow as thirty yards—often was shallow but alive with wildlife and glistening in ice. Each day we hustled to make bridge openings and tried to forget that we could no longer feel our hands or feet. If we'd left Newport a month earlier, we'd probably revel in the American landscape. But, because we were impatient to be farther afield, the snail's pace seemed endless.

Thanksgiving arrived; my dad and stepmother, who were supposed to meet *Ithaka* in the Bahamas for the holiday, went anyway and stayed in a hotel.

In Beaufort, North Carolina, we sniffed for a weather window and tuned into Herb Hilgenberg's SSB weather-routing net. He offered nothing but gloom: Cold front after cold front was pummeling the coast, making a Gulf Stream crossing nutty. By then, Douglas and I were two months behind our imagined schedule. Instead of sipping margaritas under the Exumas sunshine, we were swaddled in fleece and forced into a slow march down the Magenta Line.

Finally, in Southport, North Carolina, we got a small crack in the weather—not big enough to cross the Stream, but good enough to make some miles offshore. Despite the prospect of two below-freezing nights at sea, we busted out into the Atlantic. After three days, like moles crawling from darkness, we peeled off our layers and sailed into Saint Mary's inlet on the Florida border, anchoring in blazing sunshine behind Georgia's Cumberland Island. For two days Douglas and I hiked through the forest hung with Spanish moss and crawling with armadillos, and waded along the miles of white beach on the island's Atlantic shore. Then, with our weather window for the Bahamas still shut, we puttered past wall-to-wall monster houses on the Florida leg of the ICW. Many bridges open only on schedule, so we often cooled our heels waiting an hour here, an hour there, gaping into picture windows. Three days before Christmas, we were in Key Biscayne's No Name Harbor, about as far south as we could go, listening to the weather and hoping.

"You people in Florida waiting to cross to the Bahamas," Herb Hilgenberg said, "you're getting another cold front and staying put for at least five more days."

Douglas cursed. I screamed. We brooded. This was Christmas! It would've been fine if we'd been in the Bahamas having a big old adventure. But being stuck in Biscayne Bay made me long to be home for the holiday and preparing a big dinner for our friends, as Douglas and I had done every year. On Christmas Eve, as the north winds climbed to twenty-five knots, a dinghy motored up, and a woman called out, "Hello, *Ithaka*!" Diane and Harold Clapp, from Nova Scotia, introduced themselves. "If you're not doing anything," she said, "make an appetizer and come over to *Sea Camp*."

For a small group of bummed sailors stuck in No Name, Christmas Eve ended up being full of music. Bob from *C-Note* and Harold played their guitars, and we sang, told stories, and laughed about the goofy things catching us by surprise in the cruising life. As the boys talked diesels, amps, and volts, the girls talked families, food, and feelings. On Christmas Day, Douglas and I had to face facts: There was no way now to cover all the destinations we'd put on our dance card before next hurricane season. What we needed was a radical change in plan.

❧   ❧   ❧

A few days later, I woke Douglas for his 4:00 A.M. watch as a nearly full moon set.

"Look! There to the southeast."

He stared at the first glow of lights on the horizon. Havana. We'd embraced the north winds that we'd been cursing, bagged the Bahamas, provisioned to be self-sufficient for several months, then set sail with *Sea Camp* for Cuba. From the moment we'd made the decision and spread out the charts, the pressure had lifted, and our excitement soared. At dawn, the jagged mountains of Pinar Del Río cut through the haze, and we searched the coast for the sea buoy marking the narrow entrance through the reefs. This had been a voyage of only ninety-two miles, but already we felt light-years away from our old lives.

We'd started cruising.

"Welcome to Cuba, my friend," said the voice on the VHF, in English, as we made landfall. Many officials boarded *Ithaka* for formalities. Our cell phone and handheld GPSs were sealed in a bag, to be inspected upon our departure. At Marina Hemingway, guards patrolled the docks, and cameras were trained on the boats to prevent cruisers from smuggling Cubans out of the country. With our boats safe at the quay, we set out on foot to explore Havana—a faded beauty that, since the 1959 revolution, has been a culture suspended in time. The hot streets thronged with people—women of every age and size poured into neon spandex, men in guayabera shirts, kids in school uniforms. Prerevolution American Edsels and

Studebakers, repowered with Soviet diesels, careened around horse-drawn buggies and bicycle taxies. Sexy salsa, rumba, and Afro-Cuban music poured out of every window, and bars and restaurants had live bands; in one, we noticed the cook dancing around the kitchen striking a cheese grater with a knife.

"This ain't Boca," said Douglas as the four of us walked the streets, followed by starving dogs searching for food.

On Havana's waterfront, Douglas and Harold befriended a fisherman named José, who went with us to a Cuban Baseball League game—a passion among Cubans. Seats behind the first-base dugout each cost a nickel. Harold, a Canadian, paid; José handled the transaction. Otherwise, the cost would've been about U.S. $2 each. This disparity in charges, sometimes called tourist apartheid, is commonplace as Cuba tries to amass hard currency; the Cuban peso holds virtually no value in world trade.

One day, on the backside of La Habana Vieja—Old Havana—an old woman walked with a shopping bag while shimmying to a private beat. "These people have rhythm!" said Diane, as she and I tried to imitate the step. People pointed, and the woman whirled around, amused. She shimmied slowly till we got the hang of it, and that's how we made the acquaintance of Elia, a seventy-seven-year-old grandmother on a tiny pension living in a three-room windowless flat on the third floor of a dilapidated house in Old Havana. Would we like to come to her home for coffee, she inquired?

"*Si,*" we said. "*Mucho.*"

We visited with Elia's family, shared a meal, listened, and talked—about their lives and ours. Like most older people we

met, Elia holds an unshakable devotion to Fidel—only his ene-
mies call him Castro—and how he's improved their lot since the
1959 revolution that overthrew Batista and routed out the American mafia. Where there were no hospitals or schools for the
poor, she said, now there are good education and medical systems and a thriving pharmaceutical industry. But younger
Cubans, such as Elia's grandsons, who took us dancing one
night, say they're proud of their history but frustrated by "the
bearded one," the skimpy ration books, and the armed *Guarda
Frontera*, who watch and hassle them from every street corner.
They say they need more money (professionals typically make
about twenty dollars a month). They want passports. They hope
for change. They dream, they admit, of leaving.

After two weeks in Havana, a weather window opened, and we
sailed westward to Bahía Honda, one of the pocket bays lined with
mountains on the northwestern coast. We visited lush tobacco
plantations where Cuba's famous Cohibas are produced, strolled
the dusty towns, then flew downwind at almost nine knots to the
Archipelago de los Colorados, that string of sandy islets and palm
trees once loved by Ernest Hemingway, while protected from swells
inside the barrier reef. For a few weeks, we lived near a pretty cay,
surrounded by a massive crescent of reef, and snorkeled the coral
beds, watching four-foot hawksbill turtles swim by on their migra-
tion to lay eggs on the Mexican beaches of their birth. Douglas
learned to spear fish and lobster and to clean conch, living a dream
of his to feed us from the sea, and transforming himself from desk
jockey into honest-to-god hunter-gatherer.

❦   ❦   ❦

Early one morning, two makeshift rafts cobbled together from tractor inner tubes and scraps of wood approached from the distant shore. Two boys paddled each one. When they arrived at *Ithaka*, the boys burst into a comical Spanglish version of "Happy Birthday," presented me with yucca and tomatoes, then along with Douglas, who'd gone diving with them the day before and mentioned my birthday, they whooped and gave each other high fives. Most of us don't remember many of our birthdays. I'll never forget this one.

We'd gotten to know these young fishermen and their families through Harold and Diane, who'd spent time here on previous visits to Cuba, when they'd all become as close as parents to sons.

On the day of their reunion, as the boys arranged an impromptu seafood feast for us in their homes, Harold opened a duffel of used wetsuits he and Diane bought for forty-five dollars in a thrift store in the States, and presented them to the young men, who all day free-dive fifty feet for fish and lobster from their illegal rafts. They'd stared at Harold, at the gift, at Diane, overwhelmed to realize their days of shivering were over.

Harold and Diane reminded me of a time when I was growing up and my family lived in a duplex that shared an enclosed front porch with our neighbors. My mother died when I was thirteen. Right after that, a U.S. Navy couple from Tennessee, Bobby and Nikki, moved next door and enveloped my father, my little brother, and me. We'd leave the front doors of our apartments open onto the porch, and while our meat-and-potatoes Irish family feasted on country cooking,

Bobby and Nikki developed an ear for jigs and hornpipes. After she saw that my father had gotten me an electric can opener for Christmas, Nikki commandeered our Christmas shopping, and the next year my dad gave me an outfit fit for Dolly Parton. I hadn't thought of Bobby and Nikki in ages, but that's one of the gifts of cruising: The upheaval from your familiar world stirs a lifetime of buried memories, then gives you the time to relive them.

Traveling with *Dharma III* in Virginia, and now with *Sea Camp*, I felt the same easiness I felt as a child, when our front door was open to our neighbors. Cruising friendships are like this. Every day, Douglas and Harold dived for dinner, noodled mechanical dilemmas, and blew off steam together. Since we'd moved aboard, Douglas, a tenacious fellow, was always on alert and anxious about his mechanical responsibilities for the boat's systems, despite the fact that he cared for *Ithaka* the way he does most things: thoroughly and conservatively. I was so proud of how well he'd figured out solutions to complicated problems and planned our sparse inventory. Time and again he was my hero in that regard, if damn difficult to deal with at times. But it was really in Cuba with Harold—eight years more experienced, and the essence of Buddha—that Douglas began to lighten up on himself and mellow.

Diane and I liked the same books and had the same sense of what was funny. If she baked bread or I cooked a sweet-potato tart, we doubled the recipe. She showed me how to repair our awing and grow sprouts and countless other things, and we took strolls on the beach and talked about our dads—larger-than-life Irishmen whom we adored. While the guys hunted, we snorkeled the reef and, on the way back to the boats, hovered over giant starfish on the sand banks; in a few weeks, we'd see them made into pathetic lamps for sale in Mexico.

The summer and fall had been boot camp for Douglas and me in terms of ramping up our boathandling and mechanical skills and learning the intricate rumba of living together twenty-four hours a day in thirty-nine feet without throttling each other. Diane could relate: "The first year is high anxiety, like trying to take a drink from a fire hose. Then things click." Already I could see she was right. When I got the call from my brother about Hannah, Diane said, "Go home for a week. Cruising isn't about being chained to a boat. You've got to know you can be there for your family."

❦   ❦   ❦

With our visas expiring, we reluctantly hauled up our anchors and set sail west through the turquoise shallows inside the massive reef. There was still so much to see in Cuba, but for us, for now, it was time to go. At Cabo de San Antonio, we waited for a window to shoulder our way across the Gulf Stream to Mexico. When it arrived, *Sea Camp* and *Ithaka* set off. The night held none of the fifteen-knot, east-south-east conditions advertised in the forecast. Instead, we got twenty-five from the northeast, gusting to thirty, with stacked, fifteen-foot rollers. Exhilarated and wiped out, Douglas and I landed a day and a half later at Isla Mujeres; three days after, I kissed my partner good-bye-for-now and was airborne over the same stretch of boiling water, heading home to our godchild. We'd been gone half her life.

Hannah's operation was a success; our family celebrated together, and the doctor said she should go on to lead a completely normal life. *Whatever that is*, I thought, looking down at her asleep in her hospital crib. Is it living on a boat traipsing over the ocean like a gypsy? Or is it going to work every day and contributing to the greater whole? Douglas and I have learned it can be both, that one enhances the other.

Someday, when she's older, I hope I'll teach Hannah how to sail and tell her about my own heart surgery as a teenager. I want to tell her a little about what Douglas and I have learned on *Ithaka*, about making every mistake in the book and still rejoicing in small victories, about committing to a dream and being open to wherever that takes us. I want her to know that cruising is more about making choices, opening your eyes, and forging friendships than it is about boats or sailing. Mostly, I look forward to showing Hannah what it's like to take a course less traveled, then watching her chart her own.

In Harbor

DODO DANZMANN

We'd come to greet 1988 onboard the *Antoinette*, a former steamship now owned by friends and moored in a canal off the Hamburg Harbor. We had brought a picnic; two Spanish friends were prepared to supply everyone with twelve grapes to follow the Spanish tradition of swallowing one grape with each stroke of the bell at midnight, accompanied by a wish. There were also, of course, bottles of champagne, and Greek friends had brought two stacks of playing cards, keeping up with their country's belief that playing cards on New Year's Eve will ensure good luck the following year. A very appropriate way to celebrate New Year's Eve, I thought as we all left the subway, crossed a bridge, and showed our IDs and various passports to the border police stationed there to mark the entrance to the free harbor. Hamburg has been a port city for over one thousand years and still has one of the most active international harbors in the world. The city calls it "Our Gateway to the World."

I had loved that harbor ever since I moved to Hamburg in 1973. I had spent many a melancholy hour sitting on some wall staring out—no, not to sea, but what definitely felt like the sea. In reality the harbor is part of the Elbe River, and the North Sea is still some sixty miles away from Hamburg, but the harbor area is vast, and where the Elbe River flows out to the west, it widens out to almost two miles from bank to bank. That's a lot. All the big ships busy getting in and out of the harbor add to the feeling of being quite close to the wide-open seas. I remember how once in my early Hamburg years, feeling exceptionally blue and full of wanderlust, I had tried to persuade a good friend to come and live with me in Paris for a bit. She had refused most emphatically and had told me she needed to be by the sea. "But you aren't!" I had cried. "We never go—it's too far away!" "I know it's there, though," she replied. "I just have to look at the Elbe."

The *Antoinette* was expecting us, her engine already chugging beautifully, lights in the cabin lit. In order to board her, we had to climb down a steep metal ladder and take a bold step forward into the somewhat unknown. Excitedly I jumped on board—what an adventure!

The *Antoinette* belonged to a group of friends who had only bought her the previous year, and I'd heard a lot about her. She was a forty-two-foot, fifteen-ton steel launch, powered by a four-cylinder diesel engine and her draught measured four feet. She had been built in 1922 as a steamboat and she could do up to seven knots. She was painted blue and white, the traditional colors of the launches working the harbor; her hull was painted black with a thin red line marking the water level.

She was not a working ship any longer but, as she had been one for the greater part of her life, she came with moorage rights for the harbor proper, a vintage spot, dead cheap. She had been made over to be used for recreational purposes: she slept six people, had a nice little galley with a gas stove and cute cupboards intricately fashioned so that things would not fall out in a storm, and she even had a toilet that you flushed with a pail on a string.

I remembered hearing from my friends that the ship was in a sorry state on acquisition and it had taken considerable time to get her into working order. The ancient diesel engine in particular—built in 1937 by Hamburger Motorenfabrik C. Jastram—was reported to be a handful; fortunately another friend, an expert on diesel engines, had begun devoting his spare time to the overhaul of *Antoinette*'s inner life. Patiently and painstakingly he had taken major parts of the motor apart, closely watched by whichever of the ship's owners could spare the time. It had taken them all the better part of summer to get sufficiently acquainted with the engine, but now they all felt comfortable with it. Everything had been declared well under control, all the ship owners had gone and obtained their pilot licenses for motorized yachts, and both ship and crew were ready to tackle the legendary waters of the Elbe.

Until then I had never much thought about boats, much less about what owning one right in the middle of a working harbor might entail. I had listened to my friends' stories of the *Antoinette* with respect, a bit of awe, and not much understanding—why would anyone want to own an old launch? What would one do with it? That New Year's Eve my feelings changed and I started becoming intrigued with the idea of being part of the harbor.

After a bit of excitement casting off, we made our way out of the canal and onto the proper river and the harbor. We were not the only ship around that night and I admired our captain for steering us quite calmly through what to me felt like rush-hour traffic on one of the more popular highways. We passed shiploads of drunken tourists, admired from afar the brilliantly lit *Cap San Diego*, an old cargo freighter now used as a museum, crossed the proper shipping channel normally used by giant container ships and tankers, and turned into one of the smaller canals alongside the petroleum harbor. I could not tear myself away from the wheelhouse; it was dreadfully cold out there as only the "salon" downstairs was heated by a small petroleum stove, but I was dressed warmly enough, and I doubt I would have felt cold even if I hadn't been. I wanted to enjoy every minute of the journey.

It was getting close to midnight. We found a small pier used on workdays by the harbor ferries but now quite deserted. We docked, our captain killed the engine, and everyone climbed ashore. Glasses and grapes were handed around, champagne bottles opened. We awaited the magic hour in full view of our city's most beautiful panorama: the harbor and behind it the silhouettes of old warehouses, three famous churches, and Hamburg's skyline. A bell began to chime, I popped the first grape into my mouth and just one wish came to my mind: "I want to do this more often!"

When the clock struck twelve, all hell broke loose. All the ships, including ours, sounded their sirens, and then, fortunately quite a distance away, the fireworks began. Many Hamburgers take their fireworks to the harbor on New Year's Eve. Imagine 20,000 people, most of them not overly sober, standing packed like herrings, trying to toast each other and set their fireworks off at the same time! Once I was foolish enough to go and ended up quite beside myself when a firecracker exploded in the hood of my windbreaker. But from where we were now, what a beautiful sight the fireworks were! Quite safe, where even the noise was subdued and distant, we watched from our pier and everything was splendid, the fireworks something to be marveled at, not afraid of.

We remained on the pier as long as it was possible in the cold, watching, talking, reminiscing, the way you do on New Year's Eve, and then we chugged slowly back to where the *Antoinette* had her proper home. We docked, got all our things together, and spent a last few minutes on the walkway, looking fondly at the old ship that had taken us on such a nice trip. I slapped our captain for the night on his back. "Now I understand why you bought her," I said. "You had to—she is so beautiful!"

But she wasn't, of course, at least not in a classical way. She had none of the sleekness, the elegance, of old sailing vessels; she was a working ship, staunch, solid, dependable—no beautiful white swan, no ugly duckling, either, but something altogether different. A home on the water, perhaps, a floating caravan—but one floating on one of the most difficult waterways of the nation. Being one of her owners for a while—from 1990 to 1998—taught me a lot and left me with fond memories. Owning her felt like owning part of the harbor; she became my key to the "Gateway."

My sister and I joined the group of *Antoinette*'s owners at the same time. We had great plans for becoming able-bodied seawomen and started out by studying for the necessary papers. If you want to take a motorized yacht anywhere on the Elbe River, you have to have two licenses: one for going upstream from Hamburg, where the river is considered an inland waterway, and one for going downstream, on what is then a waterway for seagoing vessels.

In order to get these documents the fastest and easiest way, we enrolled at the maritime school of one Captain Buhlheller. A novel experience in learning, Captain Buhlheller promised to get his students through all the necessary practical and theoretical studies in two weeks time, and he did. I remember nothing, really nothing about the nightly lessons I attended at his institute, apart from the fact that I quite liked how he talked condescendingly about certain types of modern yachts—calling them "yogurt containers"—and about the men operating them with the help of the latest state-of-the-art technical equipment. He called them "yachties." "Yachtie sure likes his little gadgets," I can still hear the good captain roar, "but remember: When the mast goes down and the generator dies, it's up to you and your little gray cells. So get this into your heads . . ."

And we did. We swallowed an amazing amount of information and then, after the two weeks, the captain spirited us off to the neighboring town of Lübeck, where he probably knew somebody in charge, sat us down with the exam papers, and we dutifully spat it all out again. Next we were transported to a tiny yogurt container, given a ten-minute rundown on how to start and stop this motorized vessel, did just that with an official watching, and were handed our licenses, properly sealed and stamped then and there (we had been told to bring photographs). Slightly numbed, my sister and I stood on the pontoon after having pocketed our important new possessions and stared at Captain Buhlheller. "That was it?" I asked him. "I don't really feel ready to steer a ship." "Good Lord, no," he replied. "Did you feel ready for traffic when you got your driver's license? You need to practice. No need to worry," he laughed heartily and slapped me on my back, "you are not about to take a launch out into Hamburg Harbor now, are you?" My sister and I looked at each other. "Well . . ." my sister said.

$$\text{\textcyrillic{ъ} \quad \textcyrillic{ъ} \quad \textcyrillic{ъ}}$$

Our days of official learning over, we felt we knew perhaps even less than before—or, at least we knew there was a lot we should know and didn't. We decided to take our teacher's advice and start practicing.

I felt surprisingly good on water. I loved standing at the helm of the *Antoinette*, patiently practicing how to get her in and out of her "parking spot," the place she had been allotted between two other launches in the old part of the harbor. The Elbe is a tidal river, home to many currents. Not easy to navigate. There are many things to be taken into consideration: You have to see how the wind is blowing, see how the water is flowing, pay attention to other ships, don't hit the ship docked in front, nor the one docked behind. You had to maneuver quite a bit to get her away from the wharf, going back and forth, like you would getting your car out of a narrow parking spot. A ship obviously has no brakes, and the *Antoinette* was long and heavy, so it took me a while to learn when to put her in reverse in order to make her stop exactly where and when I wanted her to. But I enjoyed the learning process.

I normally feel best on a bicycle, my favorite mode of transportation. A bicycle is quite safe, you can almost always jump off it when the going gets rough, you can shoulder it when both tires are flat, you can park it anywhere and when it breaks down, it is easy to repair. None of this was true of the *Antoinette*, but I felt strangely safe and calm with her as well.

Not my sister, surprisingly. She, who to my great admiration has, from an early age, confidently steered and repaired any motorized thing on two or more wheels, got nervous now when faced with a thing without wheels. But she was the one who felt comfortable with *Antoinette*'s engine and never seemed to be bothered by it. For me, on the other hand, our lovely old Jastram turned out to be my Achilles' heel—I always stood in awe of it. I constantly worried what might happen to it and I had terrible nightmares imagining myself stranded in the middle of the seagoing channel with a dead engine and no knowledge of what to do about it, gigantic vessels blaring their horns, threatening to kill me—all very embarrassing and even potentially dangerous.

True, I liked the look of the engine, liked the smell of it, liked to watch how the pistons went up and down, liked to grease the valves and do small maintenance things—but I always felt the Jastram to be too much for me. And in the end that kept me from ever taking the *Antoinette* out on my own, or with simply me in charge.

I always felt I had to ask somebody along who could, if push came to shove, rescue me by being able to analyze what was wrong if the engine did decide to die on me—which of course it never did.

I have often thought about this phenomenon and have felt sad about it. Had I listened too closely to all the stories about my friends' early encounters with *Antoinette* and her engine? Had these stories left me with just a bit too much respect? I can't really say, but I always regretted not having been present when they all dissected the engine, studied it, and came to know it so well.

The *Antoinette* had not always been the *Antoinette*; her name had been changed twice, something you should, according to legend, never do to a ship. It will certainly bring bad luck. And, indeed, the poor dear had sunk twice, each time after her name had been changed.

And then she almost sank again, while in our care.

A harbor means trade—and not necessarily fair trade. Hamburg is no exception, and during the 1980s and 1990s awareness of just what kind of unfair trading was done right in the middle of our city grew and the harbor became one of the focal points for the peace movement and the movements in solidarity with Third-World countries. On many occasions protests took place right on the water—under German law, a waterway is just like a street and can be used as such, provided you stick to the rules.

Although the *Antoinette* seldom was actually part of demonstrations, we were at times asked to transport journalists. Once, when things had gotten a bit out of hand and another ship, carrying some foreign defense secretary, had actually been hit by rotten eggs and tomatoes, we had our names taken down by the harbor police. It wasn't a big deal and we had forgotten all about it until one cold and dreary winter night I got a phone call from the harbor police. "We don't like people being impolite to guests of the harbor," a gruff policeman told me, "but we like your ship. If you don't want it to sink, you'd better come down fast; it's stuck in the ice and could even break."

He was right and we should have known it and seen to the problem earlier on. For some reason the Elbe, in spite of salt content and tidal activities, tends to freeze over when temperatures really drop. We immediately rushed down to the harbor to scrape the ice off the *Antoinette*. It was good the kind policeman had called that night; in the morning it would have been too late.

Apart from her political activities and use in training my sister and me, who were still learning to live up to our licenses, the *Antoinette* was busy doing other things as well. She took us and friends around the harbor on Sunday outings, called "coffee turns," as someone would invariably bring some cake and we would always make coffee. Some of these turns ended in excitement, hearts beating fast and tempers rising. Those were the times when we had forgotten about the tide and had ended up in a canal with the tide going out, and suddenly the required four feet of water no longer under our keel. How embarrassing to go aground in the middle of a canal. Not only that, sand might get into the gear unit. Sometimes we managed to break free at the last minute.

The small canals didn't just require careful navigation at low tide, you always had to steer clear of debris people had thrown into the water. But the small canals were also the most interesting part of the harbor; they often seemed to have been completely forgotten in modern times, resting and rotting there since Hamburg became a harbor somewhere in the ninth century.

Chugging ever so slowly and ever so carefully along the small canals meant chugging along derelict houses built from red brick, seeing trees growing out of the most unexpected places—it meant seeing history in front of you and sensing stories, many, many stories.

The history of Hamburg Harbor, of work in the harbor, had intrigued me for a long time, but before we owned the *Antoinette*, I had only managed once to come close to it. In the summer of 1977, while employed during university break by a temp agency, I was sent to work for one of the big dockyards, Howaldtswerke Deutsche Werft (HDW). For four weeks I was in charge of their office; the best summer job of my life. My co-workers—elderly shipbuilders and shipbuilding engineers—were very kind and introduced me to a world that even at that time was already fast fading away. These men shared not only their workplace, they shared a life. They loved their work and they respected each other, and they were quite willing to teach me, a student of languages and not even a proper Hamburger, as much as they could in such a short time. I was very sad when I had to leave them. In 1983 HDW Hamburg was closed down.

That had been my only previous venture into the world of the harbor. But I still remember the pride I had felt every morning, pushing my bicycle into the elevators of the old tunnel under the Elbe River: the pride of finally working with the smell of petrol and water in my nose, with the sound of sea gulls in my ears—working in the harbor, the famous Hamburg Harbor!

Now, as a ship owner, I spent Sundays chugging along the small canals of the harbor. Eventually we got an echo sounder to prevent embarrassment and lengthy discussions about who should have paid and who did not pay attention to the tide. My sister and I practiced mooring and other maneuvers. I kept staring respectfully at pistons going up and down, trying to really hear it when other people told me the engine was running "smooth as a sewing machine." We celebrated my lover's birthday on board the *Antoinette* and were followed by ducks that tried to enter the ship like pirates to steal the picnic. We had peaceful Sundays when we did not move from the moorage but just sat there, roasting in the sun, watching the tourists go by on the other side of the canal.

The *Antoinette*, being quite old and made of steel, had to be taken out of the water to be cleaned, repaired, and freshly painted every spring. We always tried to find a weekend close to Pentecost, with temperatures already rising, to set a date with a small dockyard a bit further upstream from *Antoinette*'s moorage to get those things done.

This small and quite old-fashioned dockyard, the Garbers Werft, was one of many fascinating anachronisms I came across while co-owning the *Antoinette*. How these people survived in the day and age of computerization, high technology, and what not, by just doing what they had done for roughly the last one hundred years, I don't know, but I do hope they will continue to be able to do it.

We always took the *Antoinette* down to the dockyard early on a Friday. She was then taken out of the water on the slipway, cleaned with a high-pressure water spray, and inspected closely for rust, thin parts, and holes. The first time I saw her out of water I was very impressed: There was so much ship normally not to be seen, and *Antoinette*'s hull came out of the river completely covered in mussels and algae, looking a bit like a huge gray bear.

When the professionals were done with what only they could do, they would go home for the weekend and leave the place to us. We did the painting ourselves, which saved us a lot of money every year.

The spring after the incident with the foreign defense secretary and the harbor police stepping in at the last minute to save the *Antoinette* from ice damage—not because they liked her owners but because they liked the ship—we got a frosty welcome at the Garbers Werft. "You have a bad reputation around the harbor," they grumbled. "Didn't really feel like taking you in this year," they continued. We were speechless: What had we done wrong?

It turned out that the harbor police had been complaining, not about us taking part in a political demonstration, but because they had given us a fair warning and thus saved our ship, and not one of us had been to see them and thank them properly. All around the harbor this was considered grossly improper behavior and quite rightly so. We were deeply ashamed. We had delegated the thank-you mission to the most undependable member of our crew, who had promptly forgotten all about it. The very next day my sister remedied our mistake and took our thank yous, apologies, and a bottle of fine cognac to the kind officers, and was graciously told there would remain no hard feelings.

The harbor, I learned during my *Antoinette* years, has its own rules and a thousand eyes. Leave a plastic bag with rubbish out somewhere and someone will neatly deposit it back on your ship: There are dustbins around, use them! People will go out of their way to be helpful but there is an etiquette you have to adhere to. Not a strict one—the harbor is a vastly tolerant place and used to eccentrics of all kinds—but an etiquette nevertheless. And we were lucky that people had relented and told us of our erring ways; the harbor can bear grudges a long time.

~ ~ ~

What else did we do? My sister and her lover once took the *Antoinette* all the way to Holland. They traveled down the Elbe and along canals and rivers, into the North Sea before entering the Dutch system of canals, rivers, and great lakes. They had an adventurous trip all the way to Holland, had to face high winds and a thunderstorm while crossing the North Sea. When I met them in Groningen to travel with them for a bit, the winds had died down and I spent the most relaxing week of my life. Leisurely we chugged along the canals, counting cows, watching the echo sounder. Whenever my sister got restless, she took the bicycle she had tied to the roof of the steering house, went ashore, and cycled a bit: much faster that way. Nights we would dock either right in the middle of a romantic Dutch town, pay a small fee to the harbor master and be entitled to use a toilet and showers; or we would just "camp wild" by docking along the bank of a canal, sometimes hammering long wooden sticks into the soil to tie the *Antoinette* up.

The tourist offices in all the places we passed provided ample information on the waterways, even handing us maps about the quality of the water. The water in some of the canals was said to be drinkable and quite often they told you to go right ahead and swim. As I have no fear of cold water, I did this several times, feeling like Jackie Onassis when I climbed down from my very own "yacht" into the bracing—albeit not exactly blue—waters. I even made my sister take documentary photographs and can now, when nostalgia hits, take out a snapshot of myself clinging to the *Antoinette*'s ladder, lips a bit blue, but grinning from ear to ear.

It was a lovely week and I became more confident steering our vessel. Taking her in and out of locks was no easy job, especially when the locks faced tidal waters. Most times our ship was the only one with a woman at the helm going in and out of a lock. The Dutch canals are full of the most wonderful and picturesque floating things: we saw an ancient, tiny wooden contraption manned by a group of Rastas and flying the rainbow flag; solid, respectable floating caravans peopled by solid, respectable families; and many things Captain Buhlheller would have dubbed yogurt containers. But however strange or "normal" the vessel might be, there was always a man at the helm when approaching a lock.

At the end of this wonderful week I found myself on a train going back, feeling decidedly sick to my stomach. The train was going much too fast.

❧   ❧   ❧

Back in Hamburg Harbor, I had simply to look at the Elbe in order to sense millions of opportunities ready to be touched, ready to be taken. Travels to faraway places, encounters with fascinating exotic people. But you need time for all that, time!

And time was what I seldom had on my hands in those years that I owned the *Antoinette*. I had become a bookseller after leaving university, always working for small, independent bookstores, and that meant always working overtime, always with a pile of things to be done and read each weekend. In the summer of 1995 I opened my own shop: Two months before that, my nephew was born. Neither my sister nor I spent much time with the *Antoinette* after that. We did go on board for the occasional birthday party, we did join the others for the yearly paint-in, but apart from that we just did not have the time and we felt guilty about it, hoping, for a while at least, that time might change us into able-bodied sea women again. It didn't, and as the other owners seemed to feel the same, and as the burden of caring for *Antoinette* came to rest more and more on the shoulders of my nephew's father, we decided to sell.

❧   ❧   ❧

The *Antoinette* now belongs to a group of delightful Third-World and environmental activists and leads an interesting life. She gets taken many places and is being well looked after. There is a sentimental spot in my heart for her. I left Hamburg for Greece three years ago, where I again live close to a fair-sized harbor. Whenever I visit Hamburg, I go see the *Antoinette*. The last time I went, she was just getting ready to take some Spanish union activists around the harbor. I listened to the engine being started and again felt a bit of regret that I had never learned to understand it properly.

Nowadays you can take courses to learn how to dissemble and reassemble an old engine like that—would I have made the time, would I have actually learned? Or was it enough for me, this knowledge that by owning the *Antoinette* I owned a small part of the harbor that I loved so much?

Survival at Sea

DEBORAH SCALING KILEY AND MEG NOONAN

"Come on! We're going!"

Someone was screaming, jolting me out of a deep sleep. Was it time to go on watch again? I felt as if I'd just closed my eyes.

"We're going! Now!" It was Brad. He had me by the arm and was dragging me out of my bunk. When my feet hit the floor, I was almost up to my knees in water.

"Go!" Brad shouted and pushed me toward the galley.

What was going on? Why was he pushing me? Then I understood: The Coast Guard must have come, or one of the merchant ships. Staggering toward the main cabin, I heard a strange rushing noise, as if the ship were right on top of us. And then I saw water cascading into the cabin through the port-side windows. My God, had they hit us? Had they smashed the windows? I saw Mark splashing through the rising water, coughing, his eyes huge. Then Meg was in the doorway, rigid with shock. She opened her mouth to scream, but no sound came out.

"Come on, Meg!" Brad yelled. John came up behind her, glanced at the flooding cabin, and shoved Meg forward toward the companionway. Then he lunged for the radio as Brad pushed me toward the stairs.

"Mayday . . . mayday . . . we're sinking, we're sunk. . . ." John was hollering. Why bother with the radio when the ship is already here? I wondered. We didn't have time to screw around; the water was nearly shoulder deep.

I crawled up the companionway behind Brad, fighting to keep my balance as the boat hurtled down the face of a wave. We both made it to the deck. But where was the ship? Where were the people who had come to rescue us? There was nothing, only the monster seas and the freight-train wind and the ugly sky. The Coast Guard wasn't here for us. No one was here—not off our port side, not off our starboard.

To stand there with the deck dropping out from under my feet and the water pouring down and seeing nothing! The blood rushed from my head, and my legs buckled. I was dizzy with the sickening truth. *Trashman* was sinking and we were alone. And then it all became a terrifying slow-motion dream.

I saw Mark dive for the compartment at the stern, where the life raft filled with emergency supplies was stowed in a fiberglass canister the size of a giant suitcase. I saw Brad on top of the cabin, waves breaking over him, struggling to untie the rubber Zodiac, which was still lashed to the deck. I saw the muscles in his arms as he dug into the iron-hard knots—knots that were being pulled tighter by the force of the sinking boat. I heard the Zodiac burst free, and I saw Brad swimming after it. He pounced on it as it stalled in the leeward shoulder of a wave.

A dark tower of water hanging above the deck came crashing down on Meg and me, dragging us into the rigging of the mainmast. I was under water and then I was up, and I could hear Meg screaming before we were both sucked back toward the stern by another surge.

In the lull between waves I managed to swim away. Treading water and riding the enormous swells, I could see Mark with his arms wrapped around the life raft canister and Meg being lifted forward by another wave. She screamed again as she slammed into the rigging. When she washed back across the deck I saw blood on her arms. The sweatpants she had been wearing were floating free.

"Meg!" I shouted. "Swim away from the boat."

"I can't!"

"Swim away. Wait for a wave to come, then swim away."

I watched her get dragged back into the shrouds. I knew she didn't understand. She didn't know enough about waves to time them so she could get away. I swam back to the boat to try to help her. When I got close, she lunged at me.

I screamed and tried to pry her hands off my shoulders. "Damn it, Meg, you're going to drown us both!" Somehow I pulled her away from the rigging and we were both in the water, free of the boat. I saw Brad holding onto the Zodiac, and I began swimming madly for it.

I grabbed onto the side of the pitching, overturned rubber dinghy, and then Meg was there, then John appeared next to Brad. The four of us clung to the line threaded around the gunwale, stunned by the sight of the sinking boat and Mark, still at the stern, fighting with the life raft canister. It looked as if it was going to pull him under.

Then, in one instant, the canister exploded and the life raft filled with air. The wind caught the raft, and Mark held on, dragged behind it like a fallen water-skier who could not let go of the tow-line. I held my breath and watched him fight for the raft. If he gets into that boat we'll never see him again, I thought. He won't come back for us. A tremendous gust ripped the raft from Mark's grasp. It blew through the rigging, skimmed the top of a wave, and vanished. Mark swam hard for the Zodiac.

"I couldn't hold it!" he sputtered when he pulled himself up next to Brad. "I couldn't hold it. . . ."

We dropped into a trough, then rose to the summit of another wave. Now we could see just the tips of *Trashman's* two masts as they went under. Finally, all that was left of her was the top of the mainmast. I watched in horror as that last bit vanished. The sinking had taken no more than two minutes. And now there was only the raging sea.

"We're all going to fuckin' die!" Mark screamed.

"Shut up, Mark," I shouted back. "Shut up."

I hung on. That was all I could do. Hang on while the dinghy rode the insane contours of the sea. Every wave threatened to yank me away from it. My palms burned. My God, my hands are on fire! I can't hold it. I can't hold it! We slid down into a trough, into a momentary calm.

Am I really here? I thought. I felt so small, so helpless, so exposed—and it had all happened in a heartbeat. Brad had dragged me from my bunk, and then what? Had the life raft really blown away? Had I really just watched *Trashman* be swallowed up by the sea?

I could still hear Mark screaming, but his voice seemed muffled and far off—as if his head was underwater and the words were bubbling up from below. Beneath the steady high roar of the wind I was conscious of the rapid-fire slamming of my heart against my chest. I pressed my forehead against the Zodiac as it climbed another moving hill. I could smell rubber and taste salt on my lips. I became keenly aware of the warmth of the water. Is the water supposed to feel this warm? Or is this what dying feels like?

I looked up again, and though I could still see Mark and John and Meg, they seemed featureless and vague, as though I was viewing them through fogged glass. An enormous wave dragged us up into the sky, and water hit me in the face, filling my mouth and nose. The salt stung my throat. I couldn't breathe. This is it, I thought. This is the end. I felt I was being drawn up into the furious, beating wings of some giant prehistoric bird, and I was powerless, limp, invisible. I was dead. No, I was still alive—but alive in the middle of the ocean with nothing to hold onto but an eleven-foot-long inflatable rubber boat—my God, my God, a boat of air!

Another wave broke over the dinghy, and I fought to keep my grip. I could see the others struggling in the turbulence. When we dropped into the quiet canyon between waves, I screamed again for Brad.

"Talk to me, Brad!" I hollered.

"What!"

I worked my way, hand over hand, to the other side of the dinghy to be next to him.

"What happened?" I asked.

"We fell," he said. He wouldn't look at me. "We fell off a wave. I saw it happen. We fell off and we landed on our side and the water came crashing through the windows."

I felt the gathering power of another wave, and the Zodiac started climbing again. Then there was an explosion of water, and the dinghy was torn out of my hands. I slammed backward into the water. When I was at last able to surface I could see the Zodiac stalled against the wall of the next huge swell. I stroked as hard as I could, but as I got close, the dinghy was picked up and flung another twenty feet away. I didn't see any of the others. I screamed for Brad and got a mouthful of seawater. Fighting panic, coughing, praying, I swam again. The muscles in my arms and thighs started to cramp. I lunged for the dinghy and caught the line with the tips of my fingers. As another wave tried to peel me off, I closed my hand around the line and the Zodiac carried me with it on its wild ride. I screamed again for Brad, then for Meg and John and Mark.

I heard Meg calling my name. She was swimming for the dinghy. Then John, Mark, and Brad came up and grabbed onto the side. We had all made it.

"Let's turn it over," Mark said, straining to be heard. "We've got to get in."

Brad and I lifted the windward side while the other three held the line and let the wind carry the Zodiac over. It slapped down onto the water with a ringing thud. We helped Meg climb in. Her legs looked as if they had been slashed by a razor-clawed tiger. Startled, Brad looked at me—I mouthed, "The rigging." The rest of us scrambled aboard. The air was much colder than the water, and I started to shake violently.

We rose up and then, just as we crested, the Zodiac flipped and again I was tumbling, being held underwater, fighting for air. When I surfaced my head hit the floor of the dinghy and I went down and came up, hitting the floor again. I was trapped! I clawed at the rubber, my lungs tightening. Then I felt the surging sea building under me and I was carried up and thrown forward. When I surfaced, my head was free.

Meg shouted my name, and I turned and saw the dinghy. I swam over and grabbed the line, then closed my eyes and prayed as I had never prayed before. We were on the wind-lashed summits and then we were in the still canyons. I would be torn from the dinghy and then swimming again, swimming for my life, swimming and praying, until I found the hard rubber and reached up and closed my hand around the lifeline.

Minutes went by, maybe forty-five. I was trembling uncontrollably. I wanted to stop—I wanted everything to stop. I could feel the heat being drawn from my body and the strength being drained from my legs.

"I'm so fucking cold," Mark said through chattering teeth when the dinghy settled into a trough.

"Me, too," Meg whispered.

"We have to get warm somehow. We can't stay like this," I said.

"We're better off in the water," Brad said.

"Yeah, the air's cold as shit," Mark said. "We have to stay in the water."

"The dinghy won't stay upright anyway," Brad said as we were carried back up into the tumult. When the Zodiac dropped back down, John said, "I want to turn the dinghy over. I want to get in."

"I'm not getting in the dinghy," Mark said.

"It's too cold, John," Brad said. "And we can't keep it upright."

"I want to get in," John insisted.

When I was fifteen, my mother had sent me to a girls' boarding school in Colorado that taught Outward Bound survival skills. Why hadn't I paid more attention? What the hell had they said about hypothermia? I knew one thing; the wind was our biggest enemy right now—whatever body heat we had would be stolen by the wind. We had to shelter ourselves somehow.

"Maybe we could go under the dinghy," I said, thinking out loud.

"You mean hang on under there?" Brad said.

"I don't know. Maybe," I said.

"We'd be out of the wind," Brad said.

"Under?" Meg asked.

"We have to try something," I said as we rose to the top of a wave and the wind blasted us once more. When we were able to talk, Brad said he thought we should try getting under the boat. Everyone agreed to try it. Brad went under, then resurfaced and said, "I think it will work. Come on."

We all ducked and came up under the Zodiac. I grabbed the line and treaded water to keep myself up. The odd reddish light made our strained faces look like ghoulish masks. I could just make out the features of the rubber boat: the aluminum floorboards, a black rubber spray cover stretched across the bow, a wire meant to secure the motor when it was being used. I could hear the waters slapping against the boat; it was strange—the waves sounded no bigger than those left in the wake of a speedboat. It was deceptively peaceful under there, like being in the clear eye of a hurricane. . . .

Each time we lifted the dinghy, we saw a little less light in the sky. Finally it was totally dark. When night overtook us, the fear and loneliness escalated. We knew it would be almost impossible for the rescue ships to find us in the dark.

Instead of concentrating on making it through the next few minutes, I had to think about living to see the sun come up again. Only with dawn could we hope that a ship would spot us. Maybe they'd send a plane again, maybe the same plane that had checked on us, when, this morning? Or yesterday?—I didn't know anymore. All that mattered was that I was in this cold, dark hell with no chance of getting out until dawn. If we could hold it together, if we could keep from going crazy, if Mark could just be quiet, if Meg would just come back under here and do what we told her to do. . . .

Poor Meg. Brad, John, Mark, and I had seen the wrath of the ocean before; we knew what it was capable of and we had chosen to come out in it. But Meg didn't have a clue. To her, sailing had been dockside parties, a way to get a tan, have some laughs. She never should have come out here, and John damn well knew it. I could hear the guilt in his voice when he talked to her. He had to deal with that guilt and with the fact that this was ultimately his failure. He would never get another boat to sail; nobody would turn over the helm of their vessel to a skipper who had sunk.

Meg was shouting something—something about a ship. We all ducked out from under the Zodiac. When I surfaced in the darkness, she was saying, "Over there, over there. There's a light!"

When the dinghy rose to the top of a wave, we could see a white light rising and falling with the sea.

"Do you think it's the Coast Guard?" Brad said.

"It looks like a spotlight," I said, straining to keep sight of it as we sank down into a trough.

"Where is it?" Meg asked.

"There," John said. "I see it over there."

"Yes!" I shouted.

Was it the Coast Guard? Or the *Exxon Huntington*? Or the *Gypsum King*? A fishing boat riding out the storm? It didn't matter—it was a boat.

"They're looking for us!" Brad said.

"Well, they're not going to see us," Mark snarled.

"They'll see us," Meg said weakly.

Again we slid down into a black canyon.

"Damn it," John said.

"Wait," Brad said.

When we rose, the light was there again. The others cheered, but my momentary euphoria was already going cold. The reality of our situation came back into focus. If it was a Coast Guard ship, it was probably using a grid system to search for us. In the darkness they would pass right by us—they might even run us over. And once they had gone by, they would probably eliminate this area from their search territory.

We watched in silence as the light appeared, then disappeared, with each roll of the sea. It grew fainter and fainter, and finally it was gone. With it went our brief joy. The night seemed blacker, the air colder, the sea fiercer. . . .

"Where does it hurt, John?" I asked

"I want to turn the boat over and get in," he said slowly. "I can't tread water anymore. It hurts too much."

"But, John . . . "

"Look, the man wants to get in the dinghy," Mark said.

Meg was in tears. "We've got to do something. He can't die."

"He's not going to die, Meg," Mark said. "You'll be fine, John. We'll turn the boat over and you'll get in and you'll feel a lot better."

"What do you think, Brad? Do you think we can keep it upright?" I asked.

Brad shrugged.

"Yeah, come on. John wants to do it," Mark said.

"It's still so rough," I said. "I don't know if we can."

"We're going to do it," Mark said.

Brad and I said we'd try it. We all helped flip the Zodiac, and Brad climbed in first. Then Mark, Meg, and I lifted John up, while Brad pulled. Eventually we got him onto the floor. Then Mark and I boosted Meg on board, while Brad balanced the boat. We all grimaced when we saw her legs. Her gaping wounds were puffy and inflamed.

Mark boosted himself into the dinghy, leaving me alone in the water. I was reluctant to climb in—the air was so much colder than the ocean. And I felt as if I had somehow become a part of the sea. It felt safe, almost amniotic. I let my legs go limp and allowed my thoughts to drift. Maybe the sun would break through the low clouds this morning . . . maybe we would feel its warmth on our puckered skin . . . maybe the sea would quiet and the Coast Guard would see us . . . maybe by tonight I'd be in a warm bed . . . after a hot shower. . . .

"It's cold as shit out here," Mark said. "Let's turn it back over."

His words were drowned out by the roar of a tremendous wave overtaking the dinghy. I shouted, and Brad jumped to the windward side as it broke over us. I gripped the line and was still hanging on when the dinghy was released from the force of the wave. It had filled with water but, amazingly, it was still upright. Brad had used his strength and bulk to keep the boat from flipping over.

"Come on, let's turn it back over," Mark said. "It was better that way. We'll freeze to death out here."

"Look, man, if you like it better in the water, then help yourself," John said. "There's a whole ocean out there."

Mark jumped into the water and held on to the dinghy directly across from me. I was getting ready to climb aboard, preparing myself for the shock of cold that I knew was coming.

"Don't kick me," Mark said.

"I'm not touching you," I said.

"You did it again," Mark said. "Cut it out."

"What are you talking about? I'm not kicking you."

"Cut it out."

I popped my head underwater to see where his feet were. I didn't think I had been kicking him, but the last thing I wanted to do was make him more agitated. I was afraid of what he might do.

I opened my eyes and felt the sting of salt water. I waited for my vision to clear. When it did, my stomach contracted. A cold sword of fear stabbed through me. I didn't believe what I was seeing. I didn't want to believe it. Now I knew what had been bumping Mark's legs. Sharks. There were sharks everywhere. Dozens, no, hundreds of them—as far as I could see. Some were so close I could see the membrane hooding their lifeless, clouded eyes. Others were just slow-moving angular shadows spiraling into the depths.

I yelled, "Sharks!" and launched myself into the dinghy, landing on top of John. A half-second later, Mark landed on top of me.

"Jesus fucking Christ!" he was screaming. "There are sharks everywhere!"

Fins broke the water all around us. For every shark that dove, two more seemed to surface. I couldn't believe I had just been in that water, spent maybe eighteen hours in that water with my legs hanging down and with Meg's open cuts. . . . If the sharks had been there all along, why hadn't they attacked? And if they hadn't been there, why had they suddenly appeared—and in such huge numbers? What drew them to us now?

We watched them circle while the Zodiac shuddered with the motion of our trembling bodies. A wave picked us up, and we listed precariously to one side before righting ourselves. It was vital that we keep the dinghy balanced. The idea of turning turtle was unbearable.

"We have to find a way to stabilize this thing," I said.

"If we had some kind of sea anchor. . . ." Brad said. But what did we have to use? Five bodies and the clothes on our backs and an open boat.

"What if we could get one of these floorboards out. . . ." I studied the three aluminum boards that covered the bottom of the dinghy. There was also a small wooden board in the bow covering a storage space. I reached into the bow and was able to pop the wooden board right out.

"All right!" Brad said.

Brad and I talked it over. If we could run the wire through the hole in the board and drag it behind us, maybe it would make the dinghy more stable—and keep us closer to the area where the Coast Guard expected to find us. Brad rigged the wire to the board and tossed it over the side. I waited for the next wave to come, eager to see how it worked. And then, *wham!*—the dinghy was yanked backward and we all went sprawling. We saw the dorsal fin of a big shark streaking away from us, dragging the Zodiac with it. The shark had gone after the board like a bluefish striking a lure. Before I could scream, the dinghy had stalled as the fin kept moving, and I knew he had spit the board out and swum away.

We all lunged for the line at the same time, almost flipping the dinghy in our panic. Mark got hold of the wire and pulled it in. The big shark surfaced again just off our port side, rising from the blue-black depths like an enemy sub. He was a monster, longer than the Zodiac.

"Get out of here, you fucker!" Mark shouted, raising the board over his head like a sledgehammer and bringing it down on the shark's back.

"Stop!" Meg and I both screamed.

"Are you crazy?" Brad said as he ripped the board from Mark's hands.

"You idiot!" I said.

"Leave it alone," John said.

"If we leave them alone, maybe they'll leave us alone. Like bees, you know?"

"Oh sure, Meg, just like bees," I wanted to say. Bees and sharks. God, we were losing it. I looked from one blue-lipped, pale, drawn face to the next. I was sure I looked as bad as they did. I closed my eyes, trying to get away from their death masks, from the sharks, from everything.

I knew a few sailors who had had to be rescued at sea. But somehow I had never imagined myself in that position. Bad things happened to other people—people who didn't know what they were doing, people who were unlucky. The boats I had been on in the past had seemed charmed somehow. I had always felt that no matter what happened, no matter how dicey things got, I would make it through.

But not this boat, I played back the chain of events in my mind. From the moment John and I left Southwest Harbor I had had misgivings. Why hadn't I just listened to my instincts? There were plenty of signs of trouble—Meg showing up and the unreliable engine and the whole thing with Mark. But I had, I had tried to get off! My God, if only I had stood my ground with Newberger. I could have just packed up and walked away. And now here we were—our legs entangled, our lives entangled . . . Brad and I at the bow, John and Meg in the stern, Mark in the middle, in a heaving rubber boat.

The Color Blue

HOLLY HUGHES

We asked the captain what course of action he proposed to take toward a beast so large, terrifying and unpredictable. He hesitated to answer and then said judiciously: "I think I shall praise it."

—Robert Hass, *Praise*

The green digits of the loran navigation system pulse our location—50°40′ latitude and 145°15′ longitude—both coordinates flickering hypnotically as we inch north and west across the North Pacific. We have been averaging only five knots, so each tenth of a degree west is hard won. The loran triangulating our position reassures me that we are moving, but it feels like a black hole, a vortex of wind and waves into which we could disappear forever.

It is just before midnight in late March, and we are held in the fist of a winter storm raging through the Gulf of Alaska. The closest land is hundreds of miles to the east, where the coastal range of mountains rears up to form the North Pacific rim. At the moment, though, the notion of land might as well not exist. Instead, the mountains here are made of water, gray slippery peaks that tower on either side as we wallow and slide, traversing the range. The radar screen is as dark as the night, no luminescent blips but ours

135

at the center; the empty screen with glowing green concentric circles echoes out one message: *alone, alone, alone.*

We are running north to Prince William Sound for the herring season on the tender *North Wind,* an eighty-six-foot power scow that, in the trough of thirty-foot waves, feels like a prop on a movie set. In fact, she is built of old-growth fir on oak frames and weighs in at close to two hundred tons, her eight-inch hull planking a testament to the vast temperate rainforests that first put the Northwest on explorers' maps. From inside the wheelhouse, the storm feels unreal, the waves surging past, curling and breaking hypnotically; step outside on deck, and reality returns with a cold slap of wind-driven rain. The black seas heave, sending us soaring up over the crest and then crashing down off the top of the wave with a bone-jarring thud.

It is undeniable: We are caught in the fury of one more installment in the saga of winter storms that sweep across the gulf. The sodium lights mounted on the crosstrees of the mast shine a fragile halo, illuminating the crests of the waves as they break and shatter in white shards across our deck. Designed to help crab fishermen locate their pots, the high wattage lights are on so we can make sure the cargo stays lashed on deck. But the deck itself is visible for only a few seconds; otherwise it is awash in green seas. If anything breaks loose, I wonder what I will do. I flick the old-fashioned electrical switch a quarter turn: lights off. Maybe the motion of the sea will feel better if I can't see. It doesn't. The bright lights give the illusion of security, even if it is only an illusion. I flick the lights back on. We're running on autopilot, so I check our position again, wedge my body into the green oilcloth-covered chair, Xtra Tuf boots bracing me against the wall, and settle in for my four-hour wheel watch. The brass clock rings two bells for midnight and the chime hangs in the air, harmonizing with the howling wind.

I click through the radio channels on the VHF, fiddle with the squelch in case I can pick up a conversation. Static fills the wheelhouse. I turn the squelch back up to block it out. We heard a garbled radio transmission on the sideband radio earlier today, weather reports from two boats traveling north off Yakutat, but that's hundreds of miles from here and of no help if anything happens. *What are we doing here?* I line up the reasoning once more, wanting logic to carry me across this uncertain sea to a predictable ending.

We had been scrubbing the last fish scales off the herring pump after an intense six-hour herring season in Sitka when we heard the weather channel calling for twenty-five-knot winds out of the southeast. That's a good forecast for the Gulf of Alaska in March, and within hours we'd put Cape Spencer on our stern, stopping only long enough for groceries and to top off the water tanks. We were still hosing down the decks with seawater when we entered the long slow roll of the open Pacific and let the seas finish the cleaning. But this morning we awoke to roiling cumulonimbus clouds and that prickly sense that a storm was brewing, confirmed by the falling barometer. The wind freshened all afternoon, waves climbed, and by late afternoon the storm was upon us. The anemometer stuck at fifty knots, though the gusts are now likely wailing up to seventy knots. When we left, the wind was out of the southeast, which meant the waves were directly on our stern, and we spent yesterday surfing, sliding down the back side of each wave with an exhilarating rush of white-frothed water. But the wind has veered to south-southwest off our stern quarter, and the waves are rolling in almost on our beam, so we're scuttling like a water beetle, wallowing in the trough until the next wave slaps our stern and sends us over its top. The autopilot whines and screeches, trying to hold us on course, and the compass needle swings maniacally in twenty-degree arcs as we scream over another wave crest.

Turning back would mean beating into these seas all the way to Sitka, and then we'd still have to make the crossing in time for the herring season opening in Prince William Sound, which could be just a week away. *All we can do is keep going*, I remind myself, trying to override my instincts, which say we should turn back. Out of nowhere, a voice begins to speak: *What if we don't make it? What if we go down here in these cold black waters?* For the first time since I began going to sea four years ago, I'm holding on to my survival suit, an insulated dry-suit that's standard safety equipment on boats that work in the thirty-four-degree waters of the North Pacific ocean. Eventually, anyone who works at sea realizes that survival is partly a matter of luck and partly a matter of time. Put your life on the line enough and it can happen to you; by definition, the nature of odds is that they aren't always with you. The rule is this happens when you least expect it, like it almost did this afternoon.

$ $ $

We were running on autopilot and I was photographing the seas thrashing our deck, an old tactic to take my mind off fear. Over the seasons, I've learned that looking through the camera lens offers a shift in perspective, forces concentration. Just as I was focusing on a frothing crest, the motion of the boat shifted, at first imperceptibly, then with an alarming decisiveness. We lurched, plummeting off the wave crest, and then began to roll, a sickeningly slow, stomach-tossing roll that threw me down onto the hard fir floor of the wheelhouse. I scrambled to my feet and could see the seas curling high above us out the wheelhouse windows. Somehow we'd made a course change and were now heading beam to the seas. The autopilot must have failed, I realized, and I stretched to kick the foot clutch out of gear and disengage the old-style "Iron Mike," or mechanical autopilot, that was steering the boat. Just then Peter, the *North Wind's* owner and captain, appeared to help me wrestle her back on course. His stateroom is right behind the wheelhouse, and he'd been thrown out of his bunk on the roll. Together, we pulled her around, timing our turn, then quartered the seas until we could get back on course and were surfing again. But a malfunctioning autopilot meant we'd have to steer manually the rest of the crossing, not an easy task on this course, for the waves would keep trying to make us broach. "Aye, now this is a *real* watch," Peter said, and disappeared to rouse Dave, my husband and our official engineer, and investigate what went wrong, the door closing behind him with a final click.

For the rest of the afternoon, I wrestled the six-foot wooden wheel as Peter and Dave somehow drained the hydraulic fluid from the steering mechanism and cleaned the lines. Meanwhile, the seas kept climbing, the wheel threatening to spin as I threw all my 125 pounds into keeping us on course, determined to keep the compass lubber line within ten degrees of our heading. *We can't broach with Dave and Peter in the engine room*, I told myself. *If we roll again, they'll be thrown against the spinning shafts or burned by the engines.* Finally, they emerged, nauseous and bruised but triumphant—the autopilot fixed, the odds on our side one more time.

§ § §

Dave relieved my watch this afternoon, but I'm back now because one thing I've learned about gulf crossings is that there's not much to do if you aren't on watch. You can't sleep, for every tenth wave tosses you into the air or onto the floor, even with sea rails on your bunk. You can't read without getting sick, and you certainly don't want to eat. Earlier today I opened the refrigerator, which I'd lashed shut, timing the roll to open the door, but I misjudged and a jar of Nalley's garlic pickles sailed out, shattered, and splashed across the floor. I mopped up the nauseating juice so we wouldn't slip but couldn't stoop to pick up the pickles without getting sick, so they still roll back and forth beneath the galley table. We have been eating pilot bread and peanut butter for a day and a half. I'd cooked Easter dinner just as we were leaving Sitka, but realizing my foolishness, I stashed the boneless Virginia ham, Parker rolls, and homemade cherry pie where I hoped they'd survive. But Easter came and went yesterday in the middle of the gulf and none of us cared if the meal survived or not.

The wheelhouse clock chimes two bells: 1:00 A.M. I have the graveyard shift, midnight to four. The wind is picking up, howling and clanging the rigging, tossing off the frothy crests of the waves, rumbling like a train as we whoosh down one wave and labor up the next, the twin Jimmy diesel engines miraculously chug-chugging on. *Imagine this is a roller coaster, I think. People pay good money for this and here I'm getting it free.* But the keening wind raises the small hairs on the back of my neck. *It's okay, it's just wind.* But how much more can it pick up? My mind can't focus on that thought for more than an instant; the notion flits in and out like a moth. Three more hours to go. I want to believe I will survive this night. I wonder what will keep me from running into Peter's stateroom, from begging him to turn back, from getting on the VHF radio and shouting *Mayday, mayday, mayday* out into this black night in case someone might hear it and rescue me? Not from the sea, but from my own mind.

The blackness swims before me, pressing against my chest so I can't breathe. I begin to pray aloud to the sea, to God, for the reassurance of a voice that can drown out this din of voices. I bargain with God, promise I'll floss my teeth, and if I live through this night, I swear I'll never go to sea again. Music. Maybe that will help. I thrust the closest tape into the empty mouth of the cassette deck. Softly, the notes of Pachelbel's *Canon in D*, fragile as crystal, begin to fill the wheelhouse. I turn it up. Lucid and trembling, the notes seem to hang in the air like water droplets. Slowly, the music builds as the full orchestra joins the violins. The waves rise, crest, and crash in time with the music, and the music grows, filling the wheelhouse until the voices in my mind are stilled and only the sea and music remain. I am breathing again without conscious thought. At last, my body surrenders to the storm. And then I see the waves are no longer oily, gray, and sinister but beautiful. They are rolling to their own relentless rhythm; they aren't trying to swamp us, they are just waves.

Only then do I see the color, though it has likely been there all along. Tucked beneath the crest of each wave is a wedge of blue, an iridescent shade like the fierce blue locked in glacial ice. As we balance on the crest of a wave, it's like peering through a window into another world, a world where blue is not a hue but fear and awe melded into one. Then the moment is gone, the blue swallowed until the next wave mounts and curls. When it reappears under the crest of the next wave, the color begins to speak: *Be not afraid. The sea loves you. You are part of her. She'll be here whether you live or die, and you will too. That's all that matters, not your body, not your life. You are a part of all this; you cannot be destroyed.*

Now I am in a bubble of calm, a place without time, and the haunting strains of *Canon in D* repeat because I can't move to change the tape. The melody soars in and out of the waves, to that other world and back. It feels like flying, like I've glided through a clearing in the clouds, like the sky and the sea are one infinitely blue world. *Maybe I've drowned*, I think, but that thought seems inconsequential. I become the music, the waves, the wind rattling the rigging. The brass clock chimes four, but the sound is distant, far off, and I'm not ready to leave this infinite blue world, to turn over my watch. Finally, at seven, when first light seeps into the tattered gray horizon, revealing waves that look only like small mountains of water, I wake Peter and stumble off to my bunk.

Shakedown

Moe Bowstern

T he first day of every salmon season's got bugs in it, even on the fanciest fishing boats, I expect. New equipment, a new net, or maybe just a green crew member or two is enough to wrench around even the finest-tuned of salmon seining operations. For us, on the fishing vessel *Thunderbird* that June 14, opening day of the 1996 Kodiak, Alaska, fishing season, it was all stacked against us and we knew it.

The annual pursuit of the five species of Pacific salmon in and around Kodiak Island in southwestern Alaska is a complicated affair. One purse seine operation requires a crew of four; a purse seine permit; a net or purse seine that runs about thirty feet deep and no more than two hundred and fifty fathoms long (more than a quarter mile); a boat large enough to carry the huge net on deck and still fit four bunks, a tiny galley, and a driving station with navigational equipment; and a skiff to tow the net around during fishing operations. Skiffs usually run about twelve to twenty feet in length, and are generally powered by either an outboard motor or a diesel engine.

Each crew member is assigned, either by fate, intention, chance, or worse, specific duties which eventually define the individual within the context of the fishery. For example, nobody cares if on land you are a sensitive artist, stockbroker, or mother of four. On the boat you are the deckhand, and respect is accorded you for the cheery efficiency with which you perform alongside others day in and day out. There are plenty of accomplished people running around leading successful lives who, on the docks in Kodiak, are still referred to as that whiny pee-hole or the hippie slacker.

There is the skipper, who maintains the boat, hires and trains the crew, establishes the market with the cannery, and decides when and where to fish. During the course of putting the net into and hauling it back out of the ocean in the eternal quest to fill it with fish (hereinafter referred to as a "set"), the skipper drives the boat, gives the signal to release the net, and tows the boat end of the net off the stern in such a way as to best encourage the migrating fish to enter the net. During the second half of the set, which involves hauling the seine back on board to be stacked neatly by the deckhands, the skipper slowly tightens or purses a long line that runs along the bottom of the net. This line, called the purse line, cinches the entire net into a bag from which the salmon cannot escape. The skipper then uses various aspects of the rigging—the system of pulleys, winches, and lines powered by hydraulics by which fishing boats move and hoist various fishing equipment—to haul the end of the net on board and dump any fish into the hold.

The entire weight of the operation rests on the skipper's shoulders alone, a burden no one should bear alone. Any mishap is immediately connected to the unfortunate person who carries the curse of loving the ocean and the fish within it. As a result, it is not unusual for skippers to routinely display various expressions of temperament in response to crew blunders that elsewhere would undoubtedly result in some sort of lawsuit. In Kodiak we blow it off and thank our general deities that it wasn't as bad as the last skipper we had.

The two deckhands are the skipper's right and left hands. During the set they wash the deck, scare fish into the net, and keep an eye out for the skipper. The salmon net is made of a cork line—two hundred and fifty fathoms of large corks attached to web or mesh with one-inch square holes, at the bottom of which runs a lead line. The lead line weighs about seven to twelve pounds per foot of line and has actual lead shot sewn into it to make the net hang straight up and down in the water, creating an impassable curtain for the fish heading for their spawning grounds.

When the set is complete and it is time for the net to come back on board, the deckhands guide an end of it through a hydraulically powered block—basically a giant pulley—that hangs off the main boom. The net comes up out of the water, through the power block, and down to the deck, where it is separated into corks and leads by the cork stacker and lead stacker. Separating and stacking the net ensures a smooth set each time, and a happy skipper.

Often the cork stacker is also the cook, and the person on leads is the engineer. Sometimes this means that the lead man is a skilled diesel mechanic, but often it just means that this person has the unenviable job of holding the flashlight in the wet bilge for a cursing skipper during an emergency midnight repair.

Of all the places I've fished, Kodiak has the most women fishing, which means that, of three hundred boats, maybe fifteen or twenty have women working on board. The prevailing mythology is that stacking leads is hard, so often women stack corks and cook, but I've stacked leads and corks and I don't think one is any worse than the other. A person ends up splattered more with stinging jellyfish when they stack leads, but other than that, it's about the same.

When I first started fishing I saw quickly that I was going to get stuck with all the cooking by default if I stayed in the salmon business, so I opted out by throwing myself into learning how to run the skiff. I really hate cooking, more than I hate being drenched with waves, blistered by a skipper's rage, or being alone with a loud diesel motor, struggling to stay awake for twenty hours a day, so skiffing was for me.

My job, the job of every skiffman, was to drive one end of the net. The boat tows the skiff and me in it off its stern. Both the skiff and the net are hooked up to quick releases, steel contraptions that can be released under tremendous pressure when one of the deckhands pulls a painter—a line used only to pop the release. At the start of a set, the skipper gives the signal, the deckhand pulls the line, and I drive away from the boat towing one end of the net. The boat drives in the opposite direction and the net unfolds neatly off the boat and stretches out between us. Usually the boat drives to the shoreline and gets as close to the rocks as possible. I stay out and curve the net into a large "C" shape. The fish swim up the shoreline, hit the net, and spend about a half hour stacking up inside our net. My job is to keep the net open enough to continue accumulating fish without being so open that they just walk out.

After thirty minutes I get the radio signal to close up and the boat and I drive toward each other, the net a big circle extending behind our sterns. When I reach the boat I hand a waiting deckhand a line connected to the end of the net and then I pop a quick release and drive around to the other side of the boat, where the other deck-hand hands me a towline. I clip this towline on to the skiff and then I tow the boat around the net while the deck crew brings the seine aboard, like a snake eating its own tail. The curtain of net hanging down in the water renders the boat temporarily immobile, as the propeller would wrap up the net if the boat were in gear, so the skiff is responsible for keeping the boat out of trouble—out of the way of other boats, off the rocks, out of the wind—until the net is safely on board again. The whole process takes about an hour.

This year it was all new. New boat, new skiff, new wife, green guy on the leads, and me in the skiff. I'd been running outboard skiffs a few years but this was my first jet skiff. A regular battleaxe—sixteen feet long, at least, and seven at the beam—she could go almost forty knots when everything was working right and she wasn't under tow. She was the only thing left of the *Miranda Rose* after the *Primus* plowed into the forty-eight-foot boat in the fog in the middle of the night the summer before. The *Miranda Rose* went to the bottom of Kupreanof Strait but the crew of four made it to safety in that skiff, which came through it all with just a few big dents and gashes. Only adding to her charm, as far as I could see.

The *Thunderbird* wasn't new either, not by a long shot. It was the former *Bill W*, a strange double-housed, flat-bottomed, green-hulled oddity that had rarely ventured far from the Larsen Bay cannery dock for the last fifteen years. Maybe old Ed fished her more to get out of the house in the summer than to make money—she was always fast to the dock long before the other Larsen Bay guys even thought about heading to the barn.

My skipper, Red, had big plans for her. I'd worked for Red on three other leased boats and I knew that the *Thunderbird* was in for some wind and some waves. Red had a lot of ideas for improvements but we needed to catch some fish before he had the money to put his schemes into action.

The new wife had been fishing so long you'd think she had a tail. Marina was a hard worker and just about the best crewmate I ever had in terms of navigation, boat safety, and fishing and island know-how, plus she was a good cook, good company, and strong as a horse. She was Norwegian, which in Kodiak means that the only thing more stubborn and hard-headed than Marina (besides her fisherman dad) was the ocean, which accounted for her extremely respectful attitude toward it.

The new crewmember was a greenhorn named Cullen, a young man stout of heart and sweetly natured. He was a drama student at Boston College—sang show tunes on deck and staged dead fish puppet shows with me in the fish hold. His dad ran Tyson Seafoods, a big cannery in town. After two years of working in the plant, Cullen finally convinced his old man to let him run off to sea, or at least to pound the docks in search of a job in the salmon fishing fleet.

The old man gave his blessing on the condition that Cullen's mom would never find out, and the two developed an elaborate system of hoodwinkery to that end. As far as I know, she's still in the dark, so don't go telling her this story.

After the usual three weeks of mechanicking and farting around in town, we were ready to hit it with the big boys. The season before, Red took us up north to Foul Bay on a reinforced hunch that we'd find the fish and we cooned 'em—I made five thousand bucks in two days, picking around in the rock piles in the sun, dumping two to three times as much kelp as fish every set.

It was hard work, but it paid off. After a week of that we were the talk of the fleet. We were the boat with the unknown skipper and two women on the crew that caught all that red salmon at a dollar thirty-five a pound. We enjoyed a brief week or so of notoriety in the fiercely competitive world of commercial fishing before our lucky streak faded and we were just another middle-liner boat toiling away in the ranks.

This season Fred's hunch was sending us down all the way past Uyak Bay to Cape Uyak. When we pulled out of our stall in the harbor and drove out of the channel to start our ten-hour journey, a rushed and frantic feeling prevailed, but Red seemed pretty philosophical about it.

"It'll be a shakedown trip," he said. "We'll get out there and find out how fishy this boat is, what works and what doesn't. If we need to change anything, we can just duck into Larsen Bay and fix up at the cannery." A cold, raw wind blew the morning of the first salmon opening of the season. Gray skies threatened as we cruised the shoreline for fish and waited for the clock to turn to noon when we could legally let go of our net and start another four months of the prolonged and elaborate circus act that is the Kodiak salmon seine season. The wind got up to a steady twenty-five to thirty knots and regular five-foot waves were shouldering the hull of the *Thunderbird*—not overly dangerous weather, but certainly a challenge for a fifty-one-foot vessel towing a half a mile of net and catching wind like a huge sail. Being shallow-drafted, the *Thunderbird* could creep around silver-laden mud holes that deeper hulled boats couldn't get close enough to sneeze in, but it made her a real kite on a blustery day, especially with an empty fish hold.

There wasn't another boat to be seen when we cut loose at noon. I drove away from the boat with my end of the net and was plenty busy for the next hour trying to figure out that squirrelly skiff. In true skiff-operator fashion, I was so absorbed in my own tiny world of radio, engine, and the tangle of lines that I didn't notice that the rest of the crew was going through hell on board the boat. We got the ends of the net together neatly enough for our first try, but that was the end of the smooth.

It turned out that the vanging winch that sat on the boom and pulled it hydraulically left or right had an undersized motor. Ed, the former owner, must have gotten away with that for years by anchoring up and taking a nap at the smallest five-knot breeze, but it was something we had overlooked in our preparations and now the crew was in a rough spot.

It was blowing a good clip still and the winch couldn't hold the boom in place above the center of the deck. The weight of the huge net hanging from a block at the end of the boom was too much for the undersized motor. As the boat pitched in the waves the vanging cables stripped backwards though the puny motor and the boom swung wildly to port and starboard. It is the deck crew's job to stack the net onto the deck as it comes out of the water and down through the block, but it was all Cullen or Marina could do to cling to the net as it whipped back and forth across the deck. Finally they got the net in, without a single fish in it, so Red had us try again for fish coming the other direction, but the wind had picked up even more.

Red cursed to himself silently as he watched his wife and crew toss about on deck like rag dolls. I came back to the boat after that set to a pale, big-eyed crew. "Wanna try another one?" I asked gamely, more out of skiff bravado than out of any desire to pitch in the waves for another hour.

Red had to swallow a couple times before answering. "We gotta go to town," he said. "We can't fish like this." I hopped to it with Marina and Cullen as we secured the deck and let the skiff out on a long towline.

Longlining the skiff is sometimes a safer bet in rough weather, though there's still a danger of swamping it. That beast of a skiff was too big for us to put on deck without it rolling us over, so we ran a line through the block and gave her about ten fathoms distance from the boat. Then we crossed our fingers and went below to put the cabin to rights.

The cabin was a mess. Every cupboard was unlatched and flapping. The floor and benches were covered with the one thousand dollars in groceries we had carefully packed away two days before. Mayonnaise, honey, ketchup, dozens of cans, salt, flour, and pancake mix everywhere. As soon as we put something away another cupboard would swing as the boat rolled. In the midst of this scramble I heard a loud *thunk* from out on deck and I raced to the galley door for a look at the skiff. The boat surfed to the top of a six- or seven-foot wave and paused for a moment at the crest before going down the other side. This pause put a little slack in the towline. As the skiff caught up and pulled tight the line, there was another loud *thunk*. I was on the verge of telling Marina all was well when the towline parted and I saw the twenty-five thousand dollar skiff spin away across the waves. Without a word, I groped across the heaving galley to my wet skiff suit and pulled it back on. As I zipped it up, Marina came down from the top house. "Moe, could you get your skiff suit on and . . ."

"I'll meet you on the bow," I said, and grimly made my way to the front of the boat.

Marina stood by and I crouched on the bow as Red pulled the boat up to the runaway skiff. The boat and the skiff were bobbing up and down in the five- to seven-foot seas as Red maneuvered over to the stern of the skiff and I jumped.

As I left the boat I saw the skiff dip away abruptly and I knew I had missed.

Somehow I grabbed the rail on the way over and clung there, hoping that the skiff was not about to crash into the bow and pop me like a zit as I hung from the side of the boat. I couldn't speak, couldn't do anything in the world except hold on and wait for Marina to rescue me. "Cullen!" she yelled, as I dipped up and down in the water like a soft serve cone, knees in the water, knees in the air. Cullen finally appeared with the boat hook and cautiously crawled toward me. This was his second day on a boat. Later he told me that he thought I was dead because I wasn't moving.

"Grab her butt, Cullen!" Marina yelled. Together they hauled me in like a halibut, and by the time Red drove up on the skiff again I was ready to give it another try. I knew that we were in Red's blind spot and that he didn't know anything about my brief trip overboard. We made an unspoken crew decision not to tell him until later because I think we all knew he'd get too freaked out.

I steadied myself for another jump. I was calm and collected, flat and even-pulsed. At the time I marveled, and still do, that I wasn't frightened at all, just ready. The worst had already happened—I missed, I went over, and my crewmates pulled me in.

I can still see the square stern of the skiff in my mind, the way the gray aluminum reflected the dull shine of the stormy sky in the wide ocean, the way time froze the second before I jumped. Then everything became a blur—I landed hard and bounced around a little, cut my hands up a little. The skiff started right up, I remember, and I guess I drove it to the boat. I had to travel alongside the boat for about a half an hour before we got far enough in the lee of the weather to safely hook her up to tow. Kept her on a short line this time. The three of us tied the net down to try and keep it from sliding around—or, worse, off—the boat, and lashed everything we could think of tight to the deck. After securing the deck, the three of us went up to the tophouse to stand by our skipper, standard procedure for bad weather. We still had the hairiest part of the day left—crossing Uyak Bay to turn in toward Larsen Bay, where the waves came at us from three directions and Red would need us where he could see us if anything else went wrong. In the tophouse, Red was driving standing up, chomping on a cigar. His skipper's chair was on the floor, broken off in the melee.

"Well that was a pretty good leap," he remarked, with the understated nonchalance that is the hallmark of the seasoned Alaskan fisherman.

"Yeah," I said, "the second one worked out better, though I didn't get too wet on the first one. Marina and Cullen pulled me up quick enough."

Red just about ate his stogie at that. "We couldn't tell you, Red," I explained. "You never would have gone back."

"You're damn right about that," he said after he recovered enough to make a reply.

"Marina said you guys didn't know if the skiff was insured. We had to get it back." I looked down at my hands. There was gray deck paint under every fingernail.

Swordfish

LINDA GREENLAW

My body recognizes dawn as the time to wake up, and I felt a surge of new energy as I skipped lightly down the stairs of the gangway. Rapping sharply on the starboard and then port stateroom doors, I called out a cheerful "Good morning, guys. Time to haul back." Voices answered immediately from behind both doors. I approached the "pit" where Carl, Kenny, and Charlie slept in the cool darkness below the boat's waterline. Calling down the stairs, I waited for some response. Within seconds a light came on, and someone called up to me that they were awake and would be ready to go in five minutes. Passing through the galley, I turned on the coffeemaker, which had thoughtfully been set up the night before, and returned to the wheelhouse to prepare myself for what would probably be a ten-hour stint on deck. I glanced out the windows; the end beeper was still bobbing peacefully off to our starboard side in the calm gray sea.

I entered the head and brushed my teeth, one of the few rituals of personal hygiene I would observe on a daily basis while fishing.

I left all of the vanity that goes along with being female on the wharf in Gloucester the morning we threw the lines. I rarely ran a brush through my hair or took the time to shower and put on clean clothes, as twenty minutes to do these would be twenty minutes less sleep I might get. Although I never much cared about my appearance offshore, I consciously avoided the small mirror that hung above my sink.

In the after part of the wheelhouse, I dug through a box of boots and oil clothes to find what would be appropriate for this warm, rainy day. Pulling on a pair of low, white rubber boots, I jerked them through the legs of my lightweight yellow oil pants. For a jacket, I chose a blue, pullover type of ocean kayaking shirt with close-fitting neoprene cuffs and collar. This suit was light and easy to work in, as opposed to the constricting traditional foul weather gear of bib overalls and hooded jacket made with a thicker and heavier rubber, which I donned only on days of extreme weather. A baseball cap would keep my hair from blowing into my eyes and face; I jammed onto my head one that I had determined to be lucky. The hat was adjusted tightly enough to prevent it from flying off and into the sea, which had stolen so many hats through the years. Last, I grabbed a new pair of gloves from the box. Fishing gear manufacturers don't make gloves small enough for women, so I use ladies' gardening gloves. The gloves I had chosen for the first haul were white, with tiny black cows printed on them; at the close of the day the palm of the right-hand glove would be worn through. By the end of the trip I would have fifteen left-hand gloves; Davy Jones's locker would have fifteen threadbare rights.

Before leaving the bridge, I turned off the RDF, marked the plotter at our present position, turned the autopilot to its "remote" setting to allow me to steer from the helm station on deck, and pushed the button to activate the deck helm's clutch and throttle controls. I then met Kenny at the bottom of the wheelhouse stairs; he was heading below to check the oil in the main engine. I stepped out onto the deck and stood at the starboard rail, waiting for the crew to join me while keeping an eye on the beeper antenna in the distance.

Peter was the first man through the fo'c'sle door. He spread his arms and burst into song exactly as he had done before every haulback of the season with the chorus of "Oh, What a Beautiful Morning" from *Oklahoma!*—but with the last line changed to reflect his beautiful feeling that we would be catching some swordfish today. His deep baritone, heavier than the moist, salt air, drifted slowly down to the level of my ears and eventually settled onto the deck, where it found its way through the scuppers and into the ocean that muffled it to silence. It was a silly little song, childish, but it had become a part of the daily ritual aboard the *Hannah Boden*, and Peter knew that I would refuse to start the haul until he sang.

"Hi, Peter! Don't let a little rain dampen your spirits!" I shouted, clapping in praise of the good luck song.

Charlie was next on deck. "Good morning, Linda. You look absolutely radiant today!" (Another part of the ritual.) "Did you get a chance to ask Bob about my raise?" he teased.

"I'll bring it up at the next board meeting," I replied.

"Thanks, beautiful!"

"Big raise, Charlie, really big." The three of us laughed; then Peter and Charlie headed to the stern, where they would spend the next ten to twelve hours in the shelter of the cart house, coiling and repairing the one thousand leaders as they came back aboard.

Kenny had gone from the engine room to the deck over my head and behind the wheelhouse. He raised the starboard bird out of the water and up tight against the end of the outrigger, where it would hang until the end of the hauling. I stood at the deck hauling station, the top of my right thigh pressing against the starboard cap rail. Reaching with my left hand, I nudged the clutch control ahead and put the engine into forward gear. I pushed the throttle ahead slightly and steered the *Hannah Boden* toward "1695" using the remote helm, a four-inch-long stainless steel rod mounted on an electronic sending unit. The remote helm is tied in with the ship's autopilot, which changes the angle of the rudder hydraulically. Pushing the rod to port steers the boat to port, and vice versa. The helm, engine controls, and hydraulic valve for the mainline spool are all located on the forward bulkhead close together so that I can reach all three with my left hand, leaving my right hand free to "feel the line" and "grab snaps."

As we neared the beeper, Kenny, Carl, and Ringo joined me on the deck. Kenny sharpened his slime knife. Carl removed a small section of the starboard rail by pulling it up and out of the grooves that held it in place, leaving a three-foot gap in the rail, called a door. Fish are pulled though the door and onto the deck, sparing the men the backbreaking work of hauling large fish up and over the rail to get them out of the water and aboard. Carl took his place beside me at the rail and adjusted the position of the ball-drop spool directly inboard of where he now stood. Poking me gently with an elbow to get my attention, Carl nodded toward the middle of the deck, where Ringo was stretching and bending to loosen up. "Hey, old fuck!" he called to Ringo, "that ain't gonna help. You'll be crippled by the end of the day. You're too damned old for this kind of work. Ma's gonna bury you and Kenny in fish."

Ringo stood up straight and yelled back. "I'm not too old to take care of a snot-nosed kid like you. How are you going to work all day without changing your diaper and taking your nap?"

"Fuck you, Grandpa."

I had been working with men long enough to know that this was the way many of them communicated, and that nothing was meant, or taken seriously, by either Ringo or Carl. The two actually liked one another; if they didn't, they wouldn't speak at all. I slowed the boat's engine and threw her out of gear as the beeper floated leisurely down the side of the hull. When the buoy was at my feet, I put the engine in reverse and backed down until the boat was dead in the water. Carl grasped the beeper's antenna in his left hand to prevent it from whacking him in the head, and, leaning over the rail, reached the steel handle on top of the canister with his right. In one smooth motion, Carl yanked the buoy from the water, over the rail, and placed it gently on the deck between us. I grabbed the mainline, which dangled over the rail and into the water, and pulled a couple of fathoms of slack onto the deck for the men to work with. Ringo unclipped the beeper's snap from the bitter end of the mainline and fed the end of the monofilament through a block that hung over the rail at my right shoulder. Pulling the slack through the block, Ringo walked aft with the bitter end to the front of the cart house, where the free end coming from the spool hung through a block secured to the roof of the cart house. Tying the two ends together with a barrel knot, Ringo cinched the knot tight, dropped the line onto the deck, and gave me a thumbs-up. As Kenny secured the beeper, turning it off and stowing it in the rack, I started to haul.

I twisted the handle of the valve control for the spool, opening it slightly. Turning slowly, the spool wound the slack mainline out of the water to a point where the line had some tension on it and entered the water at about a thirty-degree angle. Twenty feet ahead of me, and six feet off the side of the bow, the line was pulled from the water, into the block over my shoulder, through the block on the cart house, and was spun up onto the spool, or drum, as it turned. Putting the boat in gear, and increasing both throttle and spool speed to maintain this angle and tension on the line, I steered the boat, paralleling the gear. Like a giant game of connect-the-dots, I followed the orange floats to the west.

My right hand hung on the line just ahead of the block at my shoulder, my fingers working to gauge the tension of the line as it passed through them. The first leader snap broke the surface ahead of me. It hung slack, indicating no fish. When the snap hit my right hand, I grabbed it, preventing it from traveling through the block with the line, pinched it open, and popped it free of the line. Working quickly with both hands, I wrapped the top of the leader around the "clothesline" that led from the hauling station to the stern. I clipped the snap onto the mono of the same leader, forming a loop around the clothesline, and let the motion of the boat through the water drag the leader to the stern, where Peter stood waiting for it. When the leader reached the starboard stern, Peter unclipped the snap and walked the leader around the corner of the cart house, where he handed it across the transom to Charlie. Charlie stood on the port side of the stern and swiftly coiled the leader into his box, pulling with right and then left until all seven fathoms were out of the water. Stopping to rip the light-stick off and toss it into a bucket, and again to pull the squid from the hook and drop it into the ocean, Charlie and Peter would coil in this fashion all day, pushing themselves to keep up with the speed of the haul.

I grabbed the second snap and sent it down the clothesline to Peter. The third snap was a ball-drop, which I handed to Carl, who stood beside me at the rail. Carl turned inboard to face the ball-drop spool and clipped the drop's snap into the loop of mono that hung from the small aluminum drum. Turning the hand crank, Carl spun the drop onto the spool until the float came over the rail. When the float reached him, Carl stopped cranking, unclipped the float from the drop, hung the float on the ball storage line, and returned to my side.

I continued to haul, and soon the angle at which the line exited the water increased. I felt the tension of the line intensify as it slid through my right hand, and as the angle sharpened and the line tightened, so did my excitement. I had been through this drill thousands of times, landed thousands of fish, and each was as exciting as the first. Just a hint of weight on the mainline was enough to wind me up tight.

I slowed the engine to an idle and threw it out of gear with my left hand, still hauling the line that was now bar-tight. The line was coming out of the water at my feet, straight up into the block, when I pulled the engine into reverse and backed down with some throttle to stop the boat before we ran by what was probably a fish on the next leader. When the boat runs beyond the fish, the weight of the boat going ahead against the weight of the fish can easily tear hook from flesh, allowing the fish to swim away. And waiting to back the engine until the fish is down by the stern can result in a fish chopped up by the propeller. When fish and steel blades turning at one thousand RPMs meet, the fish loses—and we lose. What's left of a fish after tangling with the propeller is seldom enough for a barbecue.

I slowed the spool to a crawl, easing mainline aboard until a snap broke the surface. The mainline was pulled into an "L" shape with the weight of the leader. As the boat came to a stop, I nodded to Carl, who leaned over the rail and grabbed the leader just below the snap. Standing up straight, Carl leaned into the rail with the tops of his legs and hauled the leader, hand over hand, twisting his upper body to pull with his back and shoulders. Kenny and Ringo appeared at either side of Carl, each with a sixteen-foot-long gaff. The gaff poles were two-inch-diameter oak dowels, and each had a large shiny hook secured to one end. The gaffers were poised and staring into the water, looking for the fish that we all anticipated. Carl gave a long steady pull with his right hand, and the fish came into view a few feet below the surface. It was a sword. It was big. And it was alive. My pulse quickened. Swordfish are the most magnificent of all ocean creatures. A streamlined and muscular missile with a bayonet, the swordfish is strong, swift, and agile.

The fish circled, swimming under the boat as they often do. Carl held the leader, no longer pulling; he waited. When the fish swam out from under us, Carl pulled in another fathom of leader. A dorsal fin cut the surface; then hell broke loose as the fish slashed wildly with its three-foot-long sword. The fish's bill and back were lit up in blue and purple, and its sides flashed in silver and pink. With two short jerks, Kenny and Ringo sunk their gaff hooks into the head of the fish and pulled it toward the door in the rail. The fish thrashed, and the water flew. Grabbing a twenty-four-inch steel meat hook, I reached through the door and placed the hook into one of the fish's eye sockets. Peter came from the stern with a second meat hook, and placed it in the eye socket with mine. Ringo grabbed the bill to prevent it from slashing as we all pulled together to drag the fish onto the deck. The fish slid through the door easily, and I stood and admired it for a minute. "Nice start, about one fifty," Kenny said as he zipped the bill from the fish with a push and pull of the meat saw.

"A hundred and thirty," I said, returning to the hauling station. I used an old half of a pencil to start my tally on the white-painted bulkhead ahead of me, and wrote "130" in inch-high numbers. Unclipping the leader that had caught the fish from the mainline, I tossed the snap onto the deck and started hauling again. Kenny cleaned the fish as Ringo coiled the leader, removed the hook from the fish's lower jaw, and took it aft for Peter to deal with. A few slack leaders went down the clothesline, and another live marker was pulled through the door. The next time I backed the boat down resulted in a pair of fish on two leaders tangled together in a twisted knot of mainline, a "doubleheader" of nice pups, eighty to ninety pounds each. Both fish, barely alive, had only a shake or two of their tail fins left for fight. Carl and I each hauled a leader, while Charlie and Peter came from the stern to gaff the pups through the door and onto the deck, where Ringo and Kenny went to work on them.

Cutting the twisted leaders from the snarl with a pair of mono scissors, I handed the snaps to Peter and tossed what was left of the leaders into a garbage bin on the port side. Carl and I worked to loosen and untangle the wad of mainline and wind it back onto the drum. If pushed for time, this snarl would have simply been cut out of the line, the two clear ends tied together, and we would be hauling again within seconds. All cut snarls would be stored, to be straightened out when the crew had time. I preferred to work the snarls out as they came aboard rather than chop up the mainline. When fishing among the fleet, and racing the clock, hauling back becomes a daily ten-hour panic scene, and snarls are quickly cut and tossed aside. Eventually, as a result of rushing and scurrying, the amount of line on the spool decreases significantly as the mountain of discarded snarls grows. The miles of line that remain on the drum become full of knots, which are undesirable because they prevent the leaders heavy with fish from sliding along the mainline as the fish swim. A snap jammed up against a knot will often result in the "pulling off," or losing, of a lightly hooked fish. As Carl and I shook, pulled, and unwound the ball of mono, the butchers each cleaned a fish and the coilers built new leaders to replace what I couldn't untangle and had cut from the snarl.

Ringo has cleaned so many swordfish through the years that he has the procedure down to a science. His technique is smooth and routine; he wastes neither time nor motion. Bill, fins, and head are severed with as many strokes of the meat saw. As these parts are cut from the fish, they are thrown overboard, the second fin in the air before the first one hits the water, and the third in the air before the second one splashes. The belly of the fish is then laid open with one long smooth slice with the slime knife, from anus to between where the pectoral fins had been. Two jabs of the knife cuts gill plates from nape. All entrails are pulled from the body cavity in one bloody mass and slid across the deck and out the nearest scupper, leaving behind a smeared trail of red goo. Next, the body cavity is scraped clean of the thick, sticky mucus "slime" that clings to the inside walls; the rounded blade of the slime knife is manufactured specifically for this use. Two shallow slices the length of the backbone, along either side of it, free the "bloodline" from the inside of the fish, allowing it to be pulled out in one brown, snakelike clotted string and flung over the rail into the water, where a flock of birds will often feast on it. The carcass is thoroughly rinsed with the saltwater deck hose, completing the cleaning, or dressing.

Kenny, who is also among the best of butchers, rinsed his fish and automatically looked around the deck for the next one. Not finding an uncleaned fish, he stood and straightened his back, which had been doubled over while dressing fish. "They'll never get ahead of us this way, Ringo," he said loudly enough for us all to hear.

"Yeah. Well, what do you expect from a girl and a snot-nosed kid? We might as well go in for lunch while they finish with that snarl. Christ, they look like a couple kittens playing with a ball of yarn. Hey, you're supposed to be untangling that, Carl," Ringo teased.

"Fuck you, Grandpa." I stole Carl's line. "Why don't you two put those fish down in the hold before they start to ferment? Or maybe Snot-nose and I can do it for you while you rest; after all, you have cleaned two whole fish apiece."

"Yeah, don't strain yourself, old-timer," Carl chimed in as we shook the last of the snarl out and wound the slack onto the drum. I started to haul again as Carl helped Ringo lower the dressed-out swords to Kenny, who had climbed the ladder down into the fish hold.

Before we reached the beeper ending the first section, we landed another sword, a small marker of about 110 pounds that was quite frisky but was quickly overcome by Carl's tenacity and Kenny's sharp gaff to the back of its head. Once on deck, the fish flopped on its side, raising head and tail into the air and slapping both down, over and over, flogging the deck soundly. The flops got fewer and less vigorous, the up-and-down motion working like a pump, pushing the life from the fish, from torrent to trickle in a matter of minutes. The colors left the fish in the same way that a Polaroid picture develops, but in reverse. Sharp flashing silver lines and vivid colors yielded to fuzzy borders of blended shades of blues and purples that gave way to mottled patches of grays, blacks, and whites as the last of life dribbled from the defeated fish.

Crossings

SUE MULLER HACKING

Clouds like lion's claws streaked the pale South African sky as my husband Jon and I lugged our duffle bags out to the Cape Town docks. I didn't know enough about clouds to worry about them. They were simply nature's artistry in the sky: in this case a tapestry of gray on a background of blue. A light breeze had stolen the heat from the summer day, and I shivered in my flannel shirt and jeans. Jon and I were facing what we then thought would be the last three months of a year-long sojourn through Asia and Africa. Instead of flying to the States, we had opted to sail: bound for the Caribbean on a fifty-four-foot sailboat, part of a crew of ten. And we didn't know how to sail. Luckily, the hired skipper did, and had promised to teach us.

Enclosed within the sea wall, the inner harbor accepted an occasional low swell like a shrug, the oil-slick water heaving beneath the small freighters, fishing boats, and our lone yacht, *Sabi Star*. The pale-blue steel sailboat with its two masts and newly finished woodwork lacked the spit-and-polished look of the other yachts in the neighboring marina, but I couldn't see that yet. To me, she was to be our home and transportation for three months.

Back in 1981, many Rhodesians sought to flee their war-torn country but the newly formed government of Zimbabwe froze their assets, and allowed each person to leave with the equivalent of only one thousand dollars. In a desperate bid for escape from a country where he was no longer welcome, the sixty-five-year-old owner of *Sabi Star* had followed shipwright plans and welded himself a boat in landlocked Zimbabwe. He filled her with a year's supply of canned meats and vegetables, stashed all his belongings below, and trucked her fifteen hundred miles overland to Cape Town. From there, he offered passage to the Caribbean and England, attracting other young travelers like Jon and me. For the price of a plane ticket to the States we bought into a three-month adventure. With cash in hand from eight paying crew, the owner was ready to set sail. The fact that he didn't know how to sail was not an impediment. To shepherd us across more than six thousand miles of open ocean, the owner had hired twenty-six-year-old Howard, a man with sun-bleached hair, an easy smile, and a mellow confidence. On our two shakedown sails on *Sabi Star* in the previous weeks, I was reassured that Howard would be an easy person to learn from. His personality and his credentials—three ocean crossings as navigator on the Cape-to-Rio sailboat race—hooked us. "Anyone can learn to sail," he said. "The most important thing about an ocean crossing is the crew— everyone needs a good sense of humor."

Now, four weeks later, *Sabi Star* was ready for her voyage. Jon and I threw our gear in the aft double cabin and went to help stow the last of the groceries in the salon. I checked the medical supplies with Richard, a slim, cheerful South African who was making this journey as a last fling before diving into his job as an accountant.

I sorted through the box of bandages, antibiotics, and sterile dressings. "I took a first-aid course years ago," I said. "But I wouldn't want to take responsibility at sea. . . . There's no doctor on board?"

"I guess I'm it," he said, with a self-deprecating smile. "I was a medic in the bush wars in Angola." Then, grinning mischievously, he held up a handsaw that lay on the salon seat next to the medical supplies. "Amputation device, I believe."

After Richard and I finished packing the medicine chest, Jon helped the owner and Howard stow away the last of the electrical tools and paint cans that had been used just that morning to put finishing touches on the doghouse, the wooden dodger with a glass window. Although it seemed strange to me that the men could still be working on the boat the day we sailed, I didn't yet appreciate that a boat is never really "done."

"Let's start her up," called Howard. Through the soles of my sneakers I could feel the vibrations of *Sabi Star*'s engine, and I could hear the clicking, throbbing hum of the diesel. It was a sound that would, over the next three months, continue to elicit feelings of both anxiety and excitement—a herald of arrivals and departures to and from places unknown. Today I felt a heavy mix of sadness at leaving Africa and anxiety about our passage. My only other sails on *Sabi Star* had ended with a return to the Cape Town harbor. Now, our next planned stop was the tiny island of St. Helena, two weeks of day and night sailing to the northwest of Africa. The voyage stretched ahead of me like a giant gray fog bank.

I had no idea of the immensity of the ocean or the grueling task of day and night sailing.

The engine revs picked up and with quiet instructions Howard told someone to cast off the lines, removing our last umbilicus to life ashore. A gap of oil-slicked water opened between the pale blue of the hull and the rubber tire fenders on the dock. I inhaled the salty, acrid scent, reluctant to bid farewell to Africa. Sadness washed through me. Though it was Jon's family, not mine, that hailed from Africa, I had come to love the land and its people. In the simple act of leaving Africa, I already yearned for it.

The gyrating tail of a crepe streamer whipped my face as it caught on the wires behind me, and I brushed it aside to watch the last wall of the harbor slip behind us. White caps decorated the slate blue of Table Bay, and *Sabi Star* rolled awkwardly in the unsettled water. I sat on the side of the cockpit, suddenly aware that the wind was in my face, and we had turned so that we faced south into the heart of dramatic Cape Town and its sentinels of Lion's Head and Table Mountain.

"Let's get the mainsail up," said Howard. Five men stepped forward and created a fray of bodies pulling on ropes, wrestling a flapping sail, and balancing on the rolling deck. I held back, unwilling to push into the middle of so much activity when I hadn't a clue what to do.

From the mast Howard called back to the owner, Reg, on the helm. "More to port. Hold her into the wind."

The words blew past me with no significance. My knowledge of nautical terms included port and starboard, bow and stern. All the men's actions seemed mysterious and strangely complex. As one of only two women on board I wondered how I would measure up. Would I ever learn what all the ropes were for? Would Jon and I find friends among all these strangers? Could I keep my sense of humor on this long crossing? I sat still, using the time to observe Howard, the skipper. He moved with cat-like grace on the rolling deck, his body fluid in response to the erratic motion. His voice was soft and clear. As skipper, Howard held more clout even than Reg, the owner. I don't know how many potential skippers Reg had interviewed in Cape Town for this job—the port was probably bustling with them—but so far, it seemed, he had made a good choice.

I watched the frothy white wake that marked a clear trail back to the coast of Africa. This journey was the last leg of a one-year trip Jon and I, newly married, had undertaken as a last lark before settling down to house, work, and maybe a family in the States. I had to keep my thoughts on the present adventure, though, and not think too far ahead—I wasn't really ready to give up the vagabond life. The ocean, now free of the protection of land, had built into hulking swells that lifted *Sabi Star* and dropped her from one wave trough to another. The engine had been off for some time, and the sails billowed to the side, taut and pulling. As the hours passed, the coast shrank into itself until it was no more than a dark line on the horizon. Then, suddenly, we were alone on a vast circle of sea. The clouds that had looked so picturesque in Cape Town had congealed into a stew of gray, and the wind blew a cool breath over our backs as we sat or stood in the cockpit. The motion of the boat was becoming more erratic and I realized there were only five of us in the cockpit.

"Where is everybody else?" I asked.

Howard wore a tightened look on his previously relaxed face. "Below," he said. Then counting on his fingers he said, "We've lost Doug, Margie, Richard, Mike, and Wynn."

"Lost them?" I asked, astonished.

"Seasick. It won't kill you but you'll, wish it would."

The mere thought of seasickness can turn my stomach in circles, and I fought a twinge of nausea as the boat pitched beneath us. Thank god, so far, the motion-sickness pills I'd taken before sailing were working. Howard stood up and glanced around the horizon. The afternoon light had faded to a dark gray and the sky and ocean shared a dense, metallic look. A strange haze muffled the horizon so that I couldn't tell where sky ended and sea began. "Is that rain?" I asked, trying to understand what my eyes could not interpret.

Howard stared a moment, then said, "No, it's the ocean swells on the horizon." I followed his gaze overhead to the dense sky then back to the increasing ocean swells. "We've got to reduce sail," he said.

"Tell us what to do," Reg said.

Howard assigned Reg to the wheel with a brief instruction to be ready to turn the boat into the wind. Then he made his way onto the foredeck followed by Sean and Jon. I stayed in the cockpit, feeling useless, but out of the way. Slowly Reg turned the boat so that the waves plowed into us from the side, and with sickening lurches we became like a toy boat in a bathtub of malevolent children. I had a fleeting moment of sympathy for the seasick crewmembers below, then concentrated on hanging on and bracing my feet to avoid falling off the cockpit seat.

"Keep her going round. More into the wind, Reg," called

Howard. The motion changed again as we took each swell straight on the bow, and spray rose like a fan, then fell across the deck. Jon, Sean, and Howard clawed at the mainsail, pulling, tying, and working with it as it slapped and snapped madly in the wind. Everything, it seemed, was out of control. For minutes we lurched and dropped and rose on the sea, buffeted by the water and wind, but making no headway. Finally, at Howard's command, Reg turned the boat again. The sails pulled taut, and I felt us pick up speed as the boat found an easier gait over the seas.

When the men returned to the cockpit, Reg announced he was going below to heat up soup for any of us who could stomach it in "this bloody shit weather," then handed the wheel to Jon.

I finished the broth and crackers just as twilight gave way to the pressure of darkness, and despite the warmth in my stomach I felt the ancient despair of the loss of day. Out on the ocean there were neither streetlights to brighten the dark nor a campfire to warm and cheer me. The cloud-blackened sky settled around us like a shroud soaked in a coal-black ocean. I clung to the boat as the only base of physical reality. Where earlier I had been able to see waves rising and falling to the side of the boat, now there was only blackness, a constant swooshing sound of wind on water, and an occasional churning watery rush. In the darkness I was startled to see a white line of foam pressing down on us from behind. Then the boat lifted from the stern and the wave slid beneath us.

"Better climb into those oilies, Sue," said Howard. "You're on watch at eight."

I went below and pulled on rubber boots and bright orange

foul-weather gear. As I emerged from the companionway we nose-dived into a wave and spray flew from the bow spattering me with a patina of cold, oyster-flavored ocean. Baptized, I took the helm—a waist-high stainless steel wheel—for my first night watch at sea.

Just the week before, on placid Table Bay, I had been able to hold the compass steady within a degree or two. Now the wheel jerked and pulled and I fought to hold the black needle within ten degrees of our course. "How do you ever get to your destination when you're this erratic all the way across the ocean?" I asked.

Howard laughed. "Just try to average the course I give you," he said. "It works out."

By the end of an hour at the helm, my arms ached from the weight of the wheel. Salt water dripped down my neck and soaked my cotton flannel shirt. Jon, Howard, and I nursed the ship along while seven other crewmembers slept. By 10:00 P.M., when the next watch came on, I ached for some rest. The wind and stress of steering had depleted me. I climbed below decks and was shocked by the stench of diesel fumes and the stale smell of cigarette smoke. Luckily the air in our aft cabin was fresher. Bracing against the built-in dresser, I stripped to my underwear. With half the crew sick, there were only four hours to sleep before I was called for watch again. The tossing of the boat and the still air below tight-ened my chest, and I fought a wave of nausea. I took another motion-sickness pill, then crawled onto the bunk, praying that the wind would lessen soon. I had barely dozed off when I felt Jon crawl into the bunk beside me.

"How was your watch?" I asked.

"Bloody miserable." His voice seemed tight and anxious. Then as we rolled together again he added, "You're sticky."

"You too," I said in a half-sob, half-laugh, trying to inject levity into a situation over which we had no control. Water pounded the metal hull like a drum, the boat lurched, and slammed me sideways against Jon, then against the cold metal hull. "What's that noise? Are we okay?"

"We're okay, love. Just the metal hull." He spoke strongly, as though the strength of his conviction could bring order to this chaos.

I doubted that we were okay, but found reassurance in his tone. The boat motion was chaotic, thunderous. I wanted to hug him, to be comforted, but the boat flung us from side to side too violently to snuggle. The most we could manage was a quick touch of hands. Sleep eluded me. The South Atlantic—cold, unfathomably deep, and alien—tossed the steel sailboat from wave crest to trough, beating on us in a merciless cacophony of thuds, bangs, bongs, and sloshing sounds. The dark side of my imagination engulfed me. What if the boat sank? How would I escape this metal coffin? Could I swim up through the surging, frigid water to air? And then what? Tons of ocean water, suffocating, pounding, dragging me down. And the last thought, the regret, of dying where my body would never be found, my parents never knowing what had happened.

A loud *bong* shocked me out of my worries and I grabbed for Jon. I wanted to ask if we had made a mistake coming on this trip, but the only words I could find were, "It's pretty wild."

And wild it was. More powerful and inescapable than anything we had experienced before. In the previous ten months we had traveled alone throughout Japan and Taiwan without knowing a word of either language. We had eaten in small shacks in Hong Kong where the dim sum concoctions resembled nothing we had ever seen on a plate before. We had put ourselves in high-risk situations—climbing in the Himalayas on crevasse-etched glaciers, and, more recently, driving alone through blistering heat across the stark Namib Desert.

But this was the first time in which the danger crushed into my nighttime web of safety. What were we doing here, inside twenty tons of metal that floated only as long as we kept the ocean out? I hadn't bargained on such fear. Although I had had moments of doubt camped at eighteen thousand feet on a glacier surrounded by crevasses, the air had been still, our tent wrapped in monsoon mist, and the glacier perhaps temporarily halted in its downward motion. Months later, in our nylon tent in the Namib Desert, we slept soundly, trusting that the creatures of the desert would find other distractions more interesting than two humans. But tonight, this endless motion and tossing and noise shrouded my efforts to find beauty in adventure.

The night wore on interminably. The boat buffeted us and my emotions slid from fear to desperation as I grasped for ideas of how to survive should the boat go down. On board we had one life raft, rated for six, and an open rowboat, which would tip, fill, and sink in seconds. *Sabi Star* rolled and I pitched into Jon again, aware suddenly of the foolishness of signing onto a cross-Atlantic voyage with total strangers. I regretted the way we had so impulsively jumped at a new adventure. What did we know about sailing or the ocean? Didn't we have enough adventure in our mountain backpacking, skiing, and just everyday fun? Questions and fear mixed into a sickening miasma as I lay on the bunk, assaulted by the sounds of water on steel. What I didn't know, and could never have believed, was that this was the first of not ninety nights, but two thousand nights aboard a boat. And that this gale blowing us off the coast of South Africa was like God's hand stirring us round and round, shifting priorities, shifting emotions, setting Jon and me on a journey that would test the essence of who we thought we were.

᛭   ᛭   ᛭

I must have dozed off, because I finally heard a male voice say, "Your watch, Sue. It's 2:00 A.M."

Grateful for the chance for action, I rolled off the bunk and struggled into my damp, cold clothes, and oilies. I buckled on my webbed harness and staggered from one bulkhead to another to the companionway, bracing myself for another onslaught of fear as I faced the ocean.

But surprisingly, when I reached the cockpit, the noise lessened and changed character. Although black waves loomed above the deck and broke against the hull I could no longer hear the war between metal and water. The air was filled with a softer sound, a wondrous, tumbling whoosh as each wave curled, frothed, and dissolved into the next. Above me, the steel rigging cables whistled an eerie song in the wind. Rain pummeled the steel decks.

"It's beautiful," I shouted.

From behind the helm Howard grinned at me, his face glistening with salt spray, his hair whipped into disarray by the wind and rain. "You're a natural sailor, if you can say this is beautiful," he said, raising his voice above the wind and rain. The look in his eyes as he glanced at me told me he was pleased.

I felt far from being a natural sailor, but I let it pass. "So what's happening?"

"We're holding our course, 325 degrees, averaging seven knots." His face twisted into a playful grin. "That's really fast for a boat like this."

I didn't know if he was teasing or not, but stored the tidbit of information away to ask him, or Jon, later. Then I slid back along the seat to be near him so we wouldn't have to shout in the wind. "The weather looks worse than it did three hours ago."

"Up to a full gale now, sixty knots or so. And the rain started about midnight."

As I listened to him talk, I stared at the seas, black and gray, streaked with foaming white. As we surfed into a valley of water, the wave behind us poised high above the stern. I had to tilt my head to see the top of it and I braced myself for a wall of water.

Howard must have seen the look of fright in my eyes but he said nothing as he deftly guided the boat so that her stern rose to allow the wave to pass beneath her. "It's the rogue waves, the ones formed from several angles at once that you have to watch. And the breaking ones from astern; they're the ones that put the water in the cockpit."

"They all look like rogue waves to me," I said. I could feel no rhythm to the desperate dance occurring beneath me. Bow up, bow down, fall to port, bow up, fall to starboard, fall to port. My body jerked one way then the other. Years before, on a brief ocean sailing vacation in the Caribbean with my family, I remember watching my father stand at the railing, body loose and swaying. "Don't fight the sea," he had said. "Let your body move. Relax. It's like a dance with nature."

A rushing, foaming wave slammed against the side of *Sabi Star* and a fountain of water plastered us and poured into the cockpit. "Whoa," I yelled, able to keep my tone light because Howard looked so unperturbed. Salt spray coated my face now, too, and I licked my lips and laughingly wiped the water from my eyes. "*Brrr.* The water's bloody cold," I yelled.

"At least it's summer," he quipped back.

I grinned and shook the water from the sleeves of my jacket. I had been giving the South Africans a hard time about their Christmas in summer and the seasons all being upside down. It was January, and it felt, right now, like a blustery winter day in San Francisco, the city Jon and I called home. I looked down at the massive green rubber boots on my feet, and watched the last of the ocean swirl away down the cockpit drains. My feet ached with the cold, as though they were immersed in a puddle of snowmelt.

"Thank goodness for the drains," I yelled.

"Right. Bad idea to fill the boat up with water," said Howard. He fought the boat onto course and a look of consternation crossed his face. "Is Jon awake?" he asked. "We've got to shorten sail again."

"He's probably not asleep," I shouted back. "Shall I get him?"

Howard nodded, and I climbed below to call Jon. At the bottom of the companionway my foot slid sideways as the boat tilted severely to starboard. In the dim light of the red navigation light I saw shimmering oil and white bits sloshing across the floor.

"Cooking oil and rice," explained Jon, who surprised me by appearing from the galley.

"What happened?"

"You didn't hear the crash? Half the galley cupboards opened up and the wooden bars holding the rice and oil in place broke." Fifty kilos of rice and five gallons of cooking oil, I thought. Jon moved like a drunk, cautiously staggering from one handhold to another across the treacherous floor. "I couldn't sleep, so I thought I'd get some fresh air."

On deck, Howard told me to take the wheel and try to steady us on course. He watched a moment while I swung the helm first one way then the other. I felt the power of twenty tons of steel trying to wrench the wheel out of my hands and slew the boat whichever way the ocean willed it to go. Waves crashed and slammed the hull, and another curling monster washed across the aft deck. "Try not to over-compensate so much," Howard said, putting his hand next to mine on the wheel. "It'll be better when we get the mizzen down."

I wasn't sure what the mizzen was, but the thought that Jon and Howard were going to leave the cockpit worried me. "Clip onto something!" I yelled to Jon who was intently listening to Howard's directions. Moments later they both crawled from the cockpit to the aft deck behind me and I could no longer see them.

Howard's voice came above the wind. "Just keep her steady, Sue. Keep your eye on the compass and feel the boat."

Rise, fall, bend, lean on the wheel, back again, hold steady, crash, soaked, rise, fall, slam. Time seemed interminable. *Please, please don't get washed overboard,* I prayed silently, thinking of the men behind me. I heard a thud and then wild fabric rustling and grunts and calls, but didn't dare turn around except once, for a microsecond, just to reassure myself there were still two bodies there.

Suddenly the helm was lighter in my arms, the swings of the wheel less severe, and I got an inkling of what Howard meant by "feel the boat." As I felt my legs lift and bend to a rising wave, and the pressure increase to either left or right, I was ready to turn the wheel to compensate. Suddenly the men were back in the cockpit with me, Howard nodding and smiling. "Good job, Sue."

When Jon went below, I nestled back on the cockpit seat near Howard. Now as I looked above his head, I saw only the bare pole of the mizzen mast. The waves towered above it, and I calculated them to be over forty feet high. How much more of this could I take?

"Can't we just sail back to Cape Town?" I asked.

Howard looked puzzled, then shook his head. He leaned hard on the wheel, squinted at me, and said, "We can't turn back. We're running with the wind."

Despite the gentleness of his voice I felt a pang of embarrassment. I wasn't quite sure what that meant, to be running with the wind, but as I looked at the waves and how the sails were set way out to the side, I began to understand. The wind was pushing us along; to turn back would mean going straight into it. How outrageously naive could I be, to not even notice which way the wind had been blowing all afternoon and night? I managed a quirky half-smile and shrugged. "Oh yeah," I said, as if I had meant to make a joke. The waves behind us were no joke, though. An undulating, pulsating wave hung above our stern, then collapsed on itself, a forty-five-foot cliff of tumbling water. It crashed on *Sabi Star*'s stern sending a white-capped froth hurtling down upon us and washing into the cockpit. Howard held the wheel as salt water poured over us both. He shook himself like a puppy and gave me a look that seemed to inquire how I was doing.

I nodded and he grimaced. "Pooped," he said.

"Pooped?" I repeated.

"Water over the poop deck," he said, gesturing with a flick of his head to the area at the back of the boat.

I shivered, glad for the completely waterproof jacket and pants I had bought in Cape Town. "What was it you told us about good oilies, Howard? They have to keep you one hundred percent dry on the bow of the boat while waves pour over you?" I laughed with the sheer insanity of our situation.

Howard's tan face crinkled into a smile, turning the edges of his blond mustache up at the ends. "Are you one hundred percent dry?"

"Ninety-eight percent. It's creeping up my wrists to my sleeves. And I think the water crept up my legs and down my boots on purpose."

He laughed again as he turned *Sabi Star* hard to port, causing her to surf a wave with exhilarating speed. "Just don't try that part about 'on the bow' tonight," he added.

I turned forward to watch a froth of white sweep the foredeck, crashing and bunching up over the hatches and slam into the glass front of the doghouse that barely protected me from the spray.

🦌 🦌 🦌

When I was called for morning watch two days later, I lay on my bunk listening to the sound of waves on steel. I reassured myself that it was less frightening outside and rolled off the bunk to dress. In the galley I braced myself against the stove and pumped hot water from the thermos into two mugs with tea bags. I spooned in sugar and powdered milk, then struggled up to the cockpit to hand Howard his first cup of morning tea. It was a small action, but I felt a quiet pride. I had survived two nights and a day, and greeted morning with a familiar ritual. We raised our tea mugs. "Cheers," we said together.

The newborn light filled me with wonder. Though still clouded and gray, the sky had a luminous, almost silver, quality. And beneath it the ocean revealed its vastness. No longer was *Sabi Star* a tiny solid object in a black boiling cauldron. Now I saw us as a speck of color, of light blue and white, with odd angles and triangles and straight lines, on a round platter of sea. Although the wind still blew streaks of white over the water, the sea wore a deeper shade of gray than the sky.

Months later, after *Sabi Star* had safely completed her trans-Atlantic crossing, I thought back to that morning off the African coast: how I let my body sway to the motion, my mind freed from fear. How I was glad there was no turning back.

Sailing with Steinbeck

ANDROMEDA ROMANO-LAX

"Ready about?" Doug called as we steered into the wind. He stood in the cockpit, hand on the tiller, long black hair flying in snaky coils.

I scrambled to uncleat the main sheet behind him. "Ready!"

"Hard a-lee!"

I let the sheet out from one direction, dashed to the other side of the boat, and prepared to pull the corresponding sheet in from the other side. But I was overstoked on adrenaline. The sail flapped angrily, stalling mid-tack. I'd made the shift too soon. I should have waited for the wind to grab the sail and ease us into the new direction. My heart throbbed in my throat. My brother-in-law glared at me. It wasn't the first time I'd made this mistake and it wouldn't be the last.

Swiftly, he dropped his head to avoid the confused swing of the boom, and hurried to reclaim control of the boat, which was slowing down. I trimmed—tightened—the jib to help the small sail catch the wind again.

"Do it again," Doug demanded, steering back into a tacking position. "Ready about?"

"Ready?" Now my own response sounded like a question instead of a response. Which way were we going now? *Hard a-what?* The noises were deafening: all that metal against metal and the whap-whap of the sails, like some giant golem beating the dust out of gargantuan carpets.

"Now what are you supposed to do?" Doug quizzed me. My mind had wandered. In the cabin below, I could hear cupboards flying open and pans rattling up and down the aisle. Aryeh, my five-year-old son, was shrieking. Or was that two-year-old Tziporah? Their father, Brian, was taking care of them both, while he simultaneously searched for a missing chart and stooped to catch the vegetable cans rolling down the aisle. More thunks and rattles. It felt like the boat was heeling far to one side, like its port side was ready to splash down into the drink at any moment.

"Are we leaning too far?" I asked. "It really feels like we're leaning too far."

"No, it's good. Get ready."

"Ready? Ready for what? For tacking again?" I prepared to let go of the main sheet, but it was no use—I hadn't uncleated it behind me.

"Ah, shit." That was Doug, noticing my error. Should I stay ready, uncleat the sheet, make it tighter to fight the luff of the sail, or just get out of his way? Or maybe he was cursing something else. A metal cup that had been resting on the cockpit bench, near the tiller, rolled the captain's direction. He snagged it angrily and chucked it into the cabin without seeing who or what it might hit. A spoon followed. Then a handheld compass. This was one of his habits: dealing with loose objects by throwing them. Anyone sitting on an inside bunk suffered a regular torrent of projectiles.

"Ready about?"

Not that again. It had seemed so easy before. We'd rehearsed this maneuver a dozen times, zigzagging across the inner bay in small, measured tacks. But now I was nervous and couldn't think at all. We were heading north, to an anchorage at the mouth of Bahía Concepción in the Sea of Cortez. The red cliffs on the bay's east side faded to pale pink—*had we sailed that far away from them?* The bay's western beaches looked darker yellow as we approached. It was hard to judge distance on a desert coast that had no trees or houses to provide visual context. *Weren't there shoals in this area? Why was he taking us so close?*

"Just tell me what to do now in plain language and I'll do it," I said to the captain.

"You should know. I already told you twice."

"Tell me again. I'm learning."

"Go ahead, learn," he said, gesturing to the flapping sails.

"But I can't," I said. "You're making me nervous."

"I'm not making you nervous. *You* are making you nervous."

"No," I said. "I'm pretty sure. It's an objective fact. *You're* the one making me nervous."

After several more tacks, I called Brian to take my place. He was better at tacking, and better at keeping his mouth shut. I ducked into the cabin to see how Aryeh and Tziporah were doing. We'd lifted anchor at dawn in a hurry, without eating breakfast. Now I wedged my body between the cupboards and hurried to make them peanut butter and jelly sandwiches.

Tziporah ate hers and immediately vomited it back up. The mess covered the bunks, the floor, my shirt, and all her clothes. Brian fished a bucket out of the hold. He filled it with saltwater and passed the sloshing container to me in the cabin. I tried to strip Tziporah clean, wash her clothes with one hand, and sop up the vomit without falling on the slippery floor. *Zuiva*, the twenty-four-foot sailboat we'd borrowed for this trip, continued to sway as we tacked relentlessly across the bay's broad, foam-specked waters.

Twenty minutes later, I'd managed to wring the clothes. I'd swabbed the stinking cabin aisle. Aryeh had finally stopped shrieking in disgust. Tziporah felt well enough to ask for food. I held her limp, sweating body in my lap and fed her a piece of cheese. Almost immediately, she vomited again.

About seasickness, a naturalist once wrote, "In first place the misery is excessive, and far exceeds what a person would suppose who had never been at sea more than a few days. . . . I often said before starting that I had no doubt I should frequently repent of the whole undertaking. Little did I think with what fervor I should do so. I can scarcely conceive any more miserable state than when such dark and gloomy thoughts are haunting the mind as have today pursued me."

That was Charles Darwin. He'd been at sea aboard the *Beagle* only three days and already he was wishing he'd stayed in England.

Dark and gloomy thoughts were haunting me, too. With Tziporah's vomit still coating my hands, I railed out loud: "This isn't any fun!"

As if in answer to that cynical outburst, dolphins suddenly appeared. A large pod of them intersected our path, heading into the bay while we struggled to sail out. Dozens of battleship-gray fins sliced through the choppy waves. Shining rounded humps arched through the water, disappeared, and then emerged again. Doug loosened his grip on the tiller and we slowed to a lurching bob. I clipped Aryeh's safety harness onto a cockpit U-bolt so he could dangle his arms over the lifelines and watch the great pod swim by. I stood in the cockpit doorway and held Tziporah high. For a few moments, at least, her eyes brightened.

We tried to capture the pod on video camera—one of the few times we'd bring out the camera at all—but quickly gave up. Through the viewfinder, the fins and waves melded into a confusing blur of spray and glinting triangles. All the water around us was churning— with wind, with life. It was better simply to look and to marvel. Then, almost as quickly as they'd appeared, the dolphins were gone.

ॐ ॐ ॐ

It had taken us weeks to physically prepare the derelict *Zuiva* for this first full sailing day. Mentally and logistically, the preparations had been much longer. My husband and I had dreamed of making this trip for ten years, since first reading John Steinbeck and Ed Ricketts's classic *Log from the Sea of Cortez*, their eclectic account of a six-week marine science expedition aboard an off-duty fishing boat called the *Western Flyer*.

During that 1940 expedition, Ricketts, owner of a biological supply company, stalked tide pools for marine animals to pickle and sell back in California. Steinbeck, struggling that year with public infamy and writer's malaise, stalked the same habitats for ideas. Both men came away changed—shaken and reawakened to the wonders of the natural world at a time when the human world was darkened by impending war.

We wanted to know more about Ricketts's life-filled shore and Steinbeck's inspiring sea—why those places affected both men so much, and whether those fertile places still existed. Those questions were enough to draw me, my husband, and our two young children into a burnt wilderness for two months, following in the *Western Flyer*'s wake.

❧   ❧   ❧

Steinbeck and Ricketts's *Western Flyer* cruised along the cool, foggy Pacific Coast for seven days. Except for their stop at San Diego, they ran nearly day and night. Their plan was to motor directly to Cabo San Lucas, where they'd begin tide pooling, then follow the Sea of Cortez north as long as the tides would allow them, to the Midriff Islands, about two-thirds of the way north along the peninsula coast. Near Isla Angel de la Guarda, they would fight racing currents and cross the narrow gulf and continue south along Mexico's more-developed mainland shore. They'd stop in Guaymas, a city even then, and explore shallow lagoons to the south, before crossing back to Baja. The circle completed, they would round the peninsula's southern tip and head home.

We hoped to cover the same ground, but—because *Zuiva*'s home anchorage gave us our starting and ending points—in a different order. Our starting point, near Mulegé, was close to their midway point. We planned to sail south first, toward the peninsula's tip. Eliza, my sister and the captain's wife, would meet us for a week in La Paz, as a break from her farming—and our sailing—routine. Then, after she headed home, we'd backtrack north, continuing as far as we could manage, given the tide's increasingly powerful flow north of Bahía Concepción. We did not look forward to crossing the gulf, or navigating the mainland's treacherous lagoons, but we hoped to see those areas, too, completing our own Cortez circle.

All day we sailed past steep beaches, backed by wrinkled, rust-red hills. We saw no signs of life on the bay's eastern side and only a few buildings (the same ones again and again, to our chagrin) on the bay's road-accessible western side. But these looked rustic and vulnerable, dwarfed by the mountains rising behind. Just north of Ecomundo, the glint of distant road traffic faded as the highway headed inland, through treeless mountain passes.

Twenty-two miles long and from two to five miles wide, Bahía Concepción is eastern Baja's most sheltered body of water. It only takes a day to drive here from the border. But proximity alone matters little where there is little to drink and hardly a scrap of shade in hundreds of scorched square miles. Southeast and across the gulf, in mainland Mexico, the Spanish conquistador Hernán Cortés managed to topple the sophisticated Aztec empire. But he and his minions failed miserably here in Baja against an aboriginal people who roamed mostly naked, lived without shelter, and ate rats and snakes when other game was scarce. The desert rewards those who live simply, even if it does not reward them with much.

From Ecomundo north to Bahía Concepción's mouth, there are a few RV-accessible beaches, but no hotels and not a single harbor or marina. Imagine California's San Francisco Bay, only six miles longer than Bahía Concepción, with one-thousandth the population and not a single dock. Most of the peninsula is desert, receiving less than ten inches of rain a year. The land is steep and bare, a thinly inhabited spine twice the length of Florida, formed by four major and many lesser mountain ranges. In some places, the mountains are knife-edged and sheer, dropping directly into the blue gulf. Elsewhere, they are worn and rolling, eroded by infrequent desert downpours. From afar the desert hills can look seductively soft, like gently-folded pleats of brown suede. But up close, the suede reveals its prickly nature. Hikers who wander inland find themselves slipping along flood-cut arroyos of sharp-edged scree and struggling through thorny scrub patches.

$$\text{\.{S} \quad \.{S} \quad \.{S}}$$

At the end of our first sailing day, we pulled into Bahía Santo Domingo, barely a dip in the tawny shoreline. Nausea had knotted our stomachs all day. Now, giddy anxiety took its place. Doug was happy to stay aboard, to be alone on a still and silent boat, but the rest of us couldn't wait to go ashore and explore our first tide pools. For the first time, we would walk where the *Western Flyer*'s crew had walked and do what they had done.

Darkness would fall in three hours. We stuffed dry bags with everything we could imagine needing: journals, identification guides, the *Log* itself, artists' pencils, sketchbooks. Then we thought of the children and packed more: water bottles and snacks, extra clothes in case we all got soaked and chilled, and a first-aid kit because accidents happened only when we didn't have one at hand. Doug watched us with a bachelor's amusement, puzzled by all the fuss.

Steinbeck and Ricketts described rounding a point, Punta Concepción, from the open gulf and collecting along Bahía Concepción's eastern shore. Bahía Santo Domingo is the only good anchorage for miles and the cove itself is small, bordered by ochre bluffs to the north and gray bluffs to the south. It was the only logical place we could imagine them stopping.

Kayaking to land from the sailboat, we surveyed the shoreline, trying to guess exactly where they would have beached their dinghy. Nature lent our act of landing a sense of timelessness. The same wavelets that might have carried Steinbeck and Ricketts, now, in recycled form, carried us the last few feet to shore. The patterns visible on the beach were enduring patterns. Sloping sheets of hard, red rock underlay the shallows, followed by cobblestones, rippling sand, and a seven-foot wide strip of large sun-bleached shells, well above the high-tide line.

To our satisfaction, the land looked just as the *Log's* authors had described: "Behind the beach there was a little level land, sandy and dry and covered with cactus and thick brush. And behind that, the rising dry hills. Now again the wild doves were calling among the hills with their song of homesickness." Sixty years later, the doves still cooed from their perches atop cardon cacti. The breathy song sounded cool and dry—like dusk itself.

If the land looked and sounded just as it had in Steinbeck and Ricketts's day, the tide pools reflected the passage of years in more complex terms. The *Western Flyer's* crew reported finding beautiful pink-and-white murex shells. Sparky Enea, one of the feisty deck-hands, collected them by the washtub-full to bring back to his friends in Monterey. We couldn't have filled a tub, but we did find a handful of specimens, as well as other shell-fancier's favorites, like olive and tulip shells. They reported finding *hachas* (also called pen shells), the axe head–shaped scallops. We didn't find living species, but above the tide line, we sifted through all kinds of empty bivalve shells, including the hachas, and also clams and cockles. The vast number of empty shells suggested that this place had been rich with shellfish and that people had partaken—perhaps too enthusiastically—in this richness. We had heard of snorkelers finding great shell middens underwater, smothering other sea floor species.

Steinbeck and Ricketts found a sandy sea floor littered with sand dollars. We didn't see a single one. Below the high-tide line, we didn't even find much sand. Our tide pools were rocky—hard, red ledges washed by gentle waves. Balancing on great slats of dimpled, quartz-veined rock, we spotted dozens of sulfur sea cucumbers. We side-stepped crusty mats of barnacles, each one of the volcano-shaped mounds no bigger than an earring stud and just as sharp.

We carefully lifted brittlestars out of rocky crevices. The slender sea star cousins have small dark bodies and five thin arms that whip around in a fire-hose frenzy. The central body disk looks innocent—like the gently rounded, unseeing button eye of a teddy bear. But the thrashing legs look evil and alien. Shifting the writhing brittlestars from palm to palm was mesmerizing, like playing with a Slinky. Both Tziporah and Aryeh insisted on holding each one and took turns replacing every star to the place where it had been found.

We found hermit crabs, a moon snail, a colonial tunicate, and some polychaete worms. We watched several species of small, bright tropical fish, including the ubiquitous sergeant majors, swim between our ankles. And we saw lots of stuff we couldn't name: purplish lumps and jellied masses that might have been tunicates or someone's lost lunch—it was too hard to call. Every new species spotted felt like a hurried introduction: *Sorry, I've always been bad with names, but I'm sure we'll be seeing lots of each other in weeks to come.*

To the west, a copper haze settled over the bay as evening approached, but we had no desire to leave the beach. Somehow, we had poked around the water's edge, never wading more than knee-deep, for three hours. The whole time it felt like a scavenger hunt: on to the next ledge; look under the next cobblestone; careful not to slip on the razor-edged barnacles; maybe a few inches deeper. The children didn't pause or flag once—not to ask for dinner, not to ask when or whether we would return to the boat. Only when it was so dark that we couldn't see from one end of the beach to the other did we sit above the tide line and scrounge through our dry bags, pulling out bags of crackers and shivering as we hurried to make notes and sketch some rough shapes.

Unlike Steinbeck and Ricketts, we weren't gathering specimens, only looking—and yet our task still felt urgent and acquisitive. What did we expect to show for it at day's end, other than abraded fingertips and sore backs? What did we expect to show for it at the end of fifty such days? We didn't know, but the not-knowing fueled us, too.

Some of the species we saw matched those noted by Steinbeck and Ricketts. But other prominent features—like the red ledges of rock—didn't match what they described at all. The *Log* itself was vague about locations. Only later, studying the original captain's log kept by Tony Berry, would we understand our error. On our very first attempt to beachcomb in their footsteps, we had overshot Steinbeck and Ricketts's tide pooling spot by ten miles.

Our biggest concern had been that we might find a sterile, lifeless beach, stripped by visitors, pollution, or some other twenty-first-century hobgoblin. Instead, we'd found more creatures than we could count or name. Sunset and the upward surge of the tides had limited us to a three-hour search, but there would always be the next tide pooling "station," as Steinbeck and Ricketts called the twenty-three collecting stops they made.

At subsequent stops, we'd choose our anchorages more carefully. But finding the same littoral explored by our predecessors would never be easy. A beach, we were reminded time after time, doesn't look the same from one hour to the next. We had arrived at the middle of the day's tidal cycle. The day's lowest tide had already passed and now the water was rising, creeping imperceptibly up the shore.

Each day's lows and highs were like a curtain rising and falling on a stage, and even the stages themselves—sea bottoms shallow or sloped, muddy or sandy or rocky—would change all along our route. No two places and no two moments could ever be identical.

Tidal ranges vary by location, by moon phase, and by season. At the northern Cortez they are, at greater than thirty feet, among the world's highest. Farther south, they are less substantial. Even so, on a single beach in the middle Cortez, full and new moon tides can rise several feet over a few hours. Or, at quarter phases, when the moon and sun are exerting less combined gravitational pull on the earth's envelope of water, they may rise just a few inches. With the aid of computer-generated tide tables, we could aim to hit a low tide on the same beach that the *Log*'s authors had explored at low tide. But depending on the day they visited, their low tide might have been inches or feet lower than ours; meaning that they might have walked or waded several more yards farther from shore.

Even if we knew precisely when and where they started collecting, this still-portrait of a place would be imperfect. Because even as Steinbeck and Ricketts collected, the water rose or fell. Over hours of collecting, they would have shuffled forward or back to keep ahead of the waves—just as we did. There was no red "X" or modern quadrat on the ocean floor to show where our Monterey duo had found every sand dollar or sea anemone. Without that "X"—without replicable conditions—we could not claim to be modern empirical scientists and did not want to be. At best, we might claim to be amateur naturalists, in league with other curious bunglers, from Darwin onward. Maybe we were nothing more than wide-eyed travelers.

Captain Lou

PAMELA POWELL

I'm walking under the coffered arch at Rowe's Wharf, my five-year-old leaping beside me.

"I used to work here on the ferry boats," I tell Foster, though it's hard to equate this elegance with the splintered pier and rutted parking lot I remember.

Then I see the sign for Mass Bay Lines on the plate glass window. I didn't think the company still existed; it's been a long time since I've lived on this coast. But now here I am, living near Boston, holding the hand of my child, about to meet a friend for lunch and a trip to the aquarium. I add up the dates in my head—twenty-four years ago. Foster tugs on my hand.

"I want to go closer to the boats," he says. We walk down a gangway and onto a dock for the Logan Airport Shuttle boats. Waves are sloshing and I grip Foster's hand. We watch as a boat makes a neat turn into the dock and a deckhand steps off and fastens her lines to a cleat. Two men in business suits step aboard and hand the woman their tickets. I'm surprised to see that the captain is also a woman and I smile. As the deckhand unties her lines I go over to her.

"I used to work here, a long time ago," I say. "You don't by any chance know Captain Louise Twitchell, do you?"

"You know Lou?" she says, stepping aboard the boat. She grins.

"Tell her Pam Powell says hello."

"All right," she nods, and winks. "Have a great day!" she shouts over the sound of the engine as they pull off the dock. I can see her going down below to tell the other woman, the captain. I'm grinning now. This is a part of my legacy. I helped create this, these women driving this boat.

$$\text{\J} \qquad \text{\J} \qquad \text{\J}$$

I knew Lou. Nearly a quarter century ago now. When she was captain of the *Nantascot* and I was working my first summer as a deckhand, the summer after I'd graduated from high school; I was eighteen. My uniform: white shirt made of some cotton-synthetic blend, navy blue khakis, brass buckle on a canvas belt—the buckle scratched from leaning over the metal railing to get the line. On my shirt pocket, a plastic nameplate stuck on with tie tacks—it hurt if the backings ever came off and you got stabbed with the metal prongs. Mine said Deckhand P. Powell; Lou's, Captain L. Twitchell.

I wore a men's undershirt under my white shirt, never a bra. The undershirts would turn gray around the neck; sometimes I'd wear a uniform shirt two or three days in a row (I only had two), but never the T-shirt or tank underneath. They reeked. We used to have to lift the gangways, big hunks of metal you'd haul up at one end, wheel them over to whatever boat you were working on that day, and drop them. I was strong, could carry six flats of soda piled up and I wasn't even 5'4", my hair in braids that curled up at the ends. Mark, one of the boss's sons, the one who talked with a lisp and hated to steer, couldn't carry more than three flats of soda or beer. The cans glinted in the morning sun, and Mark grunted as he hefted them against his skinny chest. I didn't give him a hard time, though. I liked Marky. Sitting in the captain's chair in the wheelhouse, his legs twisted one around the other, telling stories, while I stood at the helm and Lou made her rounds down below. Growing up with Norm as a father, in that family of boys and boats, his younger brother Scotty (the one we called Rabbit because he was pink and pale, and was always chasing after the girls) headed for the Coast Guard, had to be tough. I'd take Marky's wheel watches for him while he sat on top of the wheelhouse and smoked a cigarette, if the radar wasn't running. If the radar was turned on, it could make you sterile. It was one of the first things a deckhand learned. I remembered Roger, one of the other captains, showing Eddie McDevitt and me how to swab a deck, and at the same time saying, "You never want to go up there when that radar's turning; it'll fry your patooties."

Nobody seemed to know if it applied to girls, but I kept away from it even when it was switched on to standby.

Mornings, to get ready, you had to fill the water tank that was disguised as a red smokestack. I liked sitting up there with the hose running—to the south, a view of the financial district, the modern bank we referred to as "pregnant" because of the way it bulged out at the middle, and the "Venetian blind building;" to the north, the Customs tower that stood like the little engine that could, amidst all the taller, more modern buildings that had sprung up around it.

The pilings creaked and swayed as the boat surged against them; gulls careened overhead. When Lou came on board she didn't say much. Went down below to check the engine. I'd already done it—filled up the batteries, seen how much water we'd have to pump from the bilge , checked the oil—careful not to slip on the greasy metal ribs of the ferry.

She was a clunker, that boat, paint buckling on the bulkheads, the deck coming up in places. Red and white and blue, from a distance she looked cute, stubby, designed for pleasure; in reality, she rattled and shook and stank of diesel if the wind blew from astern. Deckhands had to scrub the heads with some stuff from a bottle that burned the porcelain clean and would burn your skin, too, if you got any of it on you; we had to sweep the decks and swab them at the end of the day. Cigarette butts, candy wrappers, pools of gum that had to be peeled off the blistered decks like Band-Aids.

Lou's domain was the wheelhouse. White shirt buttoned over breasts like cannons, she slid her captain's stripes on to the flaps above her shoulders and buttoned them into place, her smooth, round face red from the exertion of climbing up the stairs. Her captain's hat sunk down to her eyebrows, giving her a pinched look under gold braid that Lou called her "scrambled eggs." From the back you couldn't tell she wasn't a guy.

Mornings she had her paper, her coffee, and a grimace as if the sun were too bright, log book open for entries. She could have a parking lot full of passengers waiting to board, day-trippers heading to George's Island and Nantasket Beach, and Lou would scowl at them, waiting until exactly ten minutes before departure to board. Then together we'd hoist the gangway into position. She'd hand me the clicker, bellow to the passengers, "Nantasket Beach!" and retreat to the wheelhouse.

I'd count them as they boarded—parents clutching toddlers' pudgy hands; wheelchairs we had to lift, roll, lift onto the upper deck; women with soft flopping flesh and dangling arms spilling out of house dresses; hairy-chested men heading for the beach; greased fat squeezed into tank tops, halters and cut-offs. After the last passenger—and then usually one more—we'd push and heave the gangway off; it would land with a crash and I'd close the metal gate, slamming it into place, sidestepping with my toes. Then up to the bow to fling the bowline off the piling, then to the spring line while Mark took care of the stern. I loved the power of sending a shiver of extra line out and up to lift the loop off the piling and send it flying; I'd quickly haul it in. You had to have the exact timing just right. Louise taught us to coil the line clockwise. She'd yell at Mark if she ever caught him doing it the wrong way. When he did, we had to hang the lines off the stern to get all the kinks out—wet, heavy, trailing snakes in the polluted waters of Boston Harbor.

I rode my bike to work, an old black three-speed, up over Beacon Hill in the wee hours of the morning. At night I'd find myself tangled up in the sheets, fastening a twisted sheet around an imaginary cleat in my sleep. Once my friend's older sister walked in on me where I sat without a shirt; from the back, she thought I was a guy. I was proud of my muscular back and strong shoulders.

Mostly those days blend together, a blur of seventy-hour work weeks, punching my time card in the ravaged trailer office in the parking lot at Rowe's Wharf before climbing aboard the "Nanny boat," as we affectionately dubbed her. But some days are clear in my mind, like a course on the chart, marked out with the narrow lead of a well-sharpened pencil.

I remember one July morning. Soon as we got out of President Roads, the main channel in the inner harbor, Lou handed me the wheel. She didn't need to tell me the course anymore. Cool metal under my hands, I stood leaning forward, looking out, and watching for yahoos in their speedboats. The radio wasn't busy yet. Sunlight burned across the water; it was going to be a scorcher.

"Wrinkle run this afternoon," Lou said, looking at the schedule.

"Oh great." That meant wheelchairs, lots of them, and with the tide high all day the gangway would be at an ungainly angle.

Lou shrugged. She'd make it work. She cleared her throat and turned on the mike. When Louise made her announcements she almost sounded nice, "Good morning ladies and gentlemen, welcome aboard the *Nantascot*," though her expression was grudging. She poked her head out the door to look behind us.

"*Bay State* coming up on your starboard quarter," she said, "but they've got room. Just hold your course."

"Okay," I said, "holding course." Lou hated it if you didn't repeat what the course was. She wanted to know that you'd heard her, or if you were dozing off at the wheel. We watched as the *Bay State*, freshly painted with red and black trim, churned alongside.

"That Charlie," she laughed, as the captain stood in the doorway of his wheelhouse and saluted her. She gave him a wave. We could hear the brass band tuning up on the aft deck. They had a jazz cruise weekend mornings in the summer.

"Looks like they're getting good business," I said.

"Yep, Nick Flaherty always has known how to grow a dime."

I looked out at the water, bottle brown under the creamy froth stirred up by the *Bay State*'s twin screws. Soon we'd be heading off to starboard ourselves, past Nix's Mate and the striped buoy that marked its shifting sands. It was a hell of a place to get caught in fog. We'd been there more than once, Lou's head in the radar calling out compass courses while a deckhand steered, her face pressed so hard into the black plastic eyepiece on top of the radar screen that she'd have raccoon marks indented around her eyes when the fog burned off and she finally came up for air.

Deckhands took turns on bow watch—heads cocked, listening, staring into the white nothingness where torn shreds of fog fashioned themselves into phantasms, ghost ships drifting past. We'd point into the murk whenever we heard a whistle, a horn, a shout, or the gunning of another boat's engines. Fog was scary like nothing else. Rocks, shallow water, other boats, many of whom had no clue how to navigate in the fog, all posed hazards. When the fog lifted, there'd often be a trail of little boats following us, using our horn as a beacon. When our turn on bow watch was up we'd retreat to the wheelhouse, hair and face and skin sodden and dripping, hearing half-gone from the foghorn's blare. Taking a turn at the wheel, steering the courses Lou shouted out, repeating them, keeping the boat on course. Without anything to steer for, it was easy to get the boat veering back and forth. Lou didn't let Mark take the wheel in fog anymore. Too many times she'd barked at him, "Cut out that snake wake." Muttering about how if he weren't the boss's kid . . . but this morning a breeze kept the air clear.

A woman carrying a child, who was squeezed into a sailor suit, appeared at one of the wheelhouse doors.

"See, Honey, there's the captain." She fixed her gaze on Lou. "Would it be all right if I held him by the wheel, you know, so my husband could take a photo?"

I made as if to move over; this was commonplace, though Lou's thick neck reddened and she tried to smile, took an awkward step back.

"It'll have to be quick," she said. "We're coming up on the island."

"George's Island?" the woman gushed.

"Yep," Louise nodded, hands in her pockets. We both stood to the side as Dad clicked away at Junior. The boy didn't respond to his father's goo-goo faces.

We were passing between the curves of Gallop's and Lovell's Islands now, and George's was dead ahead. I could see the prominent brick building on the dock and the *New Boston* offloading her passengers. We would be next.

Just then, Mark showed up and peered inside the door of the wheelhouse. "Want some relief?"

"That's okay." Mark had a knack of showing up just before the end of the watch. But I didn't care. I'd much rather steer than stand out on deck giving the evil eye to anyone who dropped their candy wrappers or Coke cans on deck, or grabbing little kids, telling them to stop running, only to see them do it again as soon as they turned the corner.

"You get that stern line, Mark," Lou said. "Pam and I will handle the bow and the spring."

"Okey-dokey," Mark said, heading for the stern. He might have time for a cigarette.

I set up the bow and the spring lines, looping them over the railing just the way Lou had taught me so they'd be ready. I asked a few people to move so I'd have plenty of swinging room. When Lou got the boat close enough, I sent the spring line flying onto the piling, then hauled in the slack. With one turn around the cleat I leaned back into it, letting the boat creep up to our mark. In the door to the wheelhouse, Lou raised her fist to show that I was to make it fast, and then gave me one of those squinty smiles of hers that I lived for. I shot up to the bow and got that line on with the help of Mark, who'd hopped onto the dock after securing the stern. We were there only long enough to unload some passengers so that they could walk around inspecting the hollowed-out fort—abandoned buildings that kids swore were haunted, where they ran around inside screaming and yelling, smoking cigarettes, or writing graffiti.

Back on board, Mark came up to the wheelhouse with the clicker.

"Thirteen off on the island," he said, handing it to Lou. She tossed it in the air catching it with the same hand, and gave Mark a fake glower. Sometimes I wished she could just smile at him full-on, like she sometimes did at me.

I glanced over as Lou took out her pocket watch. She held it in her hand, feeling the weight and heft of it—its dull silver like the ship's wheel under my hands—and began winding it.

"Bud gave me this, when I came down from Vermont."

I nodded. I'd heard his name before, but didn't know too much about Bud, the man who lured her down from Vermont where her family owned a dairy. Away from cow hooves, teats, and Bag Balm, he planted the sea in her. She used to work for him, on his fishing boat, working the lines, swabbing decks, and helping the tourists to hook on bait. And then he died.

"Bud used to say, 'Lou, you're tougher than a boiled owl.' I think he liked that about me. That I was tough. A farm girl. I was strong from milking cows." She looked down at her small white hands and shook her head.

I glanced out the window to make sure the route was clear, we were passing Bumpkin Island, and then I looked back at Lou. Her eyes were full of tears, and just then one fell onto her impeccable white shirt.

"Lou," I said, wanting to reach my hand toward the smooth skin of her arm where a thick silver bracelet delineated her wrist, "you okay?"

"Yeah," she shook herself, turned her head, and wiped her eyes. "Yeah, I'm okay. Why don't you go make an engine check? I don't trust that Mark to do it right. And then get your lines ready." She pulled a men's white handkerchief out of her pocket and blew her nose.

"Okay," I said, leaving her standing behind the wheel, staring at the green curves of World's End and a single white osprey standing in the muck. I wanted to hug her but I didn't dare. Only when she'd had a few, then she'd talk.

❧   ❧   ❧

On the dock with Foster, I watch the airport boat pull away, thinking of all the things I would tell her and all the things I remember, churning around in my head like the white froth of their wake.

"Let's just check in here for Captain Lou," I say at the top of the gangway. I hold the door open for Foster and step into the office.

A young man, hair cropped like a well-kept lawn, looks up from his orderly desk.

"I used to work here," I say, "a million years ago, as a deckhand on the *Vineyard Queen* and the *Nantascot*. I doubt you have them anymore. They were pretty old then."

"*The Queen*," he laughs, "yeah, she was mothballed a while ago."

Foster pulls at my sleeve, "What's mothballed?"

"It's what happens when you get old and you're a boat," I say. "If you were a horse, people would say you'd be 'put out to pasture.'" Foster's only half-satisfied with my explanation, but gets distracted looking out at a jet taking off from Logan.

"But we've still got the '*Nan*,'" he continues. "She's down in Gloucester, hauled out."

"Wow, that's amazing. Is anyone around still from those days? Like Louise Twitchell?"

"Lou," he said. "Yeah, she's still around. Got married to her friend . . ."

Bud? I think for a minute and then I remember—Hawaiian shirt, red face. "George?" I ask.

"Yeah; he just turned ninety. So she's Louise Rialto now. She lives in Medford."

We walk down Atlantic Avenue, away from the boats, my mind still turning on Lou.

🦌   🦌   🦌

It's weeks before I pick up the phone.

"Pam!" she says. "Of course I remember you. We finally tied the knot, George and me. Now he's ninety and legally blind. But we're doing all right, busy. I'm on the *'Belle* three days a week and we got the nineteen cats to look after . . ."

"Nineteen cats?"

"And a dog," she adds.

We talk a little more and agree that I'll bring Foster for a boat ride sometime soon.

It's a bright September afternoon, wind whipping up the water like frosting on a cake, when we finally take the subway to South Station and walk down to Rowe's Wharf.

I'm wearing a sundress, and Foster jumps around on the sidewalk, running ahead of me a little, then back. When we reach the dock, we see the *Island Belle*, chugging in our direction. It's a fake paddle wheeler, and Foster's disgusted.

"That's not the boat we're going on, is it? I want to go on the *Freedom*," he says, pointing up at the modern-looking catamaran.

"Sorry," I say, "we're going with Captain Lou. Maybe she'll let you steer." Foster looks resigned.

My stomach tightens as I watch the *Island Belle* turn into the dock; I can see Lou at the helm, short brown hair, concentrating. She gives us a wave.

Once the passengers are off, she comes down to the gangway.

"Pam, it's been a long time," she says giving me a hug. "Hello, Foster, you coming for a boat ride? He's a beauty," she says to me.

Foster frowns, pulling on my hand. "I want to go on the *Freedom*."

"Come on, bunny," I whisper in his ear.

$$\text{\small ❧ \quad ❧ \quad ❧}$$

We're up in the wheelhouse chugging across the inner harbor; Foster perches on a chair by the window.

"No, they stopped those runs to Nantasket Beach a long time ago. We still go to George's, and do the harbor tours and over to the *Constitution*." A jet roars overhead and Lou pulls out the mike ready to switch it on.

"To our starboard lies Castle Island and beyond that Pleasure Bay, South Boston." She launches into a tale of card playing and murder, her words and intonation as familiar as if I'd heard them the day before. I remember this, all of this. The deep blue water splashing against the hull, the smell of diesel on the aft deck, the vibration of the stanchions, Lou's solid back in front of me.

When she clicks off the microphone I ask her the question I've been wondering.

"Lou, you must have been just a kid when we were working together?"

She laughs, "I was thirty-six, I'm coming up on sixty now."

"That's hard to believe," I say, "you don't look it. I've got more gray hair than you do." I run my hand across the top of my head.

"Yeah, I'm doing all right, and George, he isn't doing too bad for ninety. He's down below. Really, I just do it for him. He likes to get out on the water."

"It sure brings back a lot of old memories," I say, looking out over Foster's curly head at the harbor. "Remember Eddie McDevitt chatting up girls on the aft deck?"

"Yeah, and layovers at Nantasket—we had some wild times!" Lou belts out a laugh and her eyes crinkle up at the corners.

"And those crazy 'booze cruises' when we'd have to get tough with the drunken passengers; I remember you just yanking some down off the wheelhouse, making sure they didn't jump overboard. Remember the women who'd show up in high heels, and those big cracks on the dock?"

"Yeah, they were asking for it," Lou says.

"What about Mark?" I ask, when our stream of reminiscences seems to have slowed.

"He lives in Portland, gay, of course. It's Scotty who's had the hard time. Got into drugs and all that. Hard on Norm. But then Norm was always hard on him."

"Huh," I say. I always thought it was Mark who got the hard time from his father. For a moment I could hear Marky's laugh, his smoker's cough, kind of shallow in his throat. I pictured him hiking up his blue jeans or tearing the wrapper off a Three Musketeers, eating it in careful tiny bites. Once, he fell asleep curled in a corner of the wheelhouse, and when Lou saw him she just asked if I was going to take his watch. The sun was going down and it was one of those sunsets you wanted to close the blinds on, it was so goddamn pretty. At least that's what Lou might have said. I remembered steering and how cozy it was in the wheelhouse with Marky asleep on the floor.

Lou interrupted my thoughts. "So you've had your license for a while. I heard you were working for the *Hy-line*. Are you using it now?"

"Not so much since Foster," I say. "I sailed in the Caribbean for three years, working on charter boats and cruising, then I ran a harbor tour boat in Annapolis and a yacht club launch in Camden, Maine. Then I ended up teaching for Outward Bound in Maine and Florida and Washington State. A little bit here in Boston—I taught a course last summer here in the harbor, for girls."

"Oh, those little life boats," she says. "I've had to dodge them—crazy-looking things with those oars sticking out all over. Guess it's good for the kids. You have rough ones?"

"Sometimes," I smile.

"Ever think of coming to work on the ferries again?"

"Yeah, I do. Hard to work it out with my little guy, though."

"I'm lucky I guess. For me it's always just been the water. You know," she said looking straight at me, "I can still loop a piling in a gale."

"I bet you can." Truth was, I would have loved to see her get a ringer again. I remembered, morning on the commuter boat, approaching the dock at Hull Gut, tide running hard, wind blowing off the dock.

"Like this," she'd shouted, coming out of the wheelhouse and grabbing the line from me. The spring sailed free and clear and pretty coming down right over the bollard.

"Take up the slack," she'd hollered as she ran into the wheelhouse to take the boat out of gear.

"Nice job, Lou," I'd whispered

Rowing to Latitude

Jill Fredston

I left England anxious to trade confined waters for open spaces, and to leave manicured greens, black academic gowns, prescribed manners, and overcooked brussels sprouts behind. Armed with a master's degree (in glaciology from the University of Cambridge's Scott Polar Research Institute) and one trophy oar, I arrived in Anchorage during the summer of 1982. It wasn't a question of whether I would explore Alaska's coastline, which beckoned with more miles than those of the lower forty-eight states combined, only of when and how. Sea kayaking was beginning to be popular, but the five weeks I'd spent as a seventeen-year-old in Prince William Sound spinning my arms like a pinwheel had convinced me that kayaks were not for me, at least not while I had legs and an understanding of leverage. The only wilderness rower I knew rowed a heavy wooden dory that made me feel like a galley slave. It surprised me that there were no rowing boats made for touring. There were recreational "ocean" shells that were sturdier and more stable than racing boats, but they were either undecked like canoes, inviting swamping in big water, or hatched over so that there wasn't room for much more than a water bottle and car keys.

Still, I had to start somewhere, so I ordered a recreational shell by phone. The sister of a friend drove it from Maine, across the country and up the Alaska Highway, while I waited impatiently, eyes flitting from the university desk where I worked to a map of Alaska on the wall. The boat, an Alden double, was eighteen feet long, with patriotic colors—a red deck, white trim, and blue hull. With its wide-open interior, it could be rowed as either a single or a double. Eventually, I would build watertight bulkheads and deck it over, making a vast storage space accessible through removable hatches and reducing the swampable area to a cockpit large enough to accommodate only the four-foot-long track for the sliding sea. Aluminum riggers extended from the track and over the gunwales of the boat, and on the end of each arm was a brass oarlock. Nine-foot-nine-inch oars, varnished to a gloss and disarmingly light, slid into these oarlocks and were held in place by a plastic collar, called a button in rowing terminology. The bottom of the boat was flat, which I gradually learned gave the boat a tendency to slide off the waves sideways in beam seas and cause me to smash my hands together. I would also discover that the lay-up of the fiberglass was relatively thin for the abuse to which it would be subjected.

٤   ٤   ٤

Sculling is the closest I'll ever come to being a ballerina, to creating visual music. A good rowing stroke is fluid, circular, continuous. It is unmarred by pauses, lurches, arm yanks, or back heaves. The end of one stroke is the beginning of the next, the movement so smooth and graceful that it is impossible to tell exactly where the power is coming from. It should look misleadingly easy, almost effortless. Most beginners are amazed when they fall off the seat, bang their hands together, and propel themselves in circles.

To describe rowing, I find myself closing my eyes and listening for the catch, the instant when both blades enter the water at precisely the same moment, and feeling the boat run underneath me. At the catch, my chest brushes against the steep bend of my knees, and my arms are fully extended toward the stern. People reach for my biceps when they hear I'm a rower, but really my legs and back do most of the work. Lifting my hands slightly to drop the oars into the water, I instantly lock on with my legs and thrust off the foot stretchers. The oars, with little more than the blades buried, begin to arc through the water. When my legs are about halfway down, my back starts to open up, leaning toward the bow, as though I'm sinking into a favorite soft chair with my arms outstretched. Only during the last part of the stroke do my arms bend and provide the pull to bring the oar handles to my chest. Throughout the stroke, my oar handles move in a straight plane; they do not loop upward, rowboat style, or the oar shafts would dive deep into the sea. At the finish, my hands drop down to my stomach and my knuckles rotate skyward, lifting the oars, feathering the blades so that they are parallel to the water, and pushing the oar handles aft. My legs and back follow my arms up the slide, as gently as possible, lest I push the boat in the wrong direction and lose hard-won inches. That's a complete stroke, repeated about twenty times per minute, sometimes for fourteen hours a day—the equivalent of a marathon or two—most days of the week, month after month. In rowing, rhythm is everything.

§   §   §

Traveling backward, which most people think of as rowing's greatest liability, has trained me to enjoy looking at where I have been as well as to move toward objectives I can't see, ready to react to the unexpected, like a low-lying iceberg or an off-angle wave. I, of course, think this has had a beneficial influence upon my career, making me flexible, resourceful, and willing to shift in less conventional directions. My father would say that it accounts for my seasonal unemployment. With a few dramatic exceptions, though, I've rarely run into obstacles. If the shoreline is uncomplicated— that is, not cluttered with rocks or ice—I'll turn around and take a second to mentally map the next stretch of coast. I use my ears more than I ever would have guessed. They can pick up the lapping of the water against a fixed object like a rock or alert me to unexpected shallows. People walk, birds fly, I row backward to move forward.

Zen is a stroke without beginning or end. It is a sensation of being completely connected and disconnected in the same moment, a feeling of pure harmony and symmetry. It happens when my oars are just extensions of my arms and my legs seem to grow out of the boat. I am not consciously working or thinking in any disciplined way. The boat flows. I am a marionette, the boat is part of me, the water is air, the journey the ultimate magic carpet ride. Or maybe I am the boat—its heart, its motor, its spirit. My legs are pistons. I could row forever.

꒰   ꒰   ꒰

Any prolonged rowing causes a marked physical metamorphosis. Once, in Labrador, an urchin of a boy who could have been Oliver Twist clasped his thin fingers around my biceps and exclaimed in an almost incomprehensible 1800s Cockney accent frozen in time by the emigration of his ancestors, "Jeez, ye got lumps welded onto ye arms." I end a trip with my stomach muscles bunched in six neat compartments, hands as tough as walrus hide, sculpted shoulders, and a back that looks as if it has been implanted with bicycle tubes paralleling my spine. The bones of my buttocks are so thoroughly bruised by the rowing seat that, for months afterward, I squirm on unpadded chairs. Once, at a resort on the Alaska Peninsula, I was introduced to a florid-faced oil executive from Texas with initials for a name. He recoiled when we shook hands and looked at me as though I'd jetted in from Mars with the express purpose of horrifying him. "Honey," he said, "no woman deserves hands like that."

Doug and I try to break our bodies in slowly. We begin with five-to-eight-hour days and, over the course of about three weeks, work up to the double digits. After miles of rowing, my creaky knees may not let me leap tall buildings in a single bound, but I feel as if I could at least heft a skyscraper or two over my head. En route from Seattle, after weeks of battling headwinds, Doug rolled over in the sleeping bag one morning to inform me that he didn't think his heart was beating. On reflection, I decided I had the same problem. We took our resting pulses. They were only thirty-seven beats per minute; during the winter, they are normally around sixty. Our conditioning peak lasts until about the three-month mark. Then, led by overused joints, limited fresh food, and depleted body fat—despite calorie-laden snacks and a dollop of olive oil on almost everything—we begin to slide off the back side of the curve.

To my great regret, I never look as imposing as I feel. Inevitably, upon my return every fall, my friends exclaim, "You look terrible!" and compare my frame to that of an emaciated refugee. On a ferry south in 1995, after rowing twenty-five hundred miles from Sweden to Russia, we met a German tourist who said, "It must be a problem for a little woman like you to keep up with a big, strong man like Doug." While my brain flipped through a jukebox of responses, rejecting most of them as too scathing, Doug answered truthfully that, thanks to technique, I was faster than he.

As we've grown to better understand our needs and have taken on increasingly unforgiving coasts, the boats we row have undergone a physical transformation as well. It has been a long time since they resembled anything we could buy in a store. They are closer to extensions of ourselves, customized over the years to the point where they feel like a second skin. It seems appropriate that rowing boats are called shells. We are like turtles. Our boats are our homes, our safety dependent upon them.

Comparing a racing single to an oceangoing shell is like equating a toothpick with a log. The former is generally twenty-six feet long and weighs less than a pound per foot. Any rower forgetful enough to let go of the oars can flip like a pancake. Paddling in rough water or landing in surf is as unthinkable as driving a Ferrari on a road covered with deep snow. Wilderness rowing requires boats that are fast but stable and forgiving enough to let us stand in the cockpit to stretch or scout a route through ice. They must be light enough to allow us a hernia-free way of hauling them up the beach at night, sometimes hopping slimy boulders in the process. And they must have ample cargo capacity inside secure, watertight bulkheads. More room for food means greater range, more freedom to stay out longer and reach more remote, wilder country.

In British Columbia, at the dock of a fish-packing plant where several wayfaring yachts were moored, I met a rumpled man in his thirties who was very interested in our "canoes." I still remember my bewilderment that he could so differently perceive my boat, with its riggers and oars. But we kept chatting. I asked him in turn about his "canoe" and he invited me aboard. *Winter Hawk* was forty-eight feet long, with three queen-size beds, a washer/dryer, a dishwasher, a trash compactor, and a video intercom that reached into every corner of the boat. Doug later reported that the engine-room floor was clean enough to use as a plate, but I was preoccupied by the full-sized couch. It was luxuriously soft and I spent as much time as I could on it, tantalized by the idea that I could lie motionless while the boat traveled.

The man's mother graciously plied me with oranges and confessed, in a thick Oklahoma drawl, that she had thought they were "roughing it" before they met us. It was apparent to both his mother and me that though we had traveled the same coast, what we had seen and heard and felt had been shaped by our modes of travel. She knew the harbors, I looked for beaches. The distances between places seemed shorter to her—a mile was a matter of scant minutes and fuel. She saw green walls of forests while I, closer to shore, discerned individual trees. No locals along the way had taken one look at *Winter Hawk* and insisted that the owners come home with them for the night. This kind woman with a neat gray bun on top of her head couldn't fathom how we could feel comfortable moving so slowly, perched only inches above the waterline. I struggled for words to explain why, for me, that was precisely the draw. Our boats don't allow much insulation from the environment; they force us to be absorbed by it.

It's a reliable maxim that most boaters are convinced that their particular craft is the ultimate. On the Yukon, we met four Germans floating the river on a barge they'd built by lashing six rusty oil drums with fraying rope, piecing together a plywood platform from scraps, and scavenging a ratty green couch. This ragged approximation of something capable of floating didn't stop one of them from commenting on my shell, "God, that's a strange boat to find on the Yukon." Owners of big boats are especially skeptical of anything smaller. But at times our boats seem safer than their larger counterparts. When conditions get rough and the captains of forty-foot vessels are seeking anchorages and fretting about their exposure to the storm, we simply tie down our boats well above the tideline and go read in the tent.

$$\text{\textsection} \qquad \text{\textsection} \qquad \text{\textsection}$$

Traveling with rigid boats longer than your average car is not an easy proposition. Our two Amerows made their way to Sweden via barge, truck, and freighter. We rowed to Russia and ferried the boats back to Tromsø, Norway. A supply boat carried them to Bjørnøya, a dot in the Arctic Ocean, and the following spring a coast guard vessel provided a lift to Spitsbergen, east of Greenland. They made their own way around the island, with us at the oars. At the end of the trip, we were unsure how to get them home, reluctant to keep asking favors of friends of friends. So, after anxious debate, we sawed the hulls in half. While I fretted uselessly nearby, Doug and our partner, John, borrowed an electric saw in exchange for a fifth of whiskey and sliced each boat in two, right through the middle of the cockpit. It seemed a blatant act of mutilation, like sawing off a foot. The boats, which had looked so perfect minutes before, now looked deformed and pitifully fragile. I was shaken by the reminder that the indomitable craft to which I entrusted my life on cold oceans was really a mere one-eighth inch of ragged Kevlar.

The Amerows might never float again, but at least they fit on the plane. We flew with them from Spitsbergen to Copenhagen. On the next plane to Seattle, the pilot switched on the intercom and, in a crisp Scandinavian accent, apologized for the half-hour delay at the gate, explaining, "There is something jammed on the loading dock." Doug and I, surmising correctly what was stuck, slunk down into our seats behind newspapers, willing ourselves invisible.

At home, we had extra-strong fiberglass bulkheads built so that the bow and stern sections could be reattached. I wanted to bolt the stern section of my red boat to Doug's yellow bow, but he wasn't interested. We now have break-apart boats, though the process of putting them together or taking them apart takes about half a day per boat. Once they are bolted together, they do not leak a drop.

After a second summer rowing in Greenland, we flew home with all our gear rather than leaving it for another season as planned. The hitch was that we had a stopover in New York and would then be transferring to a less cooperative airline. From my parents' house, I called the airline to put a note in our reservation that we'd be traveling to Alaska with "kayaks." The agent informed me curtly, "We absolutely don't take boats of any kind. You can ship them as cargo, in which case they can travel on the same plane." I called cargo, but they quoted an outrageous price.

What to do? In the middle of a toss-and-turn night, I decided that we didn't have boats, we had "yakboards." I knew that surfboards were allowed on board for an overweight charge of fifty dollars and was quite sure that yakboards wouldn't surface on a computer list as forbidden. Doug, dubious but humoring me, went to a hardware store and bought heavy black plastic, which he wrapped around each boat section. At the airport, he asked a skycap about the procedures for checking our shotgun, which was stowed inside one of the boat sections. "Oh, don't walk through that door," the skycap cautioned, pointing toward the security gate we'd have to pass through before reaching the ticket counter. "If you do, they are going to have to call Port Authority and, Lord have mercy, you're going to wish you'd never been born. Let me get a ticket agent to come out here to check you in."

At the car, we had a conversation that could have convinced a sane man he was crazy. "We don't take canoes or kayaks," insisted the agent. "Oh," I responded in my friendliest tone, "these aren't boats, they are yakboards." After numerous iterations, the agent and her supervisor decided that our nine-foot-long, more than two-foot-thick boat sections were yakboards after all. Walking to the counter with Doug, the agent asked, "What exactly is a yakboard, anyway?" Without missing a beat, Doug described something that was a cross between a boogie board and a surfboard. The agent did not even look twice when attaching a baggage tag to the "poles," our bundled package of oars with obvious handles and blades.

At the Anchorage airport, as I was dragging one boat section across the floor toward our waiting truck, an agent of the same airline greeted me with a smile. "So, you've been kayaking? Good for you!!"

🦌   🦌   🦌

The day is colorless and cold, fog shrouds the fjord, seaweed scents the air. It is early in the morning, sadistically early, but somehow Doug and I are up and moving. From inside my hood, my field of vision is limited to Doug, kayaking about twenty feet from me. Knowing that there is no floating ice, I steer off of him, not bothering to turn around. I row with my eyes half closed, over black water that feels like silk. The oars drop into the water with a sharp, clean bite at the beginning of each stroke. I am no longer obsessing about bed. In time, Doug notices that my boat is beginning to veer gently off course. He paddles a little harder to catch up and observes me carefully. My arms and legs are working in unison, my face is peaceful, my mouth is wide open. He watches me for another half mile before he decides that it is abnormal to sleep while rowing and wakes me. Doug reports that even when I sleep in the tent at night, my arms and legs spasm as though I am rowing. He flatteringly describes it as akin to sleeping with a frog.

In wilderness rowing, I found a synthesis of my love of nature and my passion for rowing, a balance point that felt like the perfect union of body and soul. There weren't seven other people to follow or a coxswain to steer and urge me on. I was the only rower, so I didn't have to worry about being the best. I didn't even know anyone who could tell me what I needed to know. At almost every turn, there was something to figure out—what shape hull would best grip the side of a mountainous swell, how to pack gear for a hundred days, how to do surf landings, how to keep mind and body going when terrified, bored, or bones-to-dust exhausted. Along the coast of Norway in 1995, we were often told, "You are very brave to live in the nature." The implication was that we needed courage to master the storms, the sudden winds, the torrential rains, and the big seas. But these are things that can never be mastered. If what we do has required any courage at all, it is in attempting to master ourselves. Wilderness rowing is far more than sport to me; it has been a conduit to knowing and trusting myself. It is my way of being, of thinking, of seeing. My rowing has taken me north and pushed me to explore my own horizons. In the process, rowing has evolved from something I do to some way that I am. Figuratively and literally, I have spent years rowing to latitude.

Evergreen

MELINDA TOGNINI

How can you comprehend the grief someone endures with the death of a loved one, unless you too have experienced that same loss? And how do you ever come to terms with that loss? Especially when you're not there to say goodbye, when you hear of her death on the seven o'clock news, when one of the last occasions you saw her was the moment you deserted her?

But let me start at the beginning.

My love affair with the slim, sixty-foot sloop *Evergreen* began hesitantly. I was fifteen and living in a small mining town in the north of Australia. My parents had been sailing on *Evergreen* for months and had attempted, on numerous occasions, to convince me to join them. But I preferred hanging with my friends to spending the day with my parents.

Finally, on Australia Day 1987, I gave in. I figured if I went out once I could say I'd tried it and now please don't ask again. Then they'd leave me alone. The day did not go as planned. From the moment I was asked to wind a winch, I was hooked.

"You know," the owner and captain, Bill Gibson, told me on the second weekend, "if you keep sailing, you could sail in the Tall Ships Race with me."

"Okay," I replied, not comprehending the enormity of that particular race, or the opportunity he was offering. I had no idea what the Tall Ships Race was, or even whether Bill was serious.

Nevertheless, I sailed on *Evergreen* almost every weekend after that. Instead of going reluctantly, as I had that first day, I now looked forward to Sundays, for many reasons. It was partly the clear, calm waters of the Arafura Sea. And the coastline of the Gove Peninsula, with its rugged red cliffs, paper-white beaches, and isolated islands. It was the breeze in my face and drying salt on my skin. The adrenaline that surged whenever *Evergreen* tacked and heeled to increase speed. And the thrill of overtaking another yacht.

But for an insecure fifteen year old, the most important aspect of sailing on *Evergreen*—the reason I fell so in love with her—was the camaraderie I experienced. It didn't matter that I wasn't part of the "cool crowd," or wearing trendy clothes, or attending the right parties. Instead, I was appreciated for who I was and what I could contribute. As my skills developed I participated more and more, becoming an integral part of the team. Even Old Tom, suspicious of women on board, finally gave me the nod of acknowledgment that signified acceptance.

And my everyday stresses—the disappointment of adolescent crushes, the bullying at school, my parents separating—these could all be left behind the moment we rowed out to *Evergreen* and climbed aboard her mint-colored deck.

Before I knew it, it was December and time to head to Hobart where I joined the rest of the crew, some of whom had just completed the famous Sydney to Hobart Yacht Race. *Evergreen* herself had competed in that race before, winning line honors way back in 1955, under the name of *Even*.

I now realized the importance of the Tall Ships Race, being held as part of Australia's bicentennial celebrations. Yachts from all over the world were docking in Hobart. Although *Evergreen* was sixty feet long, she was dwarfed by real Tall Ships such as *Dar Mlodziezy* and *Young Endeavour*.

Part of the criteria for the race was that half the crew be between sixteen and twenty-five. Having turned sixteen only a month earlier, I was one of the youngest. But it didn't take long to make friends with those on other yachts. The upcoming race, a shared passion for adventure, and a love of the sea were enough to be included in whatever was happening. By the time race day came around I felt I'd known some of them for years, rather than a week.

January 14 finally arrived. It was at once exciting to be embarking on the journey of a lifetime and sad to be separated from new friends. The parade of sail was chaotic. *Evergreen*'s propeller refused to work effectively, so we had to sail most of the nineteen miles from Constitution Dock to the starting line. With barely a breeze blowing, we were still twenty minutes from the start when the gun sounded. Luckily for us, most of the other yachts were also at a standstill. One yacht crossed the starting line backwards. To top it off, I began to feel nauseous and realized that the one thing I'd forgotten was my motion-sickness tablets.

Then a sudden wind carried us across the line and past a number of other vessels. We were moving!

"See ya in Sydney!" I yelled to several other yachts as we overtook them.

We sliced through the water, continuing to overtake other yachts through the afternoon. The exhilaration of being part of it all chased away my seasickness. But not for long. My first watch was spent, along with another girl, Ingrid, leaning over the side, conversing with the waves.

As we headed up the Tasmanian coast and into Bass Strait, the ocean became increasingly rough, with some of the highest swells, even Bill, a veteran sailor, had experienced. I know it could have been worse—it wasn't as bad as the Sydney to Hobart Yacht Race a decade later—but I don't think a *lifetime* of sailing in the calm Arafura Sea could have prepared me for the waters of Bass Strait.

Excitement coexisted with fear. Especially when changing the sail in darkness, with the spray kicking up over the bow, needing to be attached to the mast to avoid being flung into the ocean and lost. Or when *Evergreen* rode the crest of a wave, only to smash down the other side. Even worse was when she pitched on her side. In my head, I knew it was safe, that the yacht was designed that way for maximum speed. But my inexperience, combined with being in a car roll-over several years before, kept me fearful that something similar was going to happen here in the middle of Bass Strait.

My seasickness continued whenever I moved about the cabin;

however, I was fine lying in my bunk or up on deck. So, to avoid the smell of wet, discarded sails and the desire to vomit, I often sat above deck even when it wasn't my shift. Neither the fear nor the adrenaline totally disappeared, but I began to enjoy the journey, especially at night when the darkness enveloped us.

At regular intervals, we radioed in our position and listened to find out where the other competitors were. Each time, we cheered as we discovered we'd passed even more yachts since the last check-in. On handicap we were in there with a chance.

Then just before my third shift, when the fresh air was once again more appealing than the stale smell below, I sat beside the bilge pump and began the steady rhythmic action of pumping water. No pressure. Strange. Being the youngest on the yacht, what did I know? Still, it sure didn't feel like it was supposed to.

Below, one of the crew, Woodie, checked the water level. "Shit! Water's over the engine. Can't start the electric pump. Everyone on deck! Start bailing!"

Paul, the navigator, called the race-control ship on the two-way radio.

"This is a pan situation," he stated. "A pan situation."

Ironically, it was now that my fear and seasickness completely left me. Although the situation was potentially life threatening, I was too busy concentrating on the task at hand to be scared.

Scoop, lift, dump overboard.

Scoop, lift, dump overboard.

Red flares were fired, sweeping into the air. The bucket brigade continued.

Scoop, lift, dump overboard.

Scoop, lift, down the inside of my wet weather gear. The water was icy cold.

Scoop, lift, dump overboard.

As the sky lightened, the control ship reported that *HMAS Adelaide* was on her way. A helicopter flew overhead with a media crew on board. They swung round to obtain the most effective footage. The wind from the helicopter swept up the sea so that the waves would look even higher and more dangerous on the news.

All this time we bucketed furiously. I developed arm muscles I didn't know existed.

Scoop, lift, dump overboard.

Scoop, lift, dump overboard.

A petrol-generated pump was transferred on board. We could finally stop bailing. Another navy ship, the *Stalwart*, gave us a hot breakfast and later lunch, before taking three of our male crew on board. As the situation was no longer life-threatening, neither I nor the other female crew, were permitted aboard the navy vessel.

The *Andrew Hardy*, a fishing boat with a sail, was also competing in the Tall Ships Race but abandoned its own quest for the finish line and came to our aid. Accompanied by a school of dolphins, we were towed into the fishing town of Eden, on the southeast coast of the Australian mainland. Fishermen, Channel 10, and the local newspaper were the first to greet us.

When the yacht was taken out of the water, it was determined that we'd hit a whale. Nobody had actually seen a whale, or felt it nudge the yacht, but the waves had been so rough at times, that we wouldn't necessarily have known.

Evergreen would be repaired and we'd be on our way in a couple of days. My first thought was that I only had a week and a half of holidays left, and I wanted to spend as much time as possible with my new friends. So, rather than continue on with my crew, I caught the bus to Sydney.

It was one of the last times I would ever sail aboard *Evergreen*.

My time in Sydney was fantastic. Watching Australia Day fireworks from a yacht in the harbor. Partying all night. Hanging out with new friends. A potential romance. It was one of the most memorable times of my life.

Yet, I *still* regret catching that bus, instead of completing the journey with the rest of the crew. We had come so far, working together to keep a grand old lady alive. But I gave up before the challenge was over. I failed. Not because *Evergreen* didn't win the race, but because I gave in too soon. I was too preoccupied with what I was missing out on, rather than seeing the opportunity and adventure before me.

Without that failure, however, I would never have learned about perseverance and courage. It was precisely because I was so disappointed with myself that I vowed never again to give up when things seemed tough. I realized that sometimes it's worth sacrificing temporary comfort and enjoyment, in order to experience the ultimate success of reaching a goal.

The morning after the Australia Day celebrations in Sydney, I flew home to start my final year of high school. But the Tall Ships Race was only the first leg in an around-Australia race to commemorate the country's bicentennial. And *Evergreen* was continuing on as far as Darwin in Australia's north.

She never made it.

Just off Darwin, *Evergreen* was shipwrecked. I found out via the evening news as I sat relaxing at a friend's place. *Evergreen* had actu-ally won two legs and was looking to win a third, until she hit the reef off New Year Island. There was nothing anyone could do to save her. After she rolled on her side, the waves pushed her further and further onto the reef, causing her to disintegrate.

I watched the news in disbelief, struggling to keep the tears away. I felt like I'd just been told my best friend was dead. It was as if I'd fought with a loved one the last time I'd seen her and never had the opportunity to make it up.

My friends couldn't understand the way I reacted.

"It's only a boat," one of them said dismissively.

Evergreen was never "just a boat." But how do you explain the rela-tionship you can form with a yacht? Someone who has never sailed, who has never attached herself to a yacht, can never understand the feeling of utter loss and grief. I wished desperately that I could step aboard *Evergreen* again, feel the tilt of her hull, her winch in my hand. I even missed that stale smell and claustrophobic feel of the cabin.

I have sailed again, but I will be forever drawn back to *Evergreen*. And to the Tall Ships Race. Given the opportunity, I would sail that race again, even with its Bass Strait disaster. But this time I wouldn't desert her. This time I would sacrifice a few days of partying for the satisfac-tion of sailing into Sydney Harbor knowing I'd finished the journey.

Sadly no amount of wishing will make that possible, not on *Ever-green* anyway. And so, perhaps, it would never really be the same.

But then again, maybe it's time to fall in love again.

Below Decks

JESSICA DULONG

I 'm beginning to sweat diesel. Profuse heat shakes off the five six-hundred-horsepower diesel engines that power the *John J. Harvey,* a retired New York City fireboat. I savor the breeze that greets the back of my neck on its way down the stairway from the main deck. As assistant engineer, my place is down here in the engine room. Above decks, passengers sip beers and take in the Manhattan skyline. Meanwhile I steal glimpses of the harbor through round portholes in the hull just above the water line.

At the control pedestal, my eyes dart across the thirty gauges that indicate health or trouble in the engines while I wait for the clang of the next signal from the captain. On a bell boat like this one, the captain stands in the wheelhouse. He sends signals down to the engine room with a ring and a twitch of the red arrow on one of two telegraphs—brass dials that hang like clocks on either side of my ears, one on the port side, one on the starboard. It's my job to control the spin of the propellers that steer the boat and regulate its speed.

On my first day at the controls, I had an audience of men. One of them had a video camera. Never before had a woman run these engines. The pedestal was designed for someone six feet tall. I'm five-five. When the captain signaled Full Ahead, I had to stand on my toes to swing the telegraph pointer all the way into position. Sweat pooled, sticky where the plastic earmuffs sat on my cheeks, beading up, running over my temples, and trickling off my jaw. I didn't dare take my hand off the prop levers to wipe away the drips. Between signals I stood at attention, my body rigid, my mind full of numbers. Props at 100 rpm for slow, 200 for half, 300-plus for full. Don't let the amps climb past 1,350. Run each engine at 1,100.

At the end of the trip, the captain shook my hand. "Very responsive," he said simply.

§   §   §

Words have a way of hanging suspended until you find a way to attach meaning to them. These days I find words from my childhood flooding back: camshaft, crankshaft, bearings, bushings.

I remember shop days as a slinging of names I couldn't keep track of—words for vehicles, customers, parts stores, tools. My dad is a foreign-car mechanic. Growing up, I often spent the day with him. There's a running joke in my family about how, when my older sister, younger brother, and I went to the shop, my dad had the girls, ages ten and seven, sorting nuts and bolts while the three-year-old boy worked with him fixing cars.

Sometimes he took us kids along to the machinist's shop to drop off brake drums for resurfacing or to get engine blocks rebored. The machinist, gaunt and gray-skinned, always kept quiet. The walls of his greasy shop were lined with small cardboard boxes, their facing edges angle-cut like candy bins full of screws, springs, and shims. I've since learned to name the tools that rested on workbenches above my head: drill press, milling machine, lathe.

The machine shop smells of grease, metal, and old man mixed with fumes from the donut shop next door. These visits were marathons of patience. I'd watch the machinist pivot in his swivel chair. I'd peer over the edge of a smeared bench, littered with small parts. Despite the urge to roll the metal bits between my fingertips, I kept my hands in my pockets. The "don't touch" rule was implied, though never spoken.

$$\text{\S} \qquad \text{\S} \qquad \text{\S}$$

In the six months since my first day at the pedestal I've become the fastest operator on the *Harvey*'s crew. When the boat is called to navigate tight quarters, the captain, a retired firefighter who's piloted this boat for more than twenty years, wants me at the controls.

From the time she was launched in 1931 until the department retired her in 1994, the *Harvey* served at hundreds of fires, explosions, and marine disasters. Five years later the city put her up for auction. Her current owners, a group of entrepreneurs who banded together to save her, barely outbid the guy who planned to cut her into pieces for scrap. The owners hired Tim, the chief engineer, who quickly got her running again. And after a stint in dry dock repairing some of the damage that she'd suffered while her fate hung in the balance, she was back underway with a new job: carrying people on cruises around New York Harbor to raise awareness of the river and its historic vessels. These days, while *Harvey* passengers take in the salt air, I hide in the bowels of the boat like Oz behind the curtain.

With four huge fire pumps, the *Harvey* was famous for her ability to move more than eighteen thousand gallons of river water each minute, the equivalent of twenty fire engines. When she and the George Washington Bridge were both brand new, she shot water over the bridge's roadway. Though only two pumps now work, the boat can still fire off a significant spray from her eight Morse "Invincible" deck guns. These days, instead of fighting fires, the powerful pipes shoot water in celebration, at the whim of the captain who signals me to engage the pumps.

The buzz of the vibrating engines travels through the soles of my steel-toed boots and up my feet, which swell with the heat. I stand on an upturned wooden crate that gives me the height I need. There's a particular drone of the engines at 1,100 rpms. An occasional higher-pitched whine tells me that engine five, the one with the worn-out governor, has dipped to 1,000. I nudge the throttle and settle back into the hum of balance. Any bounce tells me to even out power to the two screws so they stop fighting each other. I take the swoop and tilt of the current at the hips. And though I can't hear the slosh of bilge water over the din of rumbling engines, I can see it move under the floor. The river seeps in through a porthole on the starboard side, trickling a burnt orange trail of rust across the thick white paint inside the riveted hull. Like every vessel, the *Harvey* fights a constant, silent battle with the salt water that buoys her.

Standing at the pedestal is meditative. My head quickly fills the space. I picture my dad climbing down the narrow metal staircase from the deck. Though he's never been on a fireboat, he'd recognize the components of each engine, from the fuel lines to the flywheel. He'd understand the concept of throttling down before engaging the air-flex clutch. He's a mechanic. I'm not.

$$\text{\Large ❧ \quad ❧ \quad ❧}$$

One hot summer day when I was twelve, I convinced my dad to let me go to work with him. In our family, cars meant power. I was older by then. He'd have to let me do more than sort nuts and bolts. One of the day's jobs involved repair work on the front end of my mother's Volvo station wagon. When the work was done, Dad handed me the air gun, told me to bolt the tire back on, and walked away. I still recall the rush when I hefted the thing in my palm. I fingered the trigger with the sense of importance and risk that power tools bestow. I felt the torque in my wrist and heard the screech of the gun turn into a sputter as the nut tightened, then stiffened on the bolt. I methodically tightened each lug nut according to patterns I knew: I started in the top and worked my way clockwise around the wheel. I remember my sense of accomplishment when I was done.

The next day my father screamed at me—eyes red, spit flying.

"You could have killed your mother," he yelled. She had been cruising at seventy-five mph in the far left lane on the highway when she felt the first wobble and pulled over. "The wheel could have spun right off the axle."

My face went hot.

Then he told me I should have tightened alternating nuts, staggering turns so the wheel would sit evenly.

$$\emph{\textbf{\&}} \qquad \emph{\textbf{\&}} \qquad \emph{\textbf{\&}}$$

I land each command as the signal comes down, pushing the prop levers quickly and smoothly. The ten months since my first boat trip show in the muscles in my arms and in the calluses on my palms and fingers. I take pride in my ability to discern who's at the helm with just a few short clangs. I'm fine-tuning my docking skills—anticipating orders by watching the approach of the pier through the portholes.

As assistant engineer, I could get away with playing trained monkey, never leaving my spot at the pedestal. But I'm hungry to understand every aspect of this 130-foot, 268-ton, steel-hulled vessel that is among the most powerful fireboats ever in service. The beauty of old technology is how physical it is.

There is so much more I need to know about the power plant's complex systems. I'm waist-deep in an electro-magnetism textbook, trying to wrap my head around diesel-electric propulsion, one concept at a time.

I read and collect my questions at the pedestal while we're underway. Then, at the end of each trip, after twisting shut the valves that provide raw water to each engine, I stand in the baking, semi-dark engine room, holding a flashlight and talking shop with Tim. My dad would like him.

On my first day at the stand, Tim corrected me when I faltered, wordlessly wrapping his long fingers around my hand on the portside lever and pulling it back to Slow Astern as the captain had commanded. Now he patiently explains the mysteries of motors and magnetism. He leans over to draw soap-stone diagrams on the floor. He opens the camshaft housing to let me see the angle of the air inlet ports on a cylinder. He walks through the routine conversion from ship's power to shore power.

§　§　§

When I finally bring my dad to the boat he nearly bursts with pride. I feel a tinge of nervousness as I walk him through the paces. I describe how the engines produce the electricity that powers the two large propulsion motors. I show him the redundancy of the system—how we can operate with fewer than five engines by swapping over to auxiliary generators. I explain that the only things running direct-drive off the diesels are the water pumps. He punctuates each of my explanations with one of his signature phrases: *Wow. That's ace. That's dynamite.*

Most people who hear what I do just smile and nod, indulge in a few halted, basic questions, then switch to a more familiar subject.

My father is not only interested, he also has a grasp. Though he's a gasoline-engine mechanic who doesn't think much of diesel, he knows which questions to ask. I introduce him to Tim, whom he pelts with a barrage of questions. Once the two get to talking engines they settle right in.

Later, after I pry Dad out of the engine room and the family heads to dinner, my father asks me about the fuel system. He's been puzzling over the open drip-cups that collect unburned fuel oil.

"The runoff ends up in the sump tank below the deck plates," I explain.

"It can't be like that," he insists. "There's no opening in the system."

"It's not a closed loop," I maintain, while the rest of the family looks on. "The sump tank catches the excess and we have to pump it back into the main tanks."

I remember a night, years before, when my dad attempted to explain internal combustion to his kids at the dinner table, twisting forks into crankshafts to demonstrate how the parts moved together. I remember how desperately I wanted his makeshift visual aids to etch a comprehensible, working model into my head—to carve out understanding that would stay. Suddenly I flash back to that unmistakable *I don't get it* feeling.

I falter. "I dunno," I say, though I've emptied the sump tanks myself, fuel oil sloshing from the bucket onto my pant leg. "Maybe I misunderstood."

The next day I check with Tim.

"You're right," says Tim. "It's an open loop."

❧   ❧   ❧

I'm standing in my usual spot at the pedestal, agonizing over the fact that I'd flubbed up resealing a cylinder adapter in the number-one engine. We had to pull off the dock and run on four engines until Tim could fix my mistake. As my eyes bounce over the dials—scavenging air above three, lube oil pressure above twenty psi, starting air steady at two hundred pounds—I try to untangle the familiar knot of my own incompetence. Suddenly, a pop and a flash under the deck plates on the port side.

You can't really hear a pop over the whine of five eight-cylinder diesels. But an impact with enough force transfers sound at its most elemental level: You feel it hit.

On a boat like this, any quick change in light can make you nervous—I've often spun my head around on alert when a person on deck walks past the engine room door and momentarily blocks the sunlight from pouring down the stairs. Here, in the rush of noise and vibration, noticing any slight fluctuation is key. Tim and I joke about hyper-vigilance. But here below decks, surrounded by the pounding conversion of heat into work, combustion into power, it's not paranoia—it's prevention.

My mind races with the flash. No way that was caused by sunlight. The yellow-orange glow reflects off thick water mains below the floor. The spark lights up parts of the bilge I've never seen before. The small tornado of white smoke that follows the pop sets my heart to ricochet.

I can't find Tim. He must have slipped off to work on something in the back. I've never used the panic button before, but I reach for it now. It isn't red, but black with the word "PANIC" spelled out below it, sloppily, in Magic Marker. We'd laughed when Tim connected it to a loud siren that can be heard throughout the boat. You have to hold the button down for three seconds before it makes a sound. Right now, half a second feels too long, and I lift my finger off before it gets the chance.

I crane my neck around the number-two engine and see Tim walking toward me. Wide eyes communicate my alarm, but my outstretched finger gives direction. We peer over the edge of a deck plate into the gap beside the number-five pump. I see fire.

Urgency ripples through Tim's body, his muscles flexed, ready to move. He stretches an arm and yanks the port prop control lever into neutral. I hop in front of the pedestal and pull the starboard lever to a stop. At Tim's single-gestured instruction I slam all the throttles to idle and signal the wheelhouse: Full Stop.

Tim reaches for a long screwdriver to pull up the deck plate. He digs the flat metal tip into the corner of the plate to catch the underside. I tug the fire extinguisher off its bent metal bracket and set it within reach. We pry up the plate and flames shoot up from below. I don't want to think about the slick of fuel and lube oil sloshing in the bilge. I hand Tim the extinguisher. He yanks the pin, pulls the trigger, and with a few short sweeps, the foam suffocates the blaze. For a moment everything stops. The engine room seems suddenly suspended. There is no noise.

The Full Stop has aroused concern in the wheelhouse. Don, one of several retired firefighters who volunteer on the boat, appears in the engine room. He nearly falls into the bilge because we've removed the deck plate.

Tim waves, "Get out!"

Don swings over to my side.

I push him back, both my palms pressed flat against his chest.

"The captain wants to know what's going on," he shouts, peeling the plastic earmuff from my sweaty cheek so I can hear. The *Harvey*'s in the middle of the busy Hudson, in danger of colliding with countless other boats. The captain has nothing but manual control of the rudder. He can't steer without power.

"Tell him we had a fire, but it's out," I shout back, and Don makes his way forward again.

Tim heads to the rear of the engine room and shorts out the electricity to the whole port side. He shuts down the number-five engine then signals me to throttle the others back up. Starboard-side power is better than none at all.

Tim bends to reach the scorched contactor cover, swiping at the foam with a rag. I hustle to the other side to help him lift and slide it up and out of the way. Effortlessly, we navigate this space. For nearly a year I've been hawk-eyed, watching him work. Now, I can almost predict each step. Down on his belly, Tim reaches below the contactor with his rag. Without seeing it, I smell the source of our fire: a jet of fuel oil shooting from the pipe that supplies the engines.

Don returns again.

"I need a hose clamp and a piece of rubber," Tim shouts at me.

Maybe I actually hear him say this. It's equally possible I am reading his lips. He and I both look at Don and point. He should take the pedestal. He shrugs. He doesn't know how.

I run to the tool room. Nothing. Then I remember a box I moved to the bench behind the number one. I rush back and dig out two clamps and a stretch of hose.

With cupped fingers, Tim indicates he needs a patch. I yank the Swiss Tool off my belt and split the hose down the middle.

"This big?" I ask silently, forming a circle over the rubber with my thumb and index finger.

The patch fits. A hose clamp fastened around the leak staves off further disaster, but we call off the afternoon's voyage and limp back to the dock on two engines. The captain has minimal maneuverability, so I concentrate on my part: zero-second response time. Between calls I feel the smooth brass control levers heat up in my grip. We land at the pier with hardly a bump.

🐍   🐍   🐍

I'm shivering in the uncommon silence of the engine room. It's been two months since our last boat trip of the season. Few of us get to see the old boat this way: quiet and gently lilting in her berth. A faint drip comes from some pipe low beneath the deck plates. The familiar huff of diesel scrapes at the back of my throat. By now I can tease apart the smell the way some people discern hints of oak, cherry or chocolate in a fine wine—an exhaust-fume bouquet wedded with a richer base note of lube oil and a hint of bilge water.

A thin light glints off the shiny brass of the starboard-side tele-graph and flits across the gauges. Though it flickers like a campfire, the light is reflecting off the river water that laps at the portholes. Tim and I have drained down the engines to keep them from freezing. There's something slightly sad and embarrassingly inti-mate about seeing the boat so still. While the rest of the *Harvey* reg-ulars wait for spring, I tally off the list of repairs we hope to accomplish this winter: patching the mufflers, rebuilding the com-pressor motor, and polishing the pump shafts. All this before spring, when it's time to fire up the engines once again.

Capes of Hope

KACI CRONKHITE

Africa. After nearly a year of sailing *Tethys* in the Indian Ocean, Nancy and I were finally almost there. When I stared at our inflatable globe I could see we were moving across the opposite side of the world from home. We'd both grown up in the Midwest, far from the ocean. Yet here we were, me from a ranch in Oklahoma, and Nancy from the cityscapes of Milwaukee and Cincinnati. Together, we were heading toward the unknown.

After months of exploring new languages and foods, facing challenges like our first big damaging wave, near groundings in a couple of nasty blows, ripped sails, my first single-handing experience, and even a pirate attempt, I was now facing the biggest challenge of all: the southern tip of Africa and its many capes. The most southern is Cape Agulhas, and the most famous is the Cape of Good Hope. While either one could bear the name well, it is the Cape of Good Hope that is also called the Cape of Storms. We laughed at the irony. The eventual rounding of both capes, with their fierce winds and violent seas, is a fearsome prospect. We knew what was ahead of us and neither of us had been there before.

Nancy Erley was one of the four owners of the *Tethys*, a thirty-eight-foot custom double-ender, and its captain when they completed a circumnavigation of the globe from 1989 to 1994. On that trip around Africa, they had opted to sail up the Red Sea and through the Mediterranean Sea.

$$\text{\it \&} \qquad \text{\it \&} \qquad \text{\it \&}$$

I was sailing with Nancy on her second trip around the world. On her return to Seattle, she'd decided—after a wet Seattle winter—to take the *Tethys* out again to the tropics, and this time to teach women crew ocean passage-making skills along the way. She needed a First Mate to work with her teaching in the Pacific. My schedule fit for a portion of her trips, so after completing several deliveries, including a six-month upwind trip from Australia to Hawaii, I flew to Tahiti and joined her aboard *Tethys*. Two women learning crew were to fly from the United States to sail with us from Tahiti to the Marquesas and back, then another two would fly in to sail north from Tahiti to Hawaii. Our agreement was for me to teach aboard for two months, but I'd repeatedly renewed my commitment and lengthened my time on the boat, until I'd found myself here in the Indian Ocean.

Our small band of fellow cruising boats dwindled as the crescendo of anxiety about rounding the cape grew. In Thailand, the Maldives, and Chagos, our friends on other boats opted to head back east to Thailand or north for the Red Sea. In Madagascar, where our final decision had to be made, more boats opted not to go south around Africa. At frequent evening sundown gatherings, experienced South African sailors confirmed our worst fears of the violent winds, ship-breaking waves, and gravely limited harbors that lay between us and the cape. Then we got the news that Nancy's mother had cancer and only a few months to live. With our hearts in our throats, we made our final commitment. We headed for the closest airport so that Nancy could fly home. The closest airport and safe harbor was Richard's Bay, South Africa, just south of our first African cape, St. Lucia.

Thirteen days later, less than 200 miles from our destination, the weather turned nasty. Prudence won out over pride as we raced with two other boats to a temporary shelter behind Isla de Inhaca, just seaward of Maputo, Mozambique. We made our way into the anchorage on radar, instruments, and faith in the South African waypoints we'd been given. At two in the morning, we anchored in the cocoa-colored water as the barometer bottomed out and began the climb preceding our first South African storm. *Tethys* lay at bizarre and conflicting angles to the anchor, as the roaring tidal currents and thirty-five-knot winds battled for control. Wind and rain blew down the companionway in gusts, only to turn and blast us in the face as we renewed the bridle chafe gear a few hours later. Lightning flashed above us and reflected in the water, lighting up the night like a raging forest fire.

After sixteen hours the worst was over. No sooner had we started to relax when someone beat on the hull to say we'd gotten a thumbs-up from the Durban Sailing Academy for a weather window to Richard's Bay. In order to make it before the next storm, we had to leave immediately. Retracing our inbound path on the GPS, we struggled to motor against the two-and-a-half-knot current under the dismal dirty-gray sky. In twice the time it took us to come into the anchorage, we finally passed the Portuguese fort lighthouse and headed offshore five miles to the continental shelf where we knew the Agulhas current would be in our favor. The wind was fickle, but finally the evening land breeze kicked in and *Tethys* was making nine knots.

The wind continued to build through the night, filling in from behind us. About sixty-five miles from Richard's Bay, the barometric pressure started dropping. The good news, we told each other, was that it hadn't started to rise. We were closing in on Cape Vidal, a point we would have missed if not for our stop in Mozambique. The South African catamaran we'd met in Maputo was just ahead of us in a pod of whales and making seven knots. Miles ahead we saw, but didn't discuss, the opaque wall of storm clouds and sheet lightning to the south. We both knew we had to go faster in order to beat the storm. We headed slightly further out to sea and quickly found the swifter current.

Sweating and silent, we watched the miles to the "Rbay" waypoint count down fast on the GPS. With less than thirty miles to go, we spoke to a southbound tanker and he reported strong squalls fifteen miles ahead. Friends in Richard's Bay called to see where we were and get details of our position. The storm had arrived there, so a South African couple interrupted our radio conversation to remind us, strongly, to "close Cape St. Lucia." With a calm that belied the situation, they explained that to remain offshore ten miles we risked being swept right past Richard's Bay and caught up in violent waves that would build quickly with the onset of the storm.

Tethys was surfing at twelve knots as we put in our third reef and rolled in half the yankee to steer more dramatically for St. Lucia. The waves were nearly twelve feet when suddenly, in less than five seconds of silence and shift, a hot volcanic wind slipped through the storm clouds and slammed us head-on. I rolled in the last of the jibs and secured the fore and after guy wires on the pole while Nancy hand-steered. Incredible lightning extinguished the last orange of sunset as I noted, ironically, that nature must have known it was Guy Fawkes Day. The sky opened up in a downpour to rival the ocean, and the thunder made it impossible to hear.

The last twenty miles into Richard's Bay took us more than six hours. Wind speeds were fifty-five knots in gusts, and *Tethys* was caught in a boiling sea of southbound current against the southwest winds. Seas were nearly abeam and breaking at frequent heights of twelve to twenty feet. We struggled to maintain our course while being set as much as 135 degrees. As I plotted and replotted on charts soaked from my foul weather jacket, Nancy altered course repeatedly toward Cape St. Lucia. Finally, we got back onto the continental shelf and out of the big waves. But the current continued to shove us south until at times we felt we were sailing backwards.

Through the maze of shark nets just before the entrance, we crept into Richard's Bay at 1:30 A.M. on November 6. Our British, Swedish, American, French, and South African friends were there to take our lines.

Rounding "Lucy," as we called the St. Lucia waypoint, had driven me over the edge of fear as I had known it. In the nightmare cacophony of weather, motion, and sound in the last hours of our trip, I found a refuge inside. A hidden, rarely visited place where there were friends and a powerful, but loving "nature" that I could trust. I was reminded of how much I'd grown and how much I'd learned since the first day sailing. Then, five years earlier, I was clueless. Naive and completely ignorant of the boating world, I had stepped aboard my first sailboat with a paradoxical awareness of faith and fear. I had gone sailing because a colleague had invited me and it sounded like a wild way to celebrate the end of a work project. I didn't think about what I was doing, I just did it.

In the years since joining *Tethys*, I'd learned so much. The first two months on board spiked my learning curve. The subsequent months, then years, that Nancy and I spent together had given me a new appreciation for flexible teaching styles and provided me my first glimpse of being part of an excellent team. Our opposite approaches to action and problem-solving led to gratifying solutions that were also very educational. When the refrigerator broke down my first week aboard, we pulled out tools and I started taking it apart. Nancy pulled out the manuals and read out loud in a methodical, linear fashion while we creatively brainstormed together. We talked things through. In the end, we fixed the refrigerator together, knowing that the differences between our approaches to the problem were complimentary, and that we had both achieved the shared goal better by putting our two heads together. Our respect for each other grew from one of teacher and student to a kind of partnership. It was that sense of trust and mutual respect which empowered us both in our goal toward the cape. It was the sense of competence and confidence in myself, gained through the years of sailing with Nancy, that elicited peacefulness and deep reconnection to my childhood as we weathered the first cape.

$$\textit{\& \quad \& \quad \&}$$

The day after our arrival in Richard's Bay, Nancy flew home. A year passed before we resumed our voyage around the tip of Africa. Then, I returned to Richard's Bay, two weeks ahead of Nancy, and found the boat a mess. Fine, caustic particles of coal and aluminum had sifted into the rigging, sails, and lockers. It looked like someone had spilled black paint on the deck and it had run down the scuppers in an ugly trail. I e-mailed a list of things for Nancy to bring from the States, including two new GPS units to replace the ones that mildew and dust had killed while we were away.

Tethys was further soiled by not one, but a humiliating five varieties of cockroaches. Canned foods that had gotten wet when we took the wave the year before had burst open, then infected the good cans, creating an unidentifiable ooze of organic matter that even the cockroaches eschewed. Although friends had watched the boat during the time we'd been away, it was apparent that even the strongest, most well-kept boat can quickly become a derelict without the love of a human. It took us nearly three months to restore the boat to a safe and livable condition.

As the end of summer loomed, we knew the time had come to make a run for the cape or risk another year in Africa. While local sailors assured us that by waiting for the right weather windows we could round the cape at any time of year, we knew the better season for getting across the Atlantic and into the Caribbean was before the southern winter storms began. Despite the frightening memories of our arrival, we knew that the rest of our schedule home depended on us rounding the cape soon. We were nervous but both firmly committed to going on.

To be sure we did not jinx the trip, we spoke little of our planned departure to other people. Instead, we set a loose date for leaving and said our good-byes. Then one night, just past 3:00 A.M., we quietly slipped the lines and headed out. We'd come in during the wee hours of the morning, so we thought it only appropriate that we leave at about the same time. This dark morning, however, the weather was perfect.

We set our first waypoint five miles offshore, immediately beyond the one hundred-meter line. Less than five minutes clear of the breakwater, *Tethys* began to feel the familiar strong tug of the southbound Agulhas current. Memories of that pull conjured flashbacks of our nightmare arrival, but the radar was reliable and our course line more controlled. Mostly, the current was favorable, and the gentle night was a comfort. The current that had been our enemy was now our friend.

By noon the next day, we were a little more than halfway to Durban and the wind had picked up to thirty to thirty-five knots from astern. With the wind and current both going our direction, we were sailing comfortably and fast. Our speed with the current was a little more than nine knots. We both prayed for a miracle that we would make it to Durban before sunset.

At 4:00 P.M., we made our move back to the coast. We set a course from ten miles offshore to a promontory, Umhlanga Rocks and lighthouse. As was the case on our approach to Richard's Bay, the sweep of the current was three to four knots to the south, so we again took the advice of South African sailors and closed the coast well before the Durban breakwater. We conceded defeat in our race against darkness and slowed the boat down for the final approach. The sunset grossly obscured our view as we passed the outer Racon beacon three miles from the entrance. Ship traffic was heavy and the surf was breaking astern during the last half-mile into the channel. Despite the good weather, our nerves were on edge. At the last minute Durban Harbor patrol asked us to "hold" outside the entrance channel for a ship exiting the harbor. The wind and surf made holding dangerous, so we brought *Tethys* around in one slow circle then held our breath and surfed in just astern and in the lee of the tanker. Slowly Nancy steered us through the clear and relatively flat water while I dropped sails and prepared the dock lines, fenders, and gear for docking. We were not "in" yet.

We made our way through a maze of city and harbor lights. Nancy steered while I plotted, replotted, and alternated between binoculars and our instruments, namely the depth sounder and radar. For two hours we did circles in the hectic traffic lanes and among the shifting sands of Durban, testing our charts, waypoints, eyes, and patience trying to find the famous international jetty.

When at last we found the tiny, unlit concrete pier it was 9:00 P.M. and we were on the dock alone.

The South African couple we'd met in Mozambique lived in Durban, so they came down to visit us at daylight, and over coffee we caught up on what turned out to be a sad year for us all. Nancy told them about her mother's death and they told us how their daughter, a rising young star in the sailing community, had been killed by an unlicensed truck driver. Merle had not been sailing since her daughter's death, so we asked her to join us for the next leg, in honor and in memory of her daughter.

With only a moment's hesitation, she and Keith agreed it was a good idea, despite the fact that this next leg was potentially the most dangerous. This 250-mile section of coast, referred to as "the wild coast" had no safe harbors and boasted the largest abnormal waves in the world, "thirty-meter ship-breakers." Here, the south-bound Agulhas current was at its strongest, and most dramatically intersected with volatile contrary weather, river and tidal flows, busy shipping lanes, and a steep continental shelf.

❧   ❧   ❧

We cleared the harbor at 10:30 A.M. on March 8 with a steady bar and east-southeast to east-northeast winds from ten to twenty-five knots. As we'd done further north, we headed five miles offshore for the two hundred-meter line and picked up the current. By one-thirty in the afternoon, we were making eleven knots in gale-force easterly winds. Merle taught us to see the distinct cloud line marking the change in water temperature that also marked the strongest current. We were never more than fifteen miles offshore. At the latitude of Cape Morgan, we jibbed and headed east, beginning our approach to East London by steering for Danger Point. The boat was flying along comfortably, so I nibbled a South African appetizer, an avocado with smoked mussels and Tabasco. Merle slept and Nancy relaxed reading Michener's *Covenant*. The wind vane steered *Tethys* easily down the nine- to twelve-foot following seas. Within the hour we were back inside the two hundred-meter line, and the seas were sloppy but decreased in height. We passed Sharp Peak Light and made our way into the Buffalo River of East London just after another spectacular African sunset. By 6:15 P.M. we were tied up to the riverside pilings with a huge fender board and we toasted our arrival with peach juice and potatoes. We'd done the wild coast in record time—108 miles in twelve hours. Never did we sleep more soundly in Africa.

We tried to celebrate our halfway point in East London, but as some see the glass half full, we were all too painfully aware that our trip was only half over—half empty—and we were getting closer and closer to the cape in a season that was now beginning to change for the worse. Tied up in the river mouth we were safe from the storms, but we couldn't relax. Every few days a cold front would blow through from the southwest Atlantic, or the Indian Ocean high would pitch us gales from the other direction. We were in the southern hemisphere going south. Our weather windows were getting shorter and shorter, and we stayed ready to leave at the first good report. Eleven nerve-wracking days zipped by faster than the river current.

March 20 we sailed out of the channel under a rainbow. The barometer was 1,020 and steady after a day-long rise. The wind was southeast at ten to fifteen knots, a comfortable reach since our course was now turned more to the west, mirroring the coastal curve. Just beyond the East London breakwater and, at its closest point to the coast, we found the southbound current. The GPS showed our speed at ten knots over the ground as we pushed ourselves to Port Elizabeth, or "PE" as the locals fondly referred to this charming historically British harbor town. The wind shifted to northeast twenty knots off Point St. John's when we could see the lights off Kenton-on-Sea. At dawn we only had twenty-five miles to go as we threaded our way through fishing boats, three ships, and one hundred dolphins with babies. Just after 10:00 A.M., we surfed gently inside the breakwater and waved to the morning racers as they headed out in the opposite direction. We'd done a 140-mile trip in nineteen hours. Though it was a peaceful Sunday morning, we knew it was the end of another good weather window. We secured *Tethys*, signed into the yacht club, and slept.

That afternoon we had our best green salad in Africa, heard authentic Scottish bagpipe music, and walked among the dusty volumes of the hallowed old British library. We were the only "foreign" boat making our way south, and nearly everyone in town stopped by to share tips, strategies, and predictions about the weather. Every six hours, every day, we stared at the weather fax hoping for a break.

One week later, it came. On a dreary dull-gray watercolor day, we headed out of PE for Mossel Bay, with hopes the weather might hold for rounding the capes. The *QE2*, which we had last seen in Australia, was sailing into the harbor and the weather was benign. We opted to sail out with the locals and welcome her in, then carry on out of sloppy St. Francis Bay. Our nerves and stomachs were a jumble and it was tempting to turn around. Just then, I noticed that our heading on the GPS was 270 degrees, true west, for the first time in a year. We toasted the good news that we had very few miles left to go south on this circumnavigation, and sailed on into the night.

At dawn, we knew our weather window was closing. There were no other boats on the horizon. It was as if we were the only two people in the world. Pensively, we both watched the countdown of miles to the cape. Then, in almost whispering tones, we decided to play it safe. Reluctantly, we made the decision to delay our rounding of Cape Agulhas to another day. We headed for Mossel Bay.

The harbormaster was surprised to see us, as no other foreign boats were sailing the cape at this time of year. We tried to ignore this, and instead focused on getting his advice and explanation about the industrial-strength mooring lines even the small boats on the dock used. Within minutes of tying up, we saw our first big surging wave. Even on the calm day we arrived, the surge in the harbor was enough to topple a drink left on the galley counter below. With little warning, the next day, we saw the surge action nearly double. A southeast gale began to blow in from the Indian Ocean high, and as the waves built outside the breakwater, it sent all the boats on one side of the inner harbor hurtling into the dock and chipping away at the concrete piles. *Tethys* was on the safer side, but still needed constant attention to keep from breaking free. In addition to the weather surge, there were frequent wakes from big working tugs and fishing boats. Twenty-four hours for all ten days we were in Mossel Bay. The oil service and supply ships that work this section of the offshore plateau, maneuvered fifteen feet from *Tethys*'s stern.

After lunch, on April 9, we left the relative safety of Mossel Bay for the relative dangers of the two southernmost capes of Africa. Taking a deep breath, touching wood, and holding an optimistic weather report, we hurled our hearts and the boat toward the first of the two, Cape Agulhas. We didn't speak as the weather fax printed out line by excruciating line. Our good weather was holding, but still we didn't speak. All our energy was focused on the pine-green and gray headland in the mist ahead. The boat sailed on, spewing foam behind us like a racehorse.

Twenty-five hours after our departure from Mossel Bay, we rounded Cape Agulhas and shouted. I could taste relief. Life was good. The ocean was suddenly more alive with mammals and birds than we'd seen on the whole African coast. The surreal indigo textures in the place "where two oceans meet" slipped away to the south at four knots while *Tethys* headed north at six. Seals leapt in our wake, and hundreds of gannets, terns, and shearwaters dipped in and out of the fresh gray-green of Antarctica's frigid northbound Benguela current. Rounding the cape was, in one moment, both an end and a beginning.

It was the end of the Indian Ocean, the beginning of the Atlantic. It was the end of our journey south and the beginning of our journey north. It was the end of being on the other side of the world. We could almost see home, and to celebrate we laughed louder than the wind for the first time in months, and slapped the teak cockpit. Our thirty-knot southeaster astern eased to twenty in the lee of the continent. The dreaded southwesters we'd ducked and dodged on our eight hundred-mile journey down the east coast were no longer a threat. If it came now, the southwester would be abeam or on our quarter. It would be a favorable wind and, with the current, would only take us to Cape Town faster. We almost welcomed the thought as we rolled in the yankee from the pole to starboard and rolled it out to port, close reaching and heading north on our next and final leg around the world.

After all the anticipation, the work and investment, the scariest cape of the journey that I could imagine was passed in an instant. One moment I was approaching, and the next I was around. One moment I was before, and the next, beyond. Twelve hours later with the euphoric afterglow of "The Cape" still fresh, we muscled our way past the Cape of Storms. Despite the infamous winds of the "Cape Doctor" slipping over Table Mountain and laying us over with fifty-knot gusts, I opted to enter this cape in my journal by its other name, the Cape of Good Hope.

Whale Watching Me

JENNIFER HAHN

The kayak rode up and down in buttery swells while I considered the options. I was two days south of Addenbroke Island off British Columbia, and feeling the personality of the wide Pacific beginning to dominate the quieter channels that flagged her side. Should I leapfrog island to island in a zigzag southeast-to-south route? Or, because it was a relatively calm morning, perhaps I could be courageous and take the straightest line across, no matter the exposure? I chose to parallel a necklace of islets up the inlet, then reevaluate partway across.

What I loved most about long kayak crossings was how the sea overtook all my senses. Eventually, halfway across, I'd be completely deprived of the aroma of soil, ferns, forest, rock. Following a multi-mile crossing, the returning aroma of the land never failed to stir my heart with gratitude.

The water rimming the once-distant island on the far side of Rivers Inlet was spunky, alive. With each incoming swell, my sixteen-foot fiberglass kayak *Yemaya* danced toward the bouldered perimeter, then soared backward with the rebound wave. The rhythm was mesmerizing. And while I was watching to be sure the bow didn't puncture again, I was also playing with the energy of the sea—back paddling at just the right moment, forward stroking to get back into the dance step.

At last, tired, I paddled out of the swells to the leeward side of the forested island, removed my glasses, laid down the paddle, and drifted. A winter wren trilled its territorial symphony. Below me, a school of herring jumped at the sight of my predator-size boat. A curious seal zoomed out of sight in the dark water. Next time I looked down, it lay perfectly still in *Yemaya*'s shadow, staring up at me from three feet under the surface, its flippers folded as if in prayer.

$$\text{\textbf{\textit{\delta}} \qquad \textbf{\textit{\delta}} \qquad \textbf{\textit{\delta}}}$$

Paddling toward Kelp Head the next morning at sunrise, my heart held still while I measured the danger. I was leaving a cove of vertical trees and entering the wind's house—though no one was home right then. Even on this rare calm day I could see that outer Kelp Head was a wind-pressed country. Bushes crawled across the rocks like prostrating monks to avoid the blast of Pacific storms. Full-grown trees twisted into bonsai with mere brushstrokes for needles. Grasses grew in alert wedges like someone's blown-back hair. Every plant left me with a mistaken impression of a wind still present. I felt terror filling my heart just looking at them.

I'd dreaded this leg of the journey through Queen Charlotte Sound and around Cape Caution ever since I'd talked on the phone a year before with kayak guru Randel Washburne. He'd warned, "Wait for a weather break."

That break had come.

Place names can tell you a lot about the personality of local waters. The names along this stretch of open coast would give the most daring pause: Safety Cove, Storm Islands, God's Pocket, Cape Caution, Shelter Bay, Sorrow Island. Looking at a marine atlas, it's easy to see how the ocean can grow so nasty here. There is nothing but open ocean for forty grueling miles.

But exposure is only part of the challenge. Chaotic water conditions haunt the region, especially during ebb tides. Imagine Queen Charlotte Sound as a huge drainage ditch transporting the water from hundreds of miles of fjords out to the open Pacific, from Fitz Hugh Sound in the north to Queen Charlotte Strait in the southeast. That means the ebb flows west. Ocean swells pushed by sea winds galumph east. Everything is trying to pass in opposite directions through the same portal between Cape Scott on Vancouver Island to the south and Cape Calvert on Calvert Island to the north. The result: sumo wrestling matches under your hull.

Even with a zephyr westerly and moderate swells, the "Queen's Pond," as Queen Charlotte Sound is fondly known, can deal a dirty deck. Diesel tugs towing log booms have idled for half a month waiting for better weather in which to cross. In severe cases, hurricane-force winds have whipped the waves to almost unbelievable heights of ninety to a hundred feet. Seaworthy purse seiners have been battered to shreds near Pine Island. Cape Caution, with its fast-shoaling bottom, has wreaked havoc on many a boat and life.

All this darkened my mind as I paddled out through the placid bay and around land's end. To distract myself as I worked into the first swells, I reviewed the day's ambitious route in my head. Fourteen miles to Cape Caution, two miles around it, then seven more to Slingsby Channel. Slingsby offered the first escape route where I could turn east and travel up a fjord if I needed to.

Rounding Kelp Head, the bow vaulted up an astonishingly large wall of green water and sank softly into the wave's trough. I felt swallowed. I couldn't see the horizon inside that opaque scoop. That first big swell skittered the kayak sideways at an alarming speed. I was rushing back toward the headland. Surf pounded fifteen yards away. My heart drummed like a lovelorn grouse inside the hull of my yellow jacket.

My mind reeled. I expected to smash into the headland any second. *Do something!* Adrenaline bolted into my arms and hands. I lunged the paddle blade into the glassy wall to speed up. The kayak rose. The view returned. I emerged forty yards from the pounding surf line. Shaken, I was surprised to be so far out.

Things under water appear twenty-five percent larger than they are. Under the lens of fear, things seem even more magnified. I was rife with fear. Where did reality end and imagination begin? My worst frailty was not physical, but in my mind—shunting my fantastical imaginings of spilling over, sinking helplessly, choking in a cold frightening sea. I could drown a thousand deaths today and never leave the boat.

True, the swells were bigger than I'd expected. But were they only amplified by the headland or the ebb tide? It was too early to tell. I had to keep going to know. If I only knew then, that by the end of the day, I'd be eye to eye with a whale, the tumultuous seas would have been easier to handle. But at the time, only the next fifteen feet mattered—the distance between me and the next cresting wave.

I lost sight of the horizon again and again. I felt a tinge of relief every time the kayak rose from a trough. My eyes quickly remembered to sharpen on those upswings, to take in vital details and hold them in a gestalt before I fell back into the valley. There was only the measure of rise and fall. How many rises and falls were there between here and Cape Caution?

Receding headlands appeared in layers of mussel-shell blue, trimmed in oyster gray, toward the misty horizon, as far as I could see south down the rugged coast. A handful of island outposts lay scattered between.

My mind flicked like a Rolodex full of snapshots of solo kayakers I'd known. I recalled the names of adventurous men and women who, through luck and solid judgment, had logged years of experience under their hulls and died doing what they loved. One day, the sea embraced them and didn't let go.

Did I really need to do this section after all? Why risk my life to paddle this treacherous piece of coast? Once I committed, I might be unable to land for untold miles. What if the wind picked up? Ambling along at three or four mph, I might not have the speed to escape to safety. I'd just have to deal. God, was I loony?

I looked west to Queen Charlotte Sound and the milky Pacific warbling on the horizon. It felt as if the sea were a huge reverberating drum skin stretched across the Pacific Rim. And somewhere far beyond, where human eyes couldn't see, a huge mallet hit the surface. It shook the drum skin, sending swells out toward the edge where I paddled. What if the wind's mallet struck harder?

I glanced east to the mainland where I'd come from. Waves exploded in a spray of white manes along rock cliffs. I shuddered at the sound of their *kahh-boom!* I felt nauseated, taut-stomached.

I looked north over my stern. Blue-shouldered Calvert Island watched from the horizon like a big brother. There wasn't a boat in sight from Calvert Island south. Not a human anywhere. I was alone. Rising, falling. Atop the next swell, I glanced toward the land again. Two bald eagles, hunched on a skeleton shore pine, looked out to sea.

Other life besides me! I spoke to them.

"Eagles, I am so scared," I yelled.

I sank into another trough.

When I came up, the eagles' heads had turned. Their golden bills were arrowed right on the kayak. I felt pierced by their gaze.

I dropped into the next trough praying aloud. I need strength to make this long and difficult journey. Pleeeease, help me be strong. And as I rose over the crest I felt something powerful pass between bird and human like an invisible zap of electrical current. Immediately I felt calmer. I palpably released all of my frenetic tension and dread. Bold confidence leapt into my heart like a torch ignited by an unseen spark. I turned to the eagles and raised my paddle.

"Thank you for watching over me," I shouted. "I wish you many fish and children."

The Bella Bella people say eagles open the door to the spirit world. After praying to them, I relaxed and sank the paddle blade in deeper. I committed my everything to the journey.

Two marbled murrelets corked up beside the cockpit, inches from my paddle blade. Each bird looked no bigger than my fist. Just a brown and white swirl of feathers and a conic head. As we passed in opposite directions, their tiny feet stroked so fast—one-two-one-two—that their heads bobbed.

Ah, maybe, it wasn't size after all, I mused. Maybe it was adaptability and persistence.

Marbled murrelets are the epitome of both. Sleeping all night in old-growth forests miles inland. Winging to the coast before sunrise. Feeding all day on ocean herring. Returning to nesting sites in the mossy branches after sundown. They looked like they belonged out there. I decided, admiring their ease, that I belonged there, too.

After seeing the eagles and murrelets and realizing I was not really entirely alone, I passed over a threshold. I slipped into a state of mind as simple as this: Surrender. Whatever awaited me was okay. I was exactly where I needed to be. This life. This open coast. This body. I had been plopped into my rightful place: upright in the waves in that little grin of a kayak. The moment felt utterly full and intoxicating.

Though just minutes before everything seemed perfectly wrong, it now seemed perfectly right—even the danger. And danger was everywhere—the forty-five-degree water below my tush, the rock-buttressed shore, the no-nonsense overture of the swells hammering the rocky coast fifty yards away. Yet, I swear on forty sacred texts, I loved that tilt toward danger. It felt beautiful, because it amped my six senses. I was *alive!*

Looking around, I thought I'd never felt such a powerful place. The crashing surf now looked astoundingly beautiful. It was no longer frightening. I felt drawn to it. Tempting fate, I drifted to within a few feet of an exploding reef and watched. Glassy waves curled over the rocks and rumbled white. As the waves withdrew, I was rewarded by the song of a dozen waterfalls pouring over tiered stone and hula-dancing sea palms.

       ॐ   ॐ   ॐ

Five hours sloshed under the hull. Cape Caution's white navigation light blinked in the distance. I aimed the bow just right of it. I wanted to stay slightly offshore. "Forehead" is the Kwakiutl name for the cape. From a distance, the boulder-strewn, granite headland protrudes much like a nose from a forehead of cliffs and trees. It is a cape that stirs humility and begs patience.

"Timing is everything," Randel Washburne had warned. It took my friend Kim Kirby eight days before she and a friend found a window they could use to kayak around the frightening cape. Fog and sixteen-foot breakers nixed their safe progress. Paddling north from Seattle, they took false refuge in Slingsby Channel. They got stuck there. Waves as tall as the kayak was long blocked the channel's mouth.

I couldn't believe I was now approaching the dreaded moment.

The western swell lifted and rolled the kayak like a behemoth hand rocking a cradle. I kept squinting ahead for the tidal stream deflecting off Cape Caution's tip. Where was the typical scour-line of whitecaps that signals a tidal rip? I didn't like it that I hadn't found it. I didn't want those kind of surprises sneaking up on me.

Everywhere the sea was a not-too-threatening tumultuous gray chop. Nonetheless, hobgoblins niggled my mind. Was I too low in the water to catch approaching danger in time? Should I swing farther out to sea to avoid colliding with potential rips? Although Queen Charlotte Sound was calm by most standards, the cape itself was white-toothed, bursting with explosions of spray.

But nothing happened. Nothing! After days . . . weeks . . . months of self-aggravated, doomsday scenes played over and over, I could hardly believe my eyes. No eat-you-up and spit-you-out tide rips! No sixteen-foot breakers! Just low swell. Meager winds. Choppy surface waves. And now, after six hours, I still had tidal current running in my favor! Cape Caution is one of those rare places on the coast where the current splits because of a T-shaped oceanography. After the incoming tide enters Queen Charlotte Sound between Vancouver Island and Calvert Island, it hits the British Columbia mainland and flows in two directions along the shore. Half the flood tide bounds north up Fitz Hugh Sound. Half muddles south into Queen Charlotte Strait, sluicing behind Vancouver Island. On that morning I hitched the ebb current exiting Fitz Hugh Sound south down the open coast. At Cape Caution, the tide was changing guards. So I would again "go with the flow" and ride the flood south for six more hours—an almost unheard of timing—into the throat between Vancouver Island and the mainland. Hallelujah!

The kayak bucked up and over the waves ricocheting off Cape Caution. It rolled under the heave of the ocean swells. I didn't mind any of it. I knew that capes tend to concentrate swell and wave energy because of reflection and refraction. Without thinking, when the chop intensified, I loosened hips, leaned forward, and stroked faster. I danced with the kayak, following its lead. How many times had I instructed my kayak students: "Loose hips don't sink ships." The kayak swayed gracefully beneath me. Yet my head and spine kept vertical as if connected by a string to the sky. This technique helps maintain a crucial center of gravity. I exhaled long soothing breaths.

On the starboard side, a blast shot up. I lurched in the seat. Immediately, the boat became less stable. Beside the cockpit, the water boiled white. A dark form sank from sight. I wanted to cry. I wanted to laugh. A gray whale was accompanying me in the choppy tidal current around Cape Caution!

"Hi-ho, whale friend. Keep your eye on me," I yelled. "And please don't knock me over!"

The waves were erratic now and I could hardly turn to watch the whale, which was surfacing now on the other side of me. He dove right under! I could hardly believe it.

A voluminous cloud of mist rocketed off the bow. A barnacled forehead rose out of the sea ahead of me—big as an upturned wheelbarrow. Water poured off the whale's immense throat, and a beautiful, knobby snout appeared. The whale was spy-hopping to get a look at me. Nose pointed skyward, it gyrated slowly with its head above water while its flukes beat back and forth to keep it upright.

The whale's mottled skin reminded me of one of those curious images of the night sky taken through an astronomer's telescope. Bursts of white nebulae, sprays of starry barnacles, and shooting asteroids—the marks of scrapes—patterned the hide. But the eye— oh, that gentle eye! Just above its down-curved grin, set inside a cowry shell of folds, I met the whale's dark orb staring out from a universe of stars. Though only visible for seconds, the eye looked out wide as all curiosity. When it sank into the waves and disappeared I felt like I'd been looked at by the eye of God.

Now the whale surfaced behind. I heard the blow, and wondered, half nervous, half ecstatic, where it would come up next.

But I never saw the gray whale again.

About the Contributors

When she was eighteen years old, **Tania Aebi** sailed around the world single-handedly. She was twenty-one in 1987 when she returned and wrote a book about the experience, *Maiden Voyage*. She has since continued to sail, travel, and write to finance the raising of two boys in Vermont.

Bernadette Bernon was the Editor-in-Chief of *Cruising World* magazine for ten years before setting off in 2000 with her husband Douglas on their Shearwater 39, *Ithaka*. The Bernons sailed from their home in Newport, Rhode Island, up to Canada; then to Cuba; across to the Yucatan; down the Mexican coast to Belize, the Bay Islands of Honduras, the San Blas Islands and coast of Panama; and on to Cartagena, Colombia. In 2002, her article "Midterm Reflections," originally published in *Cruising World*, was awarded the Genmar Trophy for Best Article of the Year by Boating Writers International. Alternating with Douglas, she also writes the monthly column "Log of Ithaka" for the magazine, and for two years chronicled their preparations and cruising adventures on www.cruisingworld.com.

Moe Bowstern worked nine years as a deckhand and skiff operator in the salmon, halibut, herring, and cod fisheries of Kodiak, Alaska. She turned to writing down her fishing stories when she returned from the sea and found to her chagrin that most people don't have the patience to sit and listen to long nautical yarns. She has been published in the anthologies *Salt in Our Veins* and *Drive*, and in the *Alaska Fisherman's Journal*. She has also written for dozens of 'zines, and was nominated for a 2003 *Utne Reader* Independent Press Award. You can read all about her adventures in her 'zine, *Xtra Tuf*; issues 3, 4, and 5 are available from her for $3 at P.O. Box 6834, Portland, Oregon 97228 (no checks please).

Ginni Callahan guides and teaches sea kayaking where the weather's good—on Oregon's and Washington's lower Columbia River during the summer, and in the Sea of Cortez during the winter. In between, she drifts wherever adventure beckons and the boat floats. ginnical@yahoo.com, www.columbiariverkayaking.com

Kaci Cronkhite completed her circumnavigation and teaching work with Nancy Erley and *Tethys* in August 2001. During the trip, she earned her USCG Masters license, quit her Ph.D., single-handed the boat, dared to scuba dive, passed her Ham radio license, and co-instructed forty-six women from four countries. She now lives happily ever after in Port Townsend, Washington, where she is the coordinator of the Wooden Boat Festival, gardens with a passion, and conducts women's sailing seminars. Nancy Erley continues to teach women aboard *Tethys* from her home port of Seattle.

Dodo Danzmann is currently living in Greece, high up in the Pelion Mountains. After having been a bookseller in Hamburg, Germany, for many years, she now works as a freelance translator.

Penelope S. Duffy, Ph.D, lives with her husband in Rochester, Minnesota. Following publication of *A Stockbridge Homecoming* (Bright Sky Press, 2001), a recollection of her family's years as missionaries in China during the 1940s, she was inspired to turn from a twenty-seven-year career in neurologic communication disorders to full-time writing. She is now working on a novel set against the backdrop of schooner fishing and World War I in Nova Scotia, where she spent thirty summers sailing and racing.

Jessica DuLong lives a dual life. As an engineer she runs retired New York City fireboat *John J. Harvey*'s five opposed-piston diesel engines on trips up and down the Hudson River. As a journalist she writes for a variety of publications, from *Newsweek International, Rolling Stone,* and *Parenting,* to *Marine News, Offshore,* and *Maritime Reporter and Engineering News.*

Jill Fredston has rowed more than 22,000 miles in the Arctic and sub-Arctic, exploring the rugged coastlines of Alaska, Canada, Greenland, Spitsbergen, and Norway. She is the author of *Rowing to Latitude: Journeys Along the Arctic's Edge,* which won the 2002 National Outdoor Book Award for Literature. She writes, and works as one of North America's leading avalanche specialists, in the mountains above Anchorage, Alaska. She is currently working on a book about avalanches.

Linda Greenlaw is the author of the bestselling book *The Hungry Ocean*, the story of a trip out to sea to catch swordfish. Her latest book is *The Lobster Chronicles: Life on a Very Small Island*.

After their trans-Atlantic crossing, **Sue Muller Hacking** and her husband Jon bought an old trimaran in the West Indies. They sailed the Caribbean for six years, supporting themselves by running a day-charter boat and returning to the States to work every two years. Their son Christopher was born in Martinique and sailed with them through the Panama Canal to San Diego at two years old. The family (now including daughter Amanda) has resided in Redmond, Washington, for twelve years. Sue is author of several children's books and the Northwest guidebooks *Take a Walk*, and *Boatless in Seattle*. Recalled to the sea, the family is now cruising aboard their new catamaran, *Ocelot*, in the South Pacific. Even after twenty years and 17,000 sea miles, the full gale off South Africa remains a vivid memory, an experience she hopes never to repeat.

Jennifer Hahn, a naturalist and wilderness guide, solo kayaked from Ketchikan, Alaska, to her home in Bellingham, Washington —750 miles—over two springs and summers. This excerpt from *Spirited Waters* (Mountaineers, 2002) recalls her dicey journey around Cape Caution in Queen Charlotte Sound, otherwise known as the "punching bag" of the Pacific.

Holly Hughes has spent the last twenty-five summers working on boats in Alaska in a variety of capacities—from deckhand/cook on a salmon gill-netter to skipper of *Crusader,* a sixty-five-foot schooner for Resource Institute, a nonprofit organization that offers seminars afloat on art, native culture, natural history, and writing. She spends winters in Washington State, where she teaches a variety of writing classes at Edmonds Community College. Her poems and essays have appeared in *The Duckabush Journal, Crosscurrents, Explorations, Pontoon, Salt in Our Veins,* and *The Hedgebrook Journal,* among others. She lives in a log cabin built in the 1930s in Indianola, Washington.

Deborah Scaling Kiley was born on a ranch in west Texas and graduated from Colorado Springs School, where she participated in an Outward Bound program that later helped her survive the wreck of *Trashman.* She now lives on a farm in Massachusetts with her husband and two children.

Devorah Major is the author of two novels, *An Open Weave* (Seal Press) and *Brown Glass Windows* (Curbstone Press), and four volumes of poetry, most recently *where river meets ocean* (City Lights). She is the current San Francisco Poet Laureate (2002-2004) and is working on her next novel and a volume of essays. She is also looking forward to her next sailing adventure.

Meg Noonan has written for numerous magazines, including *Esquire, Sports Illustrated,* and *Outside.* She lives in New Hampshire with her husband and two children.

Dawn Paul has written stories for *Snowy Egret, Common Lives/Lesbian Lives,* and *North Shore Magazine,* and her poetry has been read on NPR station WBUR in Boston. Her articles on science, sports, and the outdoors have appeared in *Sojourner, Atlantic Coastal Kayaker, Sea Kayaker,* and *Explore Magazine.* Her play *The Nest* was a recent winner in the New Voices 10-Minute Play competition. She teaches poetry and short fiction. She and her partner keep a small fleet of kayaks in Beverly, Massachusetts.

Pamela Powell has worked as deckhand, first mate, cook, and captain on a variety of boats, including ferries and charter yachts. She was also an instructor for Outward Bound. While living in the Caribbean on a twenty-eight-foot gaff-rigged double-ender, she was inspired to write *The Turtle Watchers* (Viking, 1992). She's had articles published in *SAIL Magazine,* among others, and is currently working on a memoir and a novel for young adults. She lives with her husband and son in the Boston area.

Andromeda Romano-Lax is the author of several books about Baja and Alaska, including a guidebook, *Adventure Kayaking: Baja,* and a travel narrative, *Searching for Steinbeck's Sea of Cortez,* from which this essay was excerpted. She graduated with a Master of Marine Management degree from Dalhousie University and lives with her family in Anchorage, Alaska. Excerpts from her books and details of future expeditions are available on her Web site, www.booksbyandromeda.com.

Jennifer Karuza Schile, a member of a multi-generation fishing family, is a regular correspondent for *National Fisherman*. She has also been published in *Pacific Fishing*. In 2002, she was awarded an Honorable Mention in the memoir category of the *Writer's Digest* writing competition. Jennifer, who is originally from Bellingham, Washington, spent several seasons commercial fishing in Southeast Alaska to earn money for college. She graduated from Western Washington University in 1997 with an English degree. She now lives and writes at the home she shares with her fisherman husband, George, in Seattle.

Melinda Tognini is a writer and teacher who lives in Perth, Western Australia. Her work includes short stories, feature articles, and travel writing. She is currently working on a novel for young adults and has recently returned to sailing after a ten-year absence.

About the Editor

Barbara Sjoholm is the author, as Barbara Wilson, of the PEN Award-nominated memoir *Blue Windows* and comic thriller *Gaudí Afternoon*, now a film starring Judy Davis and Marcia Gay Harden. Her essays and travel narratives have appeared in *The American Scholar*, *The North American Review*, the *New York Times*, and *Smithsonian*. She is at work on a new book entitled *The Pirate Queen: In Search of Grace O'Malley and Other Maritime Women of Myth and History* due out in Spring 2004. She lives in Seattle.

Selected Titles from Seal Press

Give Me the World by Leila Hadley. $14.95, 1-58005-091-3. The spirited story of one young woman's travels by boat and by land with her six-year-old son.

No Hurry to Get Home: The Memoir of the New Yorker *Writer Whose Unconventional Life and Adventures Spanned the Twentieth Century* by Emily Hahn. $14.95, 1-58005-045-X. Hahn's memoir captures her free-spirited, charismatic personality and her inextinguishable passion for the unconventional life.

The Unsavvy Traveler: Women's Comic Tales of Catastrophe edited by Rosemary Caperton, Anne Mathews, and Lucie Ocenas. $15.95, 1-58005-058-1. Twenty-five gut-wrenchingly funny responses to the question: What happens when trips go wrong?

A Woman Alone: Travel Tales from around the Globe edited by Faith Conlon, Ingrid Emerick and Christina Henry de Tessan. $15.95, 1-58005-059-X. A collection of rousing stories by women who travel solo.

East Toward Dawn: A Woman's Solo Journey around the World by Nan Watkins. $14.95, 1-58005-064-6. After the loss of her son and the end of a marriage, the author sets out in search of joy and renewal in travel.

Gift of the Wild: A Woman's Book of Adventure edited by Faith Conlon, Ingrid Emerick and Jennie Goode. $16.95, 1-58005-006-9. Explores the transformative power of outdoor adventure in the lives of women.

The Curve of Time: The Classic Memoir of a Woman and Her Children Who Explored the Coastal Waters of the Pacific Northwest, second edition by M. Wylie Blanchet, foreword by Timothy Egan. $15.95, 1-58005-072-7. The timeless memoir of a pioneering, courageous woman who acted as both mother and captain of the twenty-five-foot boat that became her family's home during the long Northwest summers.

Seal Press publishes many outdoor and travel books by women writers. Please visit our Web site at **www.sealpress.com**.